Winds of Will

Winds of Will

Emily Dickinson and the Sovereignty of Democratic Thought

Paul Crumbley

The University of Alabama Press
Tuscaloosa

Library of Congress Cataloging-in-Publication Data

Crumbley, Paul, 1952–
Winds of will : Emily Dickinson and the sovereignty of democratic thought /
Paul Crumbley.
p. cm.
Includes bibliographical references and index.
ISBN 978-0-8173-1703-4 (cloth : alk. paper) 1. Dickinson, Emily, 1830–1886—
Criticism and interpretation. 2. Dickinson, Emily, 1830–1886—Political and social
views. 3. Women and literature—United States—History—19th century. 4. Litera-
ture and society—United States—History—19th century. I. Title.
PS1541.Z5C755 2010
811'.4—dc22

2009042883

For Lucy, Nell, and Emma

Contents

Illustrations

Author's Note

All of the illustrations, except figure 9, can be located in *The Manuscript Books of Emily Dickinson (MBED)*. Ed. R. W. Franklin (Cambridge, Mass.: Harvard University Press, 1981). The illustrations of poems that appear in this volume are numbered according to the Thomas H. Johnson numbering system, indicated by "J" before the poem number. I add the Franklin numbers (Fr) that come from Franklin's 1998 variorum edition of the poems because that is the system I use in the rest of the book.

The handwritten marks commonly referred to as Dickinson's "dashes" are presented in what follows as en dashes, rather than em dashes. This is because the en dash more accurately represents the average length of Dickinson's marks and honors Dickinson's practice of not connecting these marks to the words on either side of them. For a fuller discussion of these marks, please see my earlier book, *Inflections of the Pen: Dash and Voice in Emily Dickinson.*

Acknowledgments

I am profoundly aware of the debt I owe to others for the best features of this book. During the years I spent organizing my thinking about Dickinson and politics, I repeatedly discovered that the perceptions I considered most original, most daring, and most my own were being expressed in different form by scholars similarly interested in the political implications of Dickinson's poems and letters. As a consequence, I have come to believe that what is most valuable about my own analysis is not my distinct point of view so much as the part I play in a larger scholarly conversation. For help improving the accuracy and clarity of my contribution to that conversation, I thank Jane Donahue Eberwein and Martha Nell Smith, in particular, for their careful reading of my manuscript and for the advice that made it stronger. I am also grateful to Cristanne Miller for her comments on a portion of the manuscript and for her recommendation that I apply for a fellowship at the Rothermere American Institute at Oxford University. I thank Jed Deppman, Gudrun Grabher, Eleanor Elson Heginbotham, Mary Loeffelholz, Cindy MacKenzie, Domhnall Mitchell, and Elizabeth Petrino for the advice and support they provided as I worked through early stages of the argument that appeared in conference papers and published essays. For her many contributions to the field of nineteenth-century American poetry and her generous assessment of portions of my manuscript, I am grateful to Paula Bernat Bennett. The single greatest source of continuous support for my research has been the Emily Dickinson International Society, whose many members daily demonstrate Dickinson's power to reach beyond the narrow confines of the academy and engage the imaginations of readers around the world.

I could never have completed this book had I not enjoyed the support of Utah State University. Jeffrey Smitten, head of the English department at Utah State during the time I wrote this book, has been an invaluable ally, not only through his intellectual encouragement but also through his efforts to secure funds for travel, research, and permissions. I began the research for *Winds of Will* with a Utah State New Faculty Research Grant in 1998 and made significant progress during a 2002–2003 sabbatical year. Thanks to the suggestion of Christine Hult, who chaired the Utah State ADVANCE Committee, I applied for and received an ADVANCE Associate to Full Grant that gave me the time I so badly needed to complete a draft of the book in the spring of 2007.

The research so essential to this book was made much easier through the able and patient assistance of John Lancaster, Daria D'Arienzo, and Margaret Dakin, archivists at the Robert Frost Library of Amherst College. I also thank Leslie Morris and her staff at the Houghton Library of Harvard University. During the year I spent at the Rothermere American Institute, I benefited enormously from the expertise provided by the staff of the Vere Harmsworth Library. I will be forever grateful to the Rothermere for their generous support of my scholarship.

The poems of Emily Dickinson are reprinted by permission of the publishers and the Trustees of Amherst College from *The Poems of Emily Dickinson: Variorum Edition,* Ralph W. Franklin, ed., Cambridge, Mass.: The Belknap Press of Harvard University Press, Copyright © 1998, 1999 by the President and Fellows of Harvard College. Copyright © 1951, 1955, 1979, 1983 by the President and Fellows of Harvard College. The Dickinson letters are reprinted by permission of the publishers from *The Letters of Emily Dickinson,* Thomas H. Johnson, ed., Cambridge, Mass.: The Belknap Press of Harvard University Press, Copyright © 1958, 1986 by the President and Fellows of Harvard College; 1914, 1924, 1932, 1942 by Martha Dickinson Bianchi; 1952 by Alfred Leete Hampson; 1960 by Mary L. Hampson.

An earlier version of chapter 3 appeared as "Dickinson's Uses of Spiritualism: The 'Nature' of Democratic Belief" in *A Companion to Emily Dickinson,* eds. Martha Nell Smith and Mary Loeffelholz, Malden, Mass.: Blackwell Publishing, 2008, 235–257; I am grateful to Blackwell for permission to reprint. A portion of chapter 4 appeared as "'As if for you to choose –': Conflicting Textual Economies in Dickinson's Correspondence with Helen Hunt Jackson," *Women's Studies: An Interdisciplinary Journal* 31.6 (2002): 743–757; I am grateful to Taylor and Francis for permission to reprint. Another portion of chapter 4 previously appeared as "Dickinson's Correspondence and the Politics of Gift-Based Circulation" in *Reading Emily Dickinson's Letters,* edited by Jane Donahue Eberwein and Cindy MacKenzie, Amherst: University of Massachusetts Press, 2009; I am grateful to the University of Massachusetts Press for permission to reprint.

This book would not have been possible without the love and patience of my family. My wife, Phebe Jensen, made even our daily routines festive, despite the demands of her own scholarship; and my daughters, Nell and Emma, had the courtesy to become great readers so that the silence of solitary labor could also be intimate. My mother-in-law, Lucy Jensen, combed New England bookstores for obscure nineteenth-century texts and found each discovery a cause for celebration. My dear brother John, who passed away before this book went to press, showed me the joy of deep thinking and will forever be a part of my best work.

Winds of Will

Introduction

The Undecidability of Dickinson's Politics

It may seem self-defeating to begin a book about Emily Dickinson and democratic thought by acknowledging that her politics may never be definitively identified. But somewhat paradoxically, that very difficulty is in keeping with what I will argue is a central characteristic of the democratic discourse in Dickinson's poems. In spite of the fact that she grew up in a family with pronounced political allegiances, Dickinson rarely addressed political issues directly. When she did, it was through correspondence and poetry that scholars have mostly understood as expressions of a private self and, therefore, not examined for its political content. What I have discovered, though, is that the challenge of establishing the political meaning of Dickinson's poems and letters rests not with the absence of political content but rather with her refusal to establish a stable political position. She contradicts herself with great frequency and remains curiously disengaged from liberal causes and the sorts of female reform movements she might have been expected to participate in as an educated, white, middle-class woman whose father was a well-known political figure. The argument I make looks at even Dickinson's detachment from overt political action as the product of an ongoing democratic decision-making process, visible across the entire body of her work, which ceaselessly magnifies the role of individual choice and profoundly governs the spirit of her work.

The act of choosing is crucial throughout Dickinson's work, and what makes the identification of a consistent political position especially difficult is the fact that her writing concentrates far more on the importance of making choices than on the advocacy of specific outcomes. Dickinson elevates democratic political awareness among her readers by demonstrating that even the most insignificant seeming or "natural" behavior can mask complex thought processes through which all people translate fundamental values into actions that define them as political beings. Precisely because she insists that experience not be entered blindly and therefore articulates the multiple choices often obscured by force of habit and cultural assumption, she may be considered a democratic poet who models resistance to conformity as an expression of individual sovereignty. Dickinson scholarship has been slow to acknowledge this essentially democratic dimension of Dickinson's writing at least in part because her assertions of sovereignty so often take place on the level of epistemology, leading critics to concentrate on the implications for the interior self rather than the self's relationship to the larger world.

The Domestic Context for Democratic Thought

Despite the relative absence of overt political content in Dickinson's poems and letters, in at least one sense Dickinson's link to the larger world of public politics was undeniable. Her father's active participation in politics as a Whig candidate and officeholder meant that to some degree awareness of political debates and the principles of party affiliation must have impinged on the thought and conduct of Dickinson family members within the privacy of the family home. This is a point of particular interest to Coleman Hutchison, who draws on Lauren Berlant's concept of an "intimate public sphere" to recommend that scholars acknowledge "the manifold ways Emily Dickinson's intimate experience of everyday life managed to be both private *and* public" (8, 9). Hutchison is particularly interested in demonstrating that Edward Dickinson's Whig activism, in combination with Dickinson's brother Austin's participation in Amherst public life, meant that "Emily Dickinson's house was necessarily a *political* house; a house in which the politics of the day were, one assumes, discussed with some regularity" (10). Betsy Erkkila further confirms this position in "Dickinson and the Art of Politics" where she declares that "Whig political culture inhabited her house" (139). The question of Whig influence, particularly in terms of educational philosophy and her father's attitudes toward personal choice and political consent, is for these reasons well worth exploring, if only briefly. Doing so demonstrates that discussions of choice were very much in the air, so much so that we should take into account the probability that her personal encounters with political views had some impact on her writing. Even though we can never ascertain the precise degree that political questions informed her conscious thought, we can still identify ways broad principles register in what she wrote.

What can be said with confidence is that Whig interest in questions related to popular consent is widely acknowledged in scholarly studies of the American Whig party. Donald S. Lutz makes the case in *Popular Consent and Popular Control: Whig Political Theory in the Early State Constitutions* that the Whig party contained traditional and radical branches that differed according to emphasis on individual consent. Within the traditional view, "Whigs did not believe that the interests of the many conflicted with the interests of the wealthy few" (39). Consequently, "To say that the community can share in sovereignty through representation is to use representation in the Whig sense of electing men to dispassionately seek and serve the interest of the entire community instead of that portion of the electorate that respectively elected them" (17). Radical Whigs, however, advocated a higher level of individual political participation by treating "consent as an everyday process, one in which the people could and did intervene in every phase of government" (40). In *The Political Culture of the American Whigs,* Daniel Walker Howe also addresses these differences within the Whig party, observing that Edmund Burke's "respect for public opinion as a means of social control" (236) helped to "mediate between [Whig] conservatism and [Whig] progressivism" (235). One outcome of these ongoing tensions, Thomas Brown argues in *Politics and Statesmanship: Essays on the American Whig Party,* was the Whig conviction that democracy was best achieved through education that sought to elevate the masses by "level[ing] upward," rather than downward, and that virtue resided in individual effort (45). Such a view does indeed reflect class prejudices of the sort easily detectable in Dickinson's writing, and it also explains how a writer like Dickinson might treat the presence of democratic choice as one of the givens of daily life. By the same token, there is no way of knowing whether or not Dickinson consciously applied the Whig educational logic of leveling upward to her own poetry, thereby justifying her demands on readers as part of a larger democratic effort to elevate public opinion.

That Dickinson was familiar with debates over choice, consent, and sovereignty does seem probable, though, particularly in light of her father's active participation in politics and her own trip to the nation's capitol in 1855. Edward Dickinson's stints as a Whig politician in the Massachusetts House of Representatives for 1838–1839 and 1873–1874, in the state senate during 1842 and 1843, and in the United States Congress from 1853 to 1855 make it extremely likely that an observer as astute as Emily Dickinson would follow political events closely, even if details were not part of daily conversations within the home.[1] Alfred Habegger's account of Edward Dickinson's political career proposes that Edward placed a premium on local sovereignty and that he did not believe in concealing his political position. Habegger points out that even though "in 1840 he defended three local blacks who had abducted an eleven-year-old black orphan girl to keep her from being sold into slavery," Edward "detested abolition" because he believed "that a federal prohibition of slavery would violate state sovereignty and undo the Constitution" (293). In an effort to preserve state sovereignty, Edward vocally supported Daniel Webster, "straddling the difficulty in the classic Whig way."[2] His future in Congress was ultimately terminated when Edward steadfastly held to the Whig platform in the 1854 elections that saw the party's demise (294–298).

Further evidence that Edward maintained his insistence on political open- ness and the importance of individual choice may be found in his May 1862 let- ter to Charles Sumner. His support for the United States senator's effort to " 'rec- ognize the Independence of Hayti & Liberia' " (qtd. in Hirschorn 5) reflects the senior Dickinson's continuing engagement with questions of sovereignty and consent. By supporting legislation granting equality to black diplomats in Wash- ington, Edward openly allies himself with northern abolitionist interests while also expressing his desire that elected officials publicly declare their true political allegiances. " 'We shall all now call things by their right names,' " he declares to Sumner, and " 'so shake up the extremes of conservatism & radicalism that the veins [?] of our Republican institutions will be wide [?] & proud and enduring.' " This pronounced desire to expose political decisions to public scrutiny reflects a concern with choice directly linked not only to the decisions made by elected of- ficials, but also to the public's role in consenting to continued representation by officials whose choices may be at odds with public opinion.[3] Tempting as it may be to conclude that Dickinson seized on her father's wish to make choice a visible component of responsible political action and deliberately incorporated it as a core feature of her own democratic thought and writing, such a conclusion is at best speculative. Knowing that the Whig party debated the role of choice and that Dickinson's father magnified the importance of choice in his own public conduct merely enables us to say that Dickinson's own interest in choice is con- sistent with the intellectual environment she inhabited.

Considering choice as a component within Dickinson's characteristic habit of thought performs the useful function of connecting her to her historical circum- stance while at the same time suggesting an approach to reading her work that brings out its political content. This approach does not dismiss studies that pre- sent her speakers as either reliable lyric subjects or representations of Dickinson's own positions, but it does propose additional readings that situate the poems out- side the lyric frame. A clear example of this is a reading of "The Soul selects her own Society –" (Fr 409) that differs significantly from the critical tendency to view the speaker as applauding the self's withdrawal from the public world.[4] As I will argue on multiple occasions in what follows, the speaker who witnesses the soul's selection of one "from an ample nation" and observes her "close the Valves of her attention – / Like Stone –" might just as easily be dismayed by the soul's decision to exercise her sovereignty in this manner. More important, as readers of the poem who witness the speaker's relation to the soul we might want to as- sess for ourselves the democratic implications of being cut off from the soul's "divine Majority." Similarly, in "There is a flower that Bees prefer –" (Fr 642), I look at the way the poem poses questions about democratic sovereignty that readers are free to evaluate independently of the speaker. In this particular case, a poem that ostensibly operates as a riddle designed to fuse reader and speaker through discovery of the riddle's answer can also interrogate the riddle's unifying function as analogous to social pressures that threaten democratic independence. The oxymoronic yoking of "Purple" and "Democrat" that appears early in the poem can be interpreted as the first of many efforts to unite opposites that might easily raise questions in the minds of readers who ultimately view the speaker's use of the riddle structure as an unacceptable effort to appropriate disruptive tensions. Such a reading would question the speaker's efforts to impose a uniform voice on an unruly set of contesting impulses. As with "The Soul selects her own Society – ," this poem can be understood as encouraging reader evaluation of the speaker as part of a reading process that identifies multiple conflicting interpretations among which readers must make choices. The act of choosing one reading over another does not, however, eliminate the appeal of unselected readings; choosing instead becomes an assertion of sovereignty on the part of the reader made possible by the poem's ultimate undecidability.

The Role of Authorial Intent

As the above discussion of political influences indicates, the inability to determine Dickinson's intentions does not mean that her historical context is inconsequential. On the contrary, the precise conditions of Dickinson's historical experience gain significance as a means of answering questions that arise in connection with the way her political sensibility reflects her social status. Rather than asking whether or not Dickinson intended to be political, however, I would prefer to ask about the ways in which she can be positioned within the discussion of literature and politics that is ongoing today. In such a discussion, it is particularly important to bear in mind the distinct possibility that Dickinson may have been more aware of the political freight of her writing then we are now and that she may not have self-consciously reflected on her political position for the simple reason that she understood politics to be an inherent feature of all writing. Shira Wolosky provides a foundation for such a view when she argues that the "notion of poetry as a self-enclosed aesthetic realm; as a formal object to be approached through more or less exclusively specified categories of formal analysis; as metahistorically transcendent; and as a text deploying a distinct and poetically 'pure' language" begins to emerge only "at the end of the nineteenth century" ("Claims" 14). Accordingly, we might expect a poet like Dickinson to reflect the nineteenth-century view of poetry as "actively participating in the national life" by devoting "poetic vision to political, social, religious, and moral concerns, as well as aesthetic ones." Equally important, we can expect to find in Dickinson's work "a heightened definition and self-consciousness" of "general rhetorical constructions, in ways that may both reinforce and critique them" (15). With this in mind, the reading that I am proposing draws attention to Dickinson's engagement with political currents, many of which are visible in her use of contemporary rhetoric, without diminishing the aesthetic achievement of her work or imputing individual intent to all the many gestures that may strike modern readers as openly political.

My procedure in assessing the level of Dickinson's conscious intent is quite understandably influenced by poststructuralist theories like those associated with Roland Barthes and Michel Foucault, who have made strong arguments about the significance of texts independent of authorial intent. "Linguistically," Barthes writes, "the author is never more than the instance of writing" (145). For Foucault, this means "depriving the [authorial] subject (or its substitute) of its role as originator, and of analyzing the subject as a variable and complex function of discourse" (158). Getting at the complexities Foucault alludes to does not, however, mean jettisoning all concern with authorial intent. As Sharon Cameron has pointed out in the case of Dickinson, "the question of intention, at least on one level, is not undecidable—because we know that Dickinson intended something" (*Choosing* 18). For the purposes of this study, while assertions of intention must remain, in Cameron's words, "speculative" (7n.6), they must also be contemplated in order to achieve what Robert Scholes has described as the level of sympathetic reading necessary for "a critical distancing and examination of that intention" (169). In other words, I want to move the discussion of authorial intent from the undecidable to the debatable. The argument presented here advances on the supposition that intentionality can be approached as nonregulatory, providing what Annabel Patterson describes as the "comfort" of knowing that "we are not required to be *regulatory* on the subject" (145). Martha Nell Smith draws on Patterson's words in offering her own thoughts about a procedure for approaching authorial intent that might just as easily apply to this work: "speculating about Dickinson's intentions, we need not be regulatory and draw inflexible conclusions circumscribing her desires or literary experimentations, but, aware that our horizons of expectations are predetermined by standard histories and literary traditions, should consciously cultivate horizonal change" (*Rowing* 57). What follows in this study, then, is an analysis of Dickinson's writing that seeks to expand the critical horizon by investigating the political implications of reader choice.

To pretend that all the many elements of Dickinson's texts that promote democratic choice appear in the absence of conscious or deliberate effort on her part would, I believe, be inconsistent with the high level of intellectual awareness that pervades her writing in general. I would also be disingenuous if I did not admit that to my own way of thinking Dickinson's persistent assertion of choice, in almost all facets of her writing, so closely resembles the evidence one would gather to argue in support of author intent that to me it qualifies for precisely that, an argument for intent. At the same time, I must insist that presenting an argument that accepts some level of authorial intent does not by any means reduce or discount the significance of cultural influences that may well have shaped Dickinson's writing in ways that escaped her conscious knowledge. By arguing for Dickinson's awareness that she was building choice into her writing, I am not also arguing that she was fully aware of *all* the various ways choice surfaced in her creative life. I agree with Sally Bushell that when it comes to her holograph manuscripts especially, "Dickinson allows space within the creative process for unintended meaning and that such space, and such meaning, is an integral part of creative composition" (26). Dickinson understood that the creative process itself introduces meanings beyond those consciously selected by the author. For instance, a certain fascination with democratic choice may well have entered her thinking as a consequence of growing up in a Whig household in the years leading up to the Civil War, when Whig politicians were particularly concerned with the balance between local and federal authority and the role of the individual in the formation of popular consent. Yet knowing that these issues shaped discourse that almost certainly intruded on Dickinson's conscious experience is not the same as stating the exact level of awareness she brought to these issues each time they surfaced in her writing.

Conflicting Political Stances in Dickinson's Writing

One of the primary reasons that choice and its relationship to undecidability plays so prominent a role in my discussion of Dickinson's democratic politics is the fact that she so consistently attributes greater value to the process of making choices than to the development of a consistent political position that either resulted from or informed those choices. The written record plainly reveals that Dickinson assumed varied and frequently conflicting political postures throughout her life. The early poem "Sic transit gloria mundi" (Fr 2), for instance, humorously presents a speaker whose "country bids me go" to "the Legislature" and who bids the reader "Good bye" because "My country calleth me." In sharp contrast to such openly political sentiments, one might propose the inwardly oriented speaker of "To fight aloud, is very brave –" (Fr 138) who declares those to be "*gallanter* . . . Who charge within the bosom / The Cavalry of Wo – ." Similarly, the aristocratic speaker of "The Lamp burns sure – within –"

(Fr 247), who describes "Serfs" who "supply the Oil" and a "Slave" who "forgets – to fill – / The Lamp," might be opposed to the racially sensitive and egalitarian speaker of "Color – Caste – Denomination –" (Fr 836), who describes "Death's large – Democratic fingers" that "Rub away the Brand" of color and caste so that as "Equal Butterfly – // They emerge from His Obscuring."[5]

The letters present a like range of political postures.[6] When Dickinson protests to Susan Gilbert in June 1852 that she wants to "be a Delegate to the great Whig Convention," stating that she "knows all about Daniel Webster, and the Tariff, and the Law," she clearly presents herself as qualified for a political role she is denied on the basis of her sex (L 212). She expresses a like political impulse in her 1861 letter-poem to Austin, where she exhorts him to "[l]ook *further on!*" and not associate with "Frank Conkey," a political rival of their father's (L 381). Such direct intervention into male politics stands in sharp opposition to Dickinson's dismissal of female reform efforts, as in her January 1850 letter to Jane Humphrey, where she looks down her nose at the Sewing Society's efforts to feed and clothe the poor. "I don't attend," she writes, "notwithstanding my high approbation – which must puzzle the public exceedingly" (L 84).[7] In like manner, she writes dismissively of female reform in her 1872 letter to Louise Norcross, where she ridicules the efforts of female writers who see it as their duty to "extricat[e] humanity from some hopeless ditch" (L 500).[8]

Perhaps as a result of such contradictions, popular assessments of Dickinson's politics, as well as scholarly commentaries and responses by other poets, have expressed a broad and often contradictory array of opinions about the politics of Dickinson's poetry.[9] The poet Sharon Olds's statement that Dickinson is "intensely political" is representative of the view subscribed to by many women writers who have acknowledged Dickinson's influence on their own political writing (12). However, the broad view that literature in general can be political has been openly challenged by the comments of no less a public and political personage than first lady Laura Bush, who stated in a 2003 *New York Times* interview that Dickinson and indeed all of "'American literature is not political'" (qtd. in Bumiller 1A). Within the academic community, where there is less controversy over the potential political content of literature, there remain pronounced differences of opinion over Dickinson's relation to politics. Literary scholar Geoffrey Sanborn's recommendation that Dickinson *not* be viewed "as someone whose self-gratifying isolation is essentially at odds with democratic sociality" (1345) is consistent with the position I support. Betsy Erkkila may be understood as speaking for the opposing view when she argues that Dickinson "never conceived of taking her struggle into the public sphere" (*Sisters* 49) and that her "rhetoric" is most accurately "translated not into a dream of democracy but into a royalist dream of rule by hereditary and divine right" (51). This is a position Paula Bernat

Bennett supports, albeit from a slightly different angle, when she compares Dickinson to Sarah Piatt, another nineteenth-century American poet: "Piatt's kind of poetry—poetry wedded to social commitment, to politics—could not be more antithetical to Dickinson's largely insular and language-oriented art and should not be compared to it" (*Palace* L).

As this range of opinion suggests, central to the perception of political presence or absence is the perceiver's understanding of what constitutes writing that reaches beyond the highly personal domain of aesthetic contemplation to grapple with important social concerns. This is a point that emerges with startling force in Katha Pollitt's commentary on the political spotlight Laura Bush inadvertently directed on Dickinson when she canceled the February 2003 White House literary gathering that was to have featured Walt Whitman, Langston Hughes, and Dickinson. "Dickinson," she writes, "might seem the least political, but in some ways she was the most lastingly so—every line she wrote is an attack on complacency and conformity of manners, mores, religion, language, gender, thought" (2). As Pollitt's phrasing suggests, there is a sense in which Dickinson may "seem" at first glance not to be political and yet acquires political weight upon reflection. Part of the reason for this nearly simultaneous denial and assertion of political content has to do with the way Dickinson's writing resists containment within any single interpretive frame.

The Politics of Linguistic Undecidability

Within the terms of postmodern literary theory, the principle of linguistic undecidability usefully accounts for the propagation of multiple meanings in a manner that applies directly to the sort of reading I am advocating. As Jacques Derrida has explained, undecidability derives from the fact that the same linguistic signifier ("story") can correspond to a different meaning or signified (a form of narrative or one floor of a multistoried building), depending on context and point of view. As a consequence, no author can control the meaning of the texts he or she creates. Readers discover new meanings in literary works for the simple reason that each reader approaches the work from a different perspective, investing it with significance necessarily different from that detected by other readers. As Derrida puts it, "No context can entirely enclose it" (*Limited Inc* 9). Such an expansion of interpretive possibilities, however, potentially erodes the foundation for agreement among readers as to what a text is or what it means because it casts reading as the outcome of difference rather than sameness.

This is a matter of particular interest to Walter Benn Michaels, who points out that when the signifier has been definitively separated from what it signifies, the signifier ceases to act as a sign and instead operates as a mark. To be a sign is to signify the same meaning in each instance, whereas a mark signifies different meanings (125). Michaels expresses concern over the theoretical implications issuing from the transformation of sign to mark, concluding that literary criticism is stripped of its capacity to debate the rightness or wrongness of interpretation once it is established that no two readers attach the same meanings to the marks that appear on the literary page. Literary interpretation becomes the expression of different subject positions that cannot be debated for the simple reason that each subject position is a unique cultural expression that cannot be evaluated according to a universal standard. Because one subject position is equal to another, the outcome is the emergence of literary scholarship as a field of divergent perspectives that acquire authority on the basis of their beauty, their elegance, or some other rhetorical or stylistic feature, rather than their capacity to establish accuracy or truth. Before criticism can support debate about what a text really means, in other words, readers must acknowledge that they are reading the same thing, not something different.

The challenge of moving from difference to sameness is of central importance to this study because my aim is to establish that Dickinson's writing contains significant political content even while acknowledging that the poems and letters I examine retain a measure of difference consistent with undecidability. For this reason, the readings I present are best understood as enacting the movement from mark to sign that has special application to Dickinson purely because her intense concern with reader choice draws attention to the way reading is itself fundamentally democratic. Simply stated, all reading that yields critical insight must at some stage of the reading process both enter into and then emerge from the incomprehensible, raw sensation provoked by the mark. Derrida describes the situation of the subject when confronting the possibility of imposing order on difference as one that "calls for decision in the order of ethical-political responsibility" (*Limited Inc* 116). He further stipulates that the decision to make one's experience of the mark comprehensible to others leads to the assertion of political meaning precisely because doing so unsettles the field of sameness: "A decision can only come into being in a space that exceeds the calculable program that would destroy all responsibility by transforming it into a programmable effect of determinate causes. There can be no moral or political responsibility without this trial and this passage by way of the undecidable." In this sense, then, undecidability is part of the reading process itself that plays a larger role in the conscious experience of reading Dickinson than it does with most writers because her focus on reader choice steadfastly sustains awareness of alternative interpretive possibilities and requires that readers confront their own difference.

In this book, my aim is to illuminate the democratic dimension of Dickinson's writing by tracing some of the ways her poetry and letters enable readers to confront their own difference and then make that difference intelligible within a space shared with others. I argue that the democratic focus of Dickinson's poems emerges through the choices readers make when they encounter undecidability and choose either to affirm the beauty of isolated lyric subjectivity or invest that subjectivity with the degree of objective sameness necessary for any meaningful engagement with the larger world. If the reader decides to position the poem in the realm of isolated subjectivity, then the poem has no direct political purchase; but if the poem is understood as requiring choices that potentially change the reader's relationship to others, then the poem must be seen as political. My job is to magnify the democratic dimension of Dickinson's poems.

Scholarship Supporting Reader Choice

The interpretive slipperiness of Dickinson's poems and letters has been a subject of considerable interest within Dickinson scholarship. The poet and literary scholar Alicia Ostriker speaks for many when she observes of Dickinson's poetry, "contrary meanings coexist with equal force" (*Stealing* 40–41). Writing specifically of Dickinson's lyric voice, Margaret Dickie argues in like manner that Dickinson's voice "speaks from shifting perspectives, . . . inhabits various frequencies, . . . has no center but rather many circumferences" (27). Shira Wolosky also points to this feature of Dickinson's writing when she notes, "Dickinson texts . . . both say and unsay, claim and disclaim, desire and decline, offer and retract, assert and deny, gain and lose" ("being" 132). Wolosky then concludes that "Dickinson's texts are scenes of cultural crossroads, situated within the many and profound transitions taking place around her" (138).

Linking Dickinson's texts to multiple, frequently contesting interpretive stances has become a widely accepted approach to Dickinson's writing that I consider particularly useful in discerning the democratic implications of her writing, even though this approach further complicates efforts to state exactly what Dickinson's political position is. In my previous book on Dickinson, *Inflections of the Pen: Dash and Voice in Emily Dickinson,*[10] I drew attention to the many possible interpretations that might be sustained by one of Dickinson's most famous poems, "This is my letter to the World" (Fr 519). I argued that once the disjunctive power of Dickinson's dashes is taken into account, readers can inflect the speaker's voice in such radically contrary fashion that the poem appears both to affirm and deny key social values having to do with nature and female experience (15–18).[11]

This is my letter to the World
That never wrote to Me –
The simple News that Nature told –
With tender Majesty

Her message is committed
To Hands I cannot see –
For love of Her – Sweet – countrymen –
Judge tenderly – of Me

Given the voicing possibilities supported by Dickinson's open-ended syntax, readers can construct both the conformist voice of the reticent female speaker and
that speaker's opposite: a defiant, radically iconoclastic and disdainful woman.
The first of these voices, that of the conventional domestic female, reluctantly
and rather plaintively addresses the "World / That never wrote to Me," plead-
ing with readers to "Judge tenderly" of her because what she communicates as
"The simple News that Nature told" is not the product of her own independent
thought. Just as easily, though, the poem allows readers to imagine an altogether
different speaker: a highly unorthodox, bitter woman who loudly complains that
because "the World / . . . never wrote to Me," nature's message passed into "Hands
I cannot see," enforcing an isolation out of which she sarcastically solicits the
tenderness of "countrymen" she does not consider in the least bit "Sweet."

Precisely because the poem allows for the perception of conventional and unconventional female speakers, it may be read as both denying and proclaiming a
subversive political message. One reading proposes that nature brings "Majesty"
to the private woman, the other that the world's construction of nature has nothing to do with the actual experience of at least one woman. The initial reading
can be understood as a politically neutral affirmation of social orthodoxy, the
other a politically subversive challenge to the totalizing view of nature used to
support socially acceptable forms of female conduct. That this particular Dickinson poem should present readers with choices about voice and political content is consistent with Dickinson's poetry in general, throughout which readers
affirm their own democratic sovereignty by consenting to interpretive possibilities arrived at independent of the writer's control.

My practice of identifying the multiple voices active in Dickinson's poems
is part of an increasingly widespread scholarly adoption of dialogic theory associated most commonly with the works of Mikhail M. Bakhtin. In "Dickinson's Dialogic Voice," I argued that while voice has long been a topic of interest
in literary scholarship, the availability of Bakhtin's works in English translations
"acts as a watershed moment after which voice acquires new focus and direction

within discussions of Dickinson's poetics" (93). The following passage from that essay clarifies the way Bakhtin's analysis of voice can contribute to readings, like Wolosky's, that understand Dickinson's texts as "scenes of cultural crossroads" ("being" 138):

> Bakhtin proceeds on the assumption that all living language is social, consisting of utterances with specific speech properties, including voice. Within this framework, voice expresses the unique perspective of a speaker whose utterances generate experience through dialogue with the historical meaning of words. "Heteroglossia" is Bakhtin's term for the point where conservative, centripetal histories of words meet the centrifugal forces of the present. "The processes of centralization and decentralization . . . intersect in the utterance; the utterance not only answers the requirements of its own language . . . but it answers the requirements of heteroglossia as well" (Bakhtin, *Dialogic* 272). Words like "revolution" and "free market" that are quickly implicated in specific ideologies readily express the tensions Bakhtin describes between the centripetal histories of words and the centrifugal expansion of meanings possible in present utterances. The voice that emerges through such a dialogue with prior discourse implicitly or explicitly comments on that discourse; this commentary can then be read as the "socio-ideological position of the author amid the heteroglossia of his era" (300). (Crumbley, "Dialogic Voice" 97)

The existence of multiple voices in a single poem, as in "This is my letter to the World," is consistent with the Bakhtinian position that all language contains multiple voices, so that even a poem that falls into the category of "lyric" may display polyphonic qualities. In "The Problem of the Text," Bakhtin asks, "Is not any writer (even the pure lyricist) always a 'dramaturge' in the sense that he directs all words to others' voices, including the image of the author (and to other authorial masks)?" He then answers his own question: "Perhaps any literal, single-voiced word is naïve and unsuitable for authentic creativity" (*Speech Genres* 110).[12] Erika Scheurer's 1995 observation that "Dickinson scholarship has arrived . . . at the point where we recognize the dialogic quality of Dickinson's textual voices in their flux and play" conveys the degree that Bakhtin's latter conclusion has become a commonplace in Dickinson scholarship (90).

Scheurer's conclusion that scholarship now recognizes Dickinson's dialogic voice has important application to studies like this one that explore the centrality of choice for both Dickinson as author and for her readers. The perception of multiple voices in poems and letters has made clearer than ever before the extent that Dickinson's "vice for voices" engages readers in a form of collaboration

with the author that democratically levels reader and author functions (*L* 914).[13]
Cristanne Miller describes the way "the reader must continually stabilize the
text by choosing what belongs in it and at the same time repeatedly return to account for the other, unchosen, possibilities of the poem's meaning" (*Grammar*
49). Gary Lee Stonum argues that the "reader . . . becomes a writer—part poet,
part recording auditor" (*Sublime* 11). Martha Nell Smith, like Stonum and Miller,
identifies the particular significance of Dickinson's dialogic writing in terms of
reader collaboration with the manuscript text. "Her manuscripts," Smith asserts,
"will not let us forget that reading is a dialogic drama, always a matter of editing, of choosing what to privilege, what to subordinate" (*Rowing* 53). Choice
is most profoundly addressed as a primary issue in Sharon Cameron's *Choosing Not Choosing*, where she explores Dickinson's refusal to resolve the choices
she extends to readers. Cameron argues that "in Dickinson's poetry the apparent need to choose is countered by the refusal to choose" (*Choosing* 21), a refusal
"that results in a heteroglossia whose manifestations inform every aspect of the
poetry" (29). More recently, Domhnall Mitchell has argued that Dickinson increases reader choice through language that resists social conformity: "Dickinson reverses the assignment of heteroglossia to social discourses: it is society that
closes down meaning, and the poet who attempts to open it up again" (*Monarch*
231). In yet another recent study, Marietta Messmer seeks to specify the precise
form dialogicity assumes in Dickinson's correspondence, asserting that "Dickinson maintains a high degree of dialogicity while *simultaneously* introducing controlling focal voices that orchestrate, frame, curtail, and thus critique some of
the other 'participants' in the dialogue" (150). The question that concerns scholars most now is no longer whether or not multiple voices operate in Dickinson's
writing, but how she deploys these voices and what significance we ought to attach to the simultaneous presence of diverse points of view.

Democratic Choice in an Age of Dissensus

This acknowledgment of multiple voices in Dickinson's writing can significantly
complicate the discernment of specific political content because such a multi-
plicity of speaker positions can easily support the simultaneous perception of
conformity and resistance. Readers are free to select the voices most familiar to
them or most congenial to their particular critical approach and therefore perceive sameness and avoid encounters with the undecidable. On the face of it,
however, such a problem is by no means unique to Dickinson. Literary scholars
now debate the politics of writers like Ralph Waldo Emerson, Herman Melville,
and Walt Whitman precisely because what was seen as politically significant in an
earlier historical period no longer seems acceptably political today. To be precise,

these writers are being interrogated because their prior association with American individualism is interpreted as furthering a consensus view of American history within which individuals contributed to the achievement of a hegemonic cultural ideology. Myra Jehlen succinctly assesses this shift in scholarly orientation: "The notion of an all-encompassing American identity, in literature as in society, now appear[s] not only incomplete but, in its denial of nonhegemonic difference, actually repressive" (4). As long as Americans considered American culture exceptional and therefore deriving its distinctive character from an amalgamation of unique personalities, the literary elevation of individual experience made sense. Slogans like "E Pluribus Unum"[14] achieved and retained national currency throughout the significant historical period during which time writers as historically separated as Hector St. John de Crèvecoeur, Frederick Jackson Turner, and R.W.B. Lewis independently promoted a consensus vision of America as a democratic melting pot, replete with an infinitely renewable Adamic self widely viewed as representing the aspirations of all citizens.

However, now that American literature has expanded to include traditions that steadfastly affirm a growing spectrum of divergent cultural identities, this neat linear paradigm is increasingly defined as an expression of cultural sameness that must yield to a far more diffuse spatial model based on cultural differences that resist assimilation. As Paul Giles has argued, American literature today might more accurately be conceived as transnational, sustaining cultural ties to multiple global traditions and geographic regions. Such a transnational approach, Giles proposes, "seeks various points of intersection, whether actual border territories or other kinds of disputed domain, where cultural conflict is lived out experientially" (65). By emphasizing the ways "particular forms of individual freedom and human rights can be rendered legible only in specific historical and national contexts," this approach defines freedom as "a material condition rather than a disembodied ethical or philosophical concern" (74). The existence within American literature of distinct traditions, such as African American, Native American, Japanese American, and Chicano/a, to name just a few, tells us that America already represents itself on the page in a manner firmly rooted in specific historical conditions and therefore is harder to ethically and philosophically distinguish from the rest of the world than used to be the case. Like other countries, America increasingly represents itself in its literature as home to diverse communities whose distinctive racial and ethnic histories resist social amalgamation within a unified narrative of national identity.

An important strand of the argument I make in this book is that Dickinson's writing yields significant political content when interpreted in the context of scholarly debate over the politics of American individualism, precisely because her writing so often teeters on the boundary between individual and collective identity, between consensus and dissensus. By reading her work as a commentary on what might be thought of as the dangerous allure of nineteenth-century individualism, we discover in Dickinson an astonishingly articulate white, middle- or upper-middle-class American woman who painstakingly exposes the many pitfalls that undermine the democratic sovereignty of nineteenth-century women like her. The clear implication of this line of argumentation is that by situating Dickinson within the historical frame of her class, her race, and her gender, her political appeal to others is enhanced. Once her writing is understood as expressing a form of democratic resistance anchored in a specific socioeconomic locus, she can speak across community boundaries precisely because she is understood as giving voice to one of many sites of political struggle. Readers from diverse communities coming to Dickinson in an age of dissensus see her as modeling sensitivity to the politics of decision making that they can translate into their own particular circumstances. In this sense, her epistemological orientation helps to explain her influence on the politics of readers by requiring that they discover how the resistance she models is best expressed in their own unique contexts.

The Nonegalitarian Democratic Writer

Unlike studies of Dickinson's writing that present class as an impediment to political influence, this study approaches class as essential to the successful communication of political content. This does not mean, however, that Dickinson's writing is equally accessible to all readers. Situating Dickinson's democratic thought process in the context of her class means that the voices audible in her poems and letters nearly always register class-based limitations that necessarily restrict the democratic reach of her writings. Voice, as Robert Pinsky has argued, has a special role to play in establishing the politics of poetry: "the social realm is invoked with special intimacy at the barely voluntary level of voice itself" (22). This is to say that while the voices that proliferate in Dickinson's poems and letters do indeed represent an expansion of reader and hence citizen access to the political concerns she engages through her writing, the very intimacy of this voice injects class bias and thus militates against universal or unfettered democratic access. As Mitchell has observed, the equality conveyed in Dickinson's writing rests "on the assumption of dialogue's mutuality, its egalitarianism," an assumption belied by the demand for "a certain kind of readership" (*Monarch* 232). The natural consequence is that for Dickinson, as for all writers, reader access requires a combination of background and motivation that limits audience, thus creating a reading experience founded on what political theorists have described as "non-egalitarian classlessness" (Ossowski 107), or the imperfect embodiment of democratic principles that occurs even when the writer's aim is to address all persons, irrespective of class.[15] Another way of saying this is to state that while Dickinson is not a *populist* writer, she is a democratic writer nonetheless.

I treat Dickinson's status as an imperfect or nonpopulist democrat as central to situating her accurately in the historical context of contemporary female writers, like Catherine Beecher and Sarah Josepha Hale, both of whom Nicole Tonkovich describes as writers who define "the conduct of a woman whose identity is uniquely American" and who are therefore dedicated to the production of "American citizens, either through the embodied labor of natural reproduction or in the mind-labor of cultural reproduction" (92). Significantly, as Tonkovich points out for both Beecher and Hale—and I would argue Dickinson, as well— these writers did not argue "for a perfectly democratic state wherein all claims to social class would be equally endorsed" (95). Instead, they sought to locate social identity "in character traits most appropriate to a democracy. Not surprisingly, these are qualities already possessed by entitled ladies" (96). One of the most serious challenges writers like Beecher, Hale, and Dickinson pose for modern readers is that of seeing these writers as imperfectly democratic but democratic nonetheless.

The difficulty twenty-first-century readers face when considering Dickinson's status as a democratic writer is even further compounded by her gender and the reality of female exclusion from active participation in the nineteenth-century sphere of public politics. This concern can be addressed by a growing body of historical scholarship that supports the argument that Dickinson integrated the principle of choice into her own thought process as part of a deliberate political project directly related to democratic sovereignty and consent. Even though Dickinson was a woman at a time when women were largely excluded from direct political action, there is ample historical support for Dickinson's potential interest in the democratic politics of choice as an expression of female citizenship.

Linda Kerber's authoritative account of the emergence of Republican Motherhood in the late eighteenth century as an interim step in the historical process of female political empowerment is now widely accepted as providing a foundation for nineteenth-century female political consciousness. Kerber writes that in Dickinson's day "woman . . . claimed a significant political role, though she played it in the home. This new identity had the advantage of appearing to reconcile politics and domesticity; it justified continued political education and political sensibility" (11).[16] According to this account of female political involvement, women inhabited a transitional status located between exclusion from politics and full enfranchisement. "The triumph of Republican Motherhood," Kerber notes, "also represented a stage in the process of women's political socialization" (284). Central to this process is the concept of "deference": "In recent years, political socialization has been viewed as a process in which an in-

dividual develops a definition of self as related to the state. One of the interme-
diate stages in that process is called deference, in which a person expects to influence the political system, but only to a limited extent. Deference represents not
a negation of citizenship, but an approach to full participation in civic culture"
(284–285). Barbara Bardes and Suzanne Gossett draw from the literature published by nineteenth-century women to clarify further the specific form female
citizenship took for women like Dickinson: "According to contemporaries, free
white women in the early nineteenth-century Republic were citizens with 'equal
rights,' in theory to those of men, and they were expected to learn and transmit
the same political culture as were their husbands and fathers. The political culture espoused dual spheres of activities for the sexes; women were responsible
for educating young children in the proper moral and patriotic virtues and for
upholding the same within the home, while men represented the household in
the external political world through discussion and voting" (3). Quite understandably, the "deference" described by Kerber and the theoretical but not actual
equality described by Bardes and Gossett combined to create an uncertain political environment for women.

A key underlying tension felt by many women had to do with the inconsistent implementation of liberal values that promoted democratic sensibility in all
citizens but inhibited female public expression. Bardes and Gossett conclude that
"this tension between the core principles of the American ideology and the cultural constraints placed on women engaged the attention of authors and readers throughout the century" (5). In this context, Dickinson's efforts to illuminate
contradictions within the cultural logic of her day, particularly as that logic applied to independent female self-expression, would define her conduct as consistent with the interests of her contemporaries.

The single feature that perhaps most distinguishes the democratic style of
Dickinson's writing from that of her contemporaries is the degree with which
she persistently presents reader choice as fundamental to a poetics anchored in
democratic citizenship. As demonstrated in "This is my letter to the World" and
the many other poems that represent conflicting perspectives, Dickinson places
readers in the position of making choices about poetic meaning that parallel the
sorts of decisions citizens are expected to make in a democratic society. Dickinson required that her readers deliberate on their own allegiances by acknowledging their position among the many voices that define the social context for
choice. In doing so, Dickinson contributes to an established tradition of democratic writing that affirms the primary significance of choice in democratic culture. Nowhere is the central role of choice more clearly expressed than in the first
number of *The Federalist*, where Alexander Hamilton situates choice at the heart
of the American experiment: "It has been frequently remarked, that it seems to

have been reserved to the people of this country, by their conduct and example, to decide the important question, whether societies of men are really capable or not, of establishing good government from reflection and *choice,* or whether they are forever destined to depend, for their political constitutions, on accident and force" (3, my emphasis). Hamilton's coupling of "reflection" with "choice" points immediately to the need for resistance, or the assertion of sovereignty, that then forms the basis for free thought and action, or the assertion of liberty.[17] By posing "accident and force" as the political alternatives to reflection and choice, Hamilton effectively establishes the way sovereignty makes possible a form of government that operates on the basis of liberty and consent.

Key Political Terms and an Application

As a final introductory comment prior to reviewing the content of the chapters to follow, I want to provide a set of basic operating definitions for the key concepts of democracy, sovereignty, consent, and liberty that have already come up in this introduction and that figure prominently in the ensuing analysis of Dickinson's writing. The first of these, "democracy," is defined in Noah Webster's 1828 *American Dictionary of the English Language* as "Government by the people; a form of government, in which the supreme power is lodged in the hands of the people collectively, or in which the people exercise the power of legislation." The fundamental democratic principle, here captured in the phrase "supreme power is lodged in the hands of the people," takes a slightly different but essentially equivalent form in the *Oxford English Dictionary,* where the phrase becomes "the sovereign power resides in the people."[18] The point is that supreme power is the same as sovereign power. This is why the *OED* defines "sovereignty" as one of many forms of supremacy, including "Supremacy in respect of power." The management of sovereignty by the people is consequently complicated by the fact that supreme power must somehow be distributed among multiple citizens, each of whom possesses a distinct will.[19] In this context, Harold Laski's conclusion that the "problem of the power of a State over its own members is, very largely, a problem of representing wills" (66) makes perfect sense. What is crucial in democracies in general and representative democracies in particular, then, is that the government effectively represents the wills of independent and sovereign citizens.

Once the sovereign will of the citizen is established, consent enters the picture as the citizen's decision to accept or reject political representation.[20] Perhaps the most famous and influential articulation of political consent is that provided by Richard Hooker: "whatsoever hath been after in a free and voluntary manner condescended unto, whether by express consent, whereof positive laws are witnesses, or else by silent allowance famously notified through custom reaching beyond the memory of man" (242). Consent in a representational democracy accordingly translates into the citizen's decision to accept current changes in political representation, as well as the ongoing decision to live by the deliberations of the past.[21]

Choice then informs both sovereignty and consent as the exercise of will essential to sovereignty and the acceptance or rejection of representation essential to consent. Liberty, in its civic manifestation, may be understood as the democratic citizen's ability to arrive at and implement the choices that make sovereignty and consent possible. "Civil liberty" is defined by the *OED* as "natural liberty so far restricted by established laws as is expedient or necessary for the good of the community." Thus civil liberty forms part of a circular line of reasoning that begins with the notion that in democracies free will is essential to establishing individual sovereignty and concludes with the assertion that the free exercise of that same will must be tempered "for the good of the community."

In many of her poems, Dickinson demonstrates that she is entirely capable of grasping the various contradictions contained within this democratic juggling of sovereignty and liberty. The poem "Revolution is the Pod" (Fr 1044) is but one of many in which she draws attention to the crucial role the will plays in ensuring that social conventions or governmental institutions perform as the guarantors of liberty and not its "entomber[s]":

Revolution is the Pod
Systems rattle from
When the Winds of Will are stirred
Excellent is the Bloom

But except it's [*sic*] Russet Base
Every summer be
The entomber of itself,
So of Liberty –

Left inactive on the Stalk
All it's Purple fled
Revolution shakes it for
Test if it be dead –

By linking liberty to revolution, the poem effectively frames the uneasy relationship between the free will that makes democratic sovereignty and consent possible and the limitations imposed on freedom required to secure the common good. The implication is that in democracies liberty depends on the citizen's determination to perpetuate revolution by refusing to accept as final any of the systems previously implemented with their consent. Dickinson's use of seasonal imagery combines with the repetition of the word "Revolution" to underscore the dynamic, revolving nature of democratic politics, according to which citizens may consent to the temporary restriction of liberties for a season, while never admitting permanent infringements. The flower of liberty may pass into dormancy for a winter season, but only with the understanding that it will bloom once again in the spring. The poem's relatively infrequent use of dashes may in this context be interpreted as signaling the ease with which the syntax of representational democracy threatens to resolve itself into seamless seeming patterns that threaten to replace sovereignty with complacency. The presence of dashes after both "Liberty" and "dead" reinforces the larger message that keeping liberty alive may require rupturing the sealed seedpod of convention, thus forcing the flower out of dormancy. Liberty, in this sense, rests on the individual citizen's obligation ceaselessly to contemplate alternatives to the status quo, in order that systems of government remain impermanent.[22] For Dickinson, such contemplation equates with weighing the choices that surround any course of action.

Overview of Chapters

My opening chapter begins by examining the widespread public and scholarly tendency to both affirm and deny the political significance of American literature in general and Dickinson's work in particular. I look at scholarly analysis of Emerson as providing an important example of how this very question is contested. I then argue that Dickinson scholarship exhibits significant parallels with debates over Emerson's politics and that the political content of her writing ought to receive the same degree of scrutiny his has. To make this point, I look at the way Dickinson's use of monarchical terminology has been used to define her work as either apolitical or nondemocratic, and then argue that her use of monarchical terminology is not elitist but rather consistent with democratic discourse carried out in America during the nineteenth century. I provide close readings of "There is a flower that Bees prefer –" as a prime example of Dickinson's use of monarchical language in an effort to promote democratic thought. I also examine "Unto like Story – Trouble has enticed me –" (Fr 300) and "I play at Riches – to appease" (Fr 856) as poems that explore cultural limitations imposed on the female political imagination. I end the chapter by looking at contemporary women writers who recognize the political content of Dickinson's writing and view Dickinson as an important influence on their own political writing.

In my second chapter, I explore the presence of democratic rhetoric in Dickinson's writing as a way of demonstrating her promotion of a gymnastic self through her use of a distinctly democratic verbal register. With this as background, I contrast Dickinson's rhetorical approach to that of Emerson and Whitman, concluding that Dickinson does not model proper democratic conduct the way they do. Instead, she creates a reading environment in which her readers must evaluate for themselves the cultural context she provides and imagine appropriate action not included in her poems. Here I turn my attention to the reader's experience of thinking beyond predictable patterns of behavior and drawing on personal experience to imagine a self incommensurate with past experience. I describe this kind of reading as developing a democratic habit of thought through collaboration with the author. I then look at the ways Dickinson's relationship with readers resembles that of contemporary women writers, concentrating on specific poems by Elizabeth Oakes-Smith, Alice Cary, Lydia Huntley Sigourney, and Helen Hunt Jackson. I end the chapter by exploring Dickinson's willingness to acknowledge the difficulty of achieving the subjective reorientation required for developing a democratic habit of thought.

My third chapter examines the way principles at the core of the spiritualist movement provided Dickinson with a means to further define the democratic self as incommensurate with its own utterances. I begin by looking at spiritualism as a movement widely viewed as democratic by virtue of the authority it granted women and its interest in democratic reform. I argue that Dickinson would have been particularly intrigued by spiritualism's basic premise that communication with the spirits of the departed greatly altered the understanding of the natural world experienced by the living. By presenting earthly nature as part of a vast spiritual domain, spiritualism unsettled the boundaries conventionally imposed on the natural world and thereby brought into question the social structures founded on assumptions about nature. One of the most dramatic examples of the way the supernatural could enter into the natural and reshape social conduct came through the advent of the female medium who, by virtue of her "natural" passivity, could become the channel for male spirits and speak in public with authority ordinarily reserved for males only. I make the case that Dickinson trades on the authority of the female medium through poems that raise questions about the possibility of ever acquiring a stable understanding of nature. These poems place readers in the position of juggling possibilities about what nature might be rather than settling on fixed definitions. As a consequence, utterance is approached as never more than the transient expression of a self incommensurate with the experience of any particular place and time. I describe Dickinson's poems as modeling incomplete embodiments of experiences that invite readers to enter the process of imagining self expression not confined by a fixed understanding of the natural world. Doing so requires the democratic habit of thought essential to the assertion of democratic sovereignty.

Chapter 4 concentrates on Dickinson's correspondence as a form of gift exchange that enables her to circulate her poems outside the restrictive protocols of commercial print culture. Gift culture's demand that participants register a degree of social intransigence in order that the giving and receiving of gifts reflect and confirm nonnormative values fits well with Dickinson's insistence on choice and democratic sovereignty. I look at the letters that passed between Dickinson and Helen Hunt Jackson, Susan Gilbert Dickinson, and Thomas Wentworth Higginson because in her correspondence with these three the subjects of publication and Dickinson's relationship to a larger public are particularly pronounced. The Jackson correspondence reveals primary tensions between Jackson and Dickinson that arise from their differing views of print publication. Jackson acts as a successful female poet who openly acknowledges Dickinson's poetic ability and tries to convince Dickinson that she should seek conventional publication. Dickinson responds with poems that magnify the role of reader choice and seek to bring about the joint affirmation of individual values that is at the heart of gift culture. Dickinson's correspondence with Susan reveals a mutual understanding of the role played by gift exchange as part of a collaborative effort to create poems that unsettle readers and provoke independent thought. Within the terms of gift culture, they drew strength from each other through the affirmation of shared values while retaining independent views on the proper method for the circulation of poems. The letters that passed between Dickinson and Higginson demonstrate that Higginson responded powerfully to the unsettling power of Dickinson's writing and rapidly adapted a posture of mutual affirmation even though Dickinson's intransigence continued to baffle him. I argue that Higginson was finally willing to risk public censure by attaching his name to the 1890 first edition of Dickinson's poems at least in part because of the respect he had gained for the intransigent and democratic habit of thought he had admired over the course of his epistolary relationship with Dickinson.

In my final chapter, I examine Dickinson's innovative approach to the textual body as a democratic response to debates over copyright legislation that increasingly threatened the public circulation of thought by extending authorial control over published works. My central argument is that Dickinson seeks to escape confinement within the public definition of female privacy that predetermines what form acceptable expressions of female experience might assume on the printed page. I look at the poem "To my quick ear the Leaves - conferred -" (Fr 912) to establish Dickinson's view of female privacy as an extension of culturally established gender expectations that include the precedent established by

Eve in the Old Testament. I then analyze "Ended, ere it begun –" (Fr 1048) as a specific example of the way nineteenth-century editorial norms conspire with biblical precedent, social expectation, and medical science to establish a public expectation that women writers were compelled to validate. Central to Dickinson's aims, I argue, is her insistence that published accounts of women's lives do not communicate the actual experiences of real women; instead, they perpetuate a highly constricted view of woman that severely limits the free exercise of female sovereignty. I approach "Publication – is the Auction / Of the Mind of Man –" (Fr 788) as a poem in which Dickinson takes a strong stand in opposition to the commercialized view of female experience required by print culture. Dickinson proposes instead a form of writing that centers on reader experience and does not arise through the originating power of an isolated author. In developing her experiments with the textual body, I present Dickinson as drawing on multiple textual practices that proliferated in the popular culture of her day. These include the portfolio tradition identified by Emerson, as well as the scrapbook, the autograph album, and the commonplace book, all of which encouraged the individual appropriation of texts created by others as the expression of a communally generated subjectivity. I conclude by arguing that Dickinson's poem "That sacred Closet when you sweep –" (Fr 1385) models the sort of reading Dickinson advocates.

1
Assertions of Sovereignty

This chapter begins by looking at the ease with which American culture finds it possible to confirm and deny the political importance of its literature. I am particularly interested in the degree that current affirmations and dismissals of Dickinson's politics follow a pattern paralleling current disputes surrounding Emerson's political significance.[1] I do this to clarify further the extent that a broad cultural tendency to see and not see the political content of literature informs scholarship focusing on an influential contemporary of Dickinson's and to make the case that the kind of debate that now addresses Emerson's politics might also be applied to Dickinson. Which is to say that I do not think enough attention has been given to the political implications of Dickinson's poems and letters. I point out that one reason for this relative lack of attention can be traced to a particular tangent of Dickinson criticism that interprets her use of monarchical terminology as evidence that she is so entrenched in conservative middle-class values that her writing does not contemplate political alternatives. To counter this argument, I first demonstrate the widespread use of monarchical tropes by Americans of all political stripes and then present readings of Dickinson poems that illuminate her concern with the exercise of individual sovereignty. I conclude the chapter by identifying contemporary female writers who consider Dickinson to be a political writer, as if doing so were entirely natural. In this sense, the end of the chapter contradicts the beginning by establishing contemporary recognition of Dickinson's political importance, recognition that I earlier declared to be lacking. My point in ending this way is to argue that American culture currently supports conflicting views of Dickinson's politics and for this reason scholarship should give at least as much attention to its presence as they have to its absence.

As a first step, I want to return to press coverage of the 2003 White House literary symposium that was to have included Dickinson as evidence of mainstream America's persistent uncertainty about literature's relationship to politics. In the October 7, 2002, *New York Times* story describing Laura Bush's early efforts to establish a series of White House symposiums on major American writers, reporter Elisabeth Bumiller observes in one line that "Mrs. Bush has reached out beyond ideology" and in the very next line quotes the first lady herself as stating, " 'There's nothing political about American literature' " (*Times* A1). Here American literature's power to address and potentially subvert political ideology is almost simultaneously affirmed and denied. Bumiller implies that literature is intensely political and hence public when she links literature to ideology that significantly differs from the White House political line, while Mrs. Bush implies that literature is fundamentally private and therefore not in opposition to White House politics when she declares that American literature is not political at all. The underlying assumption is that privacy and sameness equate with political neutrality in the same way that the experience of interior lives is a form of sameness all people share that becomes a matter of politics only when connected to deliberate forms of public expression.

However, as further coverage in the international press makes clear, in succeeding months the official White House position shifted so radically that Mrs. Bush "postponed" the scheduled February 12, 2003, symposium that was to feature Emily Dickinson, Walt Whitman, and Langston Hughes. Her decision, as explained by her spokeswoman, Noelia Rodriguez, came about because the literary community's response to White House political policies threatened to " 'turn a literary event into a political forum' " (Left 6). Sameness became difference because it was connected to public action the White House opposed. This transformation of a literary event from "not political" to excessively political seems an accurate register of the unstable relationship literature maintains with politics in contemporary America. Events acquire visibility and political purchase when they are perceivable as different; that is, when they possess properties that set them apart from normative or broadly held political views, they shed the invisibility of sameness. Katha Pollitt's commentary on these developments that appeared in *The Nation* lends support to this analysis while also communicating the slippery role Dickinson plays in relation to more openly political writers like Whitman and Hughes: "Dickinson," she writes, "might seem the least political, but in some ways she was the most lastingly so—every line she wrote is an attack on complacency and conformity of manners, mores, religion, language, gender, thought" (2). As Pollitt's phrasing suggests, there is a sense in which Dickinson's political identity slips in and out of focus, so that she seems incongruously charged with political excess one minute and entirely worthy of the charge the next.

The Debate over Emersonian Individualism

Scholars concerned with American literature's contributions to a national political culture have understandably grappled with the unstable view of literature
and politics that is so clearly captured in these accounts of literature at the White
House. Nowhere has this been more apparent than in the debate over the politics
of Emersonian individualism, a debate that has excluded Dickinson primarily
because critics see her as predominantly concerned with universal features of private experience that they judge to be politically neutral due to their grounding in
apolitical sameness.[2] For many, excessive devotion to privacy equates with bourgeois indifference and is judged fundamentally undemocratic and elitist.[3] Yet
the terms most central to the debate over individualism invite consideration of
Dickinson's work precisely because the tension between private and public that
is so crucial to the liberal political tradition is an established source of scholarly interest in Dickinson studies. Scholars have long pondered, for instance, the
relationship between Dickinson's refusal to publish and her well-publicized seclusion within one of the most socially and politically prominent homes in Amherst, Massachusetts.[4] That she grew up in a family dominated by a politically
active grandfather, father, and brother, during the era when individualism first
established currency in America, might easily be understood as increasing the
likelihood that she understood the importance of individualism in the political
discourse of her day.[5]

   Teasing out this possibility encourages the view that Dickinson would have
been well aware of the political issues at stake in the discourse surrounding individualism. When the term "individualism" first appeared in the 1820s (Brown,
Individualism 2), it did so in uneasy conjunction with democratic principles. In
this passage from his 1835 work, *Democracy in America,* Alexis de Tocqueville effectively expresses the citizen's problematic relationship to the larger community
that individualism promoted: "Individualism is a calm and considered feeling
which disposes each citizen to isolate himself from the mass of his fellows and
withdraw into the circle of family and friends; with this little society formed to
his taste, he gladly leaves the greater society to look after itself" (506). The immediate cause of Tocqueville's concern—that the individual citizen will not actively participate in the social sphere but rather withdraw into the isolation of
bourgeois domesticity—appears borne out in Ralph Waldo Emerson's famous
1842 journal entry stating that "union is only perfect when all the uniters are isolated" (*Selections* 216). Emerson goes on to establish the proper role of individualism within democratic culture: "Each man, if he attempts to join himself to
others, is on all sides cramped and diminished of his proportion; and the stricter

the union the smaller and the more pitiful he is. But leave him alone, to recognize in every hour and place the secret soul; he will go up and down doing the works of a true member, and, to the astonishment of all, the whole work will be done with concert, though no man spoke. Government will be adamantine without any governor." As this passage so plainly illustrates, the difficulty of reconciling Emersonian individualism with democracy rests in the uncertain balance struck between isolated, independent selfhood and active participation in political union.[6]

Given the cultural currency of the tensions so prominently associated with individualism, it is not particularly surprising that Emerson's approach to individualism as a fusion of private and public spheres, conjoining the private self with public forms of social authority, resonates in important ways with much of Dickinson's writing. Emerson shared the same historical moment, and, as Jack Capps has pointed out in his study of Dickinson's reading, "Emerson provides the strongest and most direct connection between Emily Dickinson's verse and nineteenth-century American literature" (119).[7] Her poems "Of Bronze – and Blaze –" (Fr 319), "Strong Draughts of Their Refreshing Minds" (Fr 770), and "To earn it by disdaining it" (Fr 1445) are representative of the many poems that propose forms of individual isolation out of which the speaker ultimately communicates with a larger public, seamlessly fusing the private and the public self. In "Of Bronze – and Blaze – ," the speaker models her conduct on the aurora borealis that she describes as "preconcerted with itself" and displaying an "Unconcern so sovereign / To Universe, or me" that "my simple spirit" is infected "With Taints of Majesty." Even though the speaker goes on to describe herself as assuming her own "vaster attitudes – / And strut[ting] opon [sic] my stem – / Disdaining Men, and Oxygen," she concludes by affirming that her "Splendors," like those of the aurora borealis, "Will entertain the Centuries / When I am long ago, / An Island in Dishonored Grass – / Whom none but Daisies, know – ." In "Strong Draughts," the speaker describes her receptivity to the "powerful . . . stimulus / Of an Hermetic Mind" that "enables" hers "To go elastic – Or as One / The camel's trait – attained." We learn that even though she continues alone "Through Desert or the Wilderness," she does so refreshed by communion with another ostensibly isolated bearer of "sealed Wine." The speaker in "To earn it by disdaining it" bluntly proclaims that fame "loves what spurns him," advocating what reads like an axiom stating that renown is achieved by those who avoid it.

Considering the frequency with which Dickinson's speakers assert the public function of private experience, it makes perfect sense to position her writing within the struggle to reconcile individualism with political activism that was a central feature of nineteenth-century American culture.[8] Doing so is especially important in Dickinson's case as her increasing withdrawal from participation in the public life of her family indicates a cultivation of privacy that exceeded even the stringent gender expectations of her day. Indeed, the degree that the debate over Dickinson's politics mirrors arguments over Emersonian individualism suggests that contrary to first impressions Dickinson deserves at least some of the political consideration Emerson has received, even though achieving a scholarly consensus regarding her politics may be no more likely than it has been with Emerson.[9]

Sacvan Bercovitch and John Carlos Rowe present opposing approaches to Emerson's politics that incorporate key terms that can and have been applied to Dickinson, though scholars have not yet discussed the similarities in the two debates. In *The Rites of Assent*, Bercovitch makes the case for the political efficacy of Emersonian individualism, arguing that Emerson practices a paradoxical form of dissent according to which individual "autonomy [is] preserved, precariously but decisively, . . . within the bounds of community" (344). In sharp contrast, Rowe argues in *At Emerson's Tomb* that the "radical individualism" (22) advocated by Emerson has contributed so significantly to the flawed politics of "aesthetic dissent" (1) that the whole tradition of American literature organized around the Emersonian self has become dangerously "depoliticized" (25, 248). For Rowe, the politics of American literature must be "revaluated both in terms of its critique of ideology . . . and the discursive communities such literature helps constitute" (14). Bercovitch instead anchors political efficacy in a "distinctive type of radical thought" (345) that may remain inchoate in its outward form but nevertheless subverts the foundations of liberal thought (348). Like Rowe, Dickinson scholar Betsy Erkkila argues that "it is unclear how [Dickinson's] poetic revolution might become an agent of social change" (*Sisters* 52), while another Dickinson scholar, Geoffrey Sanborn, resembles Bercovitch when he proposes that though "Dickinson does not participate in Marxian or postcolonial discourses, she does model a practice that is a precondition of those discourses" (1345). What these parallel arguments tell us is that the academy reflects mainstream America's schizoid view of literature and politics. When it comes to the academic consideration of individualism, the differences in perception are rooted in the way privacy is perceived as either an obstacle to collective action reinforced by class-based isolation or the essential ingredient of independent thought upon which political resistance depends, regardless of class identity.

Dickinson's Monarchical Terminology

In order to make the point that Dickinson is either apolitical or openly antagonistic to democratic principles, important Dickinson scholars have focused on Dickinson's use of monarchical terminology. Rather than interpreting this lan-

guage as an extension of middle-class America's complex and troubled relationship with the politics of individualism, the practice has been to treat all monarchical terms as evidence of class-based elitism. Monarchical terms become
equated with elitist politics, which are then condemned as unacceptably de-
tached from more communally oriented expressions of political activism. Literary scholars have, for instance, taken a special interest in "The Soul selects her
own Society –" (Fr 409), a poem in which the speaker describes a "Soul" who
first "shuts the Door – / To her divine Majority – ," leaving "an Emperor" outside "kneeling / Opon [*sic*] her Mat – ," then "Choose[s] One" from among "an
ample nation" and "close[s] the Valves of her attention – / Like Stone – ." In an influential essay, Erkkila has written of this poem that "what Dickinson describes
in a monarchical language of emperors, chariots, and divine right is a rigidly
stratified social order of rank, exclusion and difference" ("Class" 8). In a similar
vein, Domhnall Mitchell has argued that "the phrase 'divine Majority' inevitably
echoes and recoils from its secular or democratic equivalent, the masses," ultimately defining a "process by which the soul comes to make a choice in terms that
simultaneously invoke and revoke the American electoral system" (*Monarch* 6).

　　Both Erkkila and Mitchell find the use of language derived from European
monarchies to be at odds with democratic sensibility. Erkkila points specifically
to Dickinson's employment of "Whig political rhetoric" as evidence that her language undermines democratic values by slipping "between the old and the new,
between an aristocratic language of rank, royalty, and hereditary privilege, and
a Calvinist language of spiritual grace, personal sanctity and divine election"
("Class" 9). Mitchell seems to take a broader view of class and politics when he
affirms that Dickinson's poems "have more to do with issues of class, immigra-
tion, ethnicity, industrialization, the mass market, and democratic politics than
first appears" (*Monarch* 111). Yet sensitivity to opposing tendencies in the writing
leads him to conclude, "The weight of historical evidence does not necessarily
enable us to fit Dickinson into a political or social scheme; she (or her speakers)
may voice conservative, even reactionary, opinions, but she also demonstrates
opposite tendencies" (109). Contemplating his conclusion in conjunction with
Erkkila's effectively locates within Dickinson studies the same political ambiguities conveyed in media accounts of Laura Bush bringing American literature
into the White House.

　　But does Dickinson's use of a monarchical vocabulary in fact justify the conclusion that she is both elitist and disengaged from the social issues of her day?
At first glance, the answer might appear to be "yes." She uses the word "purple"
fifty-six times in her poems (Rosenbaum 601–602), and in doing so confirms that
purple is both "The Color of a Queen" (Fr 875) and fashionable when "a soul perceives itself / To be an Emperor" (Fr 896). Variants of "sovereign" (always spelled

"sovreign") appear nineteen times (Rosenbaum 699–700) and other references to royalty abound in the poems and letters, including a notable poetic tribute to Elizabeth Barrett Browning, who is described as having a "Head too High – to Crown –" (Fr 600).[10] Troubling as this terminology may appear to some, readers familiar with Dickinson's reliance on the language of the King James Bible, the writing of Shakespeare, and Christian hymnody will hesitate to conclude that Dickinson's inclusion of terms linked to monarchical systems of government that also appear in those texts should automatically undermine her democratic allegiances.

Odd as it may seem to modern readers, there is substantial reason to believe that the very slippage in Whig rhetoric that Erkkila finds so undemocratic might conceivably be viewed as a normative pattern of democratic expression in nineteenth-century America. The literary historian Edmund Morgan points to the historical origins of this practice through his identification of an underlying predisposition to think in monarchical terms that emerged as part of the English movement toward popular sovereignty that provided a significant foundation for American democracy. Specifically, Morgan writes that seventeenth-century English parliamentarians had to discover that "sharing regal authority" with the monarch required that "they had to think regally" (47). The political historian F. R. Ankersmit further substantiates America's predisposition to use monarchical terminology when he describes the Anglo-American winner-take-all approach to two-party politics that surfaced in the late eighteenth century.[11] In Ankersmit's words, the political party in power functioned as the "successor of the absolute monarch" in ways that no single party could in the coalition governments of continental democracies (101). Viewed in this context, Alexander Hamilton's well-known June 18, 1787, speech at the Constitutional Convention advocating that the chief executive be "an *elective monarch*" (Madison 290) makes practical sense, not merely because of historical proximity to the English monarchy, but also because the emerging federal system retained essential features of that particular monarchical tradition.[12] Thomas Jefferson's equally famous opposition to Hamilton's "monarchism"[13] has, according to the historian Stephen E. Knott, demarcated a "contest . . . for the soul of the nation" that Americans have revisited "for over two hundred years . . . hoping to clarify their understanding of both the past and the present" (23). Knott goes on to note that the Civil War ushered in an era during which "Hamilton eclipse[d] Jefferson as a revered figure in the minds of most Americans, at least in the North" (47), but that especially for the "Ivy League – educated elite of New England," like the Dickinsons, "Hamilton's reputation . . . soared to unparalleled heights" (48). To complicate the matter even further, Jefferson himself famously advocated the political promotion of a "natural aristocracy" that to modern minds can appear to contradict democratic logic as much as did Hamilton's advocacy of an elected monarch.[14] In this context, the appearance of monarchical terminology in Dickinson's writing may signify little other than her use of an Americanism consistent with the her historical place and moment.

More to the point, even, for analysis of what Dickinson's use of monarchical terms tells us about her dedication to democratic principles, is the extent that the ostensibly democratic citizens of Dickinson's day regularly discussed "the people" who form the basis of popular sovereignty in terms that we find paradoxical if not flatly contradictory today. As Cathy Davidson has indicated in her study of literacy in the late eighteenth and early nineteenth centuries, many literate citizens appeared blind to the fact that they were surrounded by illiterate masses. She makes particular reference to John Adams's "often quoted claim that America was the most literate nation on earth. 'A native American who cannot read and write,' Adams boasted, 'is as rare as a comet or an earthquake'" (56). Davidson then proceeds to cite studies showing that "less than half of the population was literate."[15] What Adams's comments reveal may be thought of as a widespread practice of not embracing as "the people" those persons whose lives fell outside the circle of middle-class affluence.[16] Toqueville is famous for his accounts of equality in America,[17] and Emerson would write in 1860 that "all great men come out of the middle classes" (*Essays*, "Considerations" 1086).

Bercovitch has specifically addressed what he sees as a rough correspondence between American veneration of the middle-class individual and monarchical traditions of Europe. "Here," he writes of nineteenth-century America, "'self-made'" performs as "a euphoric catchall that appropriated the feudal-religious rhetoric of 'kingship' on behalf of middle-class individualism" (48). This sentiment is pointedly conveyed by Dickinson when she writes, "Who Court obtain within Himself / Sees every man a King –" (Fr 859). As in many poems, her language here identifies Dickinson as part of an established American tradition within which expressions of undemocratic or elitist seeming attitudes surface as commonplace contradictions in the middle-class political logic of the nineteenth century. Amy Schrager Lang usefully summarizes scholarly sensitivity to the problem of stabilizing the language of class identity in nineteenth-century America: "Class and its consciousness are, to quote Cora Kaplin, more polymorphous and more perverse than we once imagined them, and the language of class less stable" (7). One important implication of this instability is the distinct possibility that Dickinson actually imagined herself as inclusively embracing all Americans when she incorporates monarchic language in her writing.

Pierre Bourdieu helps to account for the presence of this apparent blindness in the literary record of nineteenth-century Americans when he explains that a major difficulty in describing the social history of literature is that "the self-evident givens of the situation . . . remained unmarked," circulating rather " 'in the air' " writers breathed and for that reason never registering as a self-conscious feature of the written record transmitted to future readers (*Field* 32). Such appears to be the case with the widespread use of socially hierarchical terminology, even by writers who deliberately promoted democratic egalitarianism. Emerson describes "the private life of one man" becoming "a more illustrious monarchy . . . than any kingdom in history" (*Selections* 76), Melville writes of "genius, all over the world" standing "hand in hand" (249),[18] and even Whitman details an "I" "waiting my time to be one of the supremes" (234, "Song" 1.1050).[19] Yet each of these writers has been approached critically as having contributed in a significant way to what F. O. Matthiessen famously described as American literature "dedicated to the possibilities of democracy" (ix).[20]

Sovereignty in Domestic Settings

In Dickinson's poetry and letters, as in the writing of other great nineteenth-century American writers, the individual citizen's exercise of sovereignty does indeed register in the vocabulary of class and rank that Erkkila and Mitchell correctly link to the patriarchal tradition of divine right. Yet for Dickinson, the presence of the regal democrat trope in many instances signals her concern with pitfalls that surround the female citizen's successful expression of democratic sovereignty. As I will shortly demonstrate, Dickinson interrogates multiple difficulties women face in the effort to exercise sovereignty responsibly, one of which has been described in contemporary terms by feminist political theorist Kathleen Jones as the "sovereignty trap" (71). In Jones's words, women who seek to exercise the sovereignty long held by men can fall into the "same dynamics of exclusion in the struggle for sovereignty" they find so easy to criticize in the patriarchal politics they oppose (71). While Jones's formulation does not apply to all of Dickinson's poems that investigate female sovereignty, it does apply to some and serves as a way to begin thinking about the manner in which Dickinson's poems address sovereignty. One reason criticism has been slow to address Dickinson's interest in the female citizen's expression of sovereignty is almost certainly due to the fact that in addition to her frequent use of the royal democrat trope Dickinson almost always situates her poems in domestic settings that reinforce the tendency to read her poems as removed from public concerns. Add to this her creation of lyric speakers who can be interpreted as mild-mannered, nonassertive females cast in the mold of true womanhood, and the problem of getting to the political part of the poems becomes even more obvious.

An essential first step, then, in seeing beneath the seemingly apolitical surfaces presented by many of her poems is to consider the possibility that Dickinson makes getting to the political message difficult because she is ambitious. The way her poems are structured suggests that her aim is not to pose quandaries that her poems and their speakers solve, but rather to stage dramas of sovereignty and consent that require her readers to think independently about the political significance of choices made in the domestic sphere. She has to thwart conventional social expectations attached to the spaces inhabited by women in order to instill in her readers the understanding that the way they think and act in those spaces has political significance. This is achieved first and foremost by challenging her readers to distrust the speakers and characters that populate the domestic spaces of her poems. Creating distance between reader and speaker is for this reason essential to the reader's independent assessment of what the speaker says and does. Once this independence is established, the experience of reading can mimic the exercise of sovereignty in the real world where responsible political action similarly requires resistance and independent judgment. When this is achieved, the separate spheres of public and private, male and female, become more porous, and domestic space becomes a site for political action.

How this takes place can be seen through a reading of "The Soul selects her own Society –" (Fr 409) that questions the speaker's relationship to what she describes. As an alternative to readings promoted by Erkkila and Mitchell, for instance, the soul's assertion of "divine Majority" that so fascinates the speaker may be understood as a tempting but dubious political objective, rather than a course of action Dickinson advocates.[21] After all, what we know about the speaker is that she passively observes the conduct of the soul who isolates herself from the speaker behind closed doors and shut valves. Reference to a "Door," a "low Gate," and a "Mat" upon which an emperor kneels collectively establish a grand domestic setting over which the soul wields queenly authority. The soul's exercise of her "divine Majority," then, presumably takes place in the domestic space beyond the speaker's field of vision, conveying the impression that the speaker is excluded from this highly restricted exercise of female power. The poem can therefore be understood as illustrating the sovereignty trap that tempts women to squander their sovereignty through expressions of exclusivity that are every bit as objectionable as the patriarchal political exclusion of women. Readers sensitive to the soul's counterproductive behavior question the speaker's equivocal position in relation to what she has observed and withhold their consent from what is at best passive resignation and at worst dumbstruck admiration.

Difficult as it may be to see through the veils of convention that at first appear to obscure Dickinson's dramas of sovereignty, doing so reveals a determination to invest domestic space with political significance that links Dickinson's political sensibility to that expressed by other nineteenth-century American women writers equally interested in female citizenship and equally engaged with the interconnectedness of individualism and sovereignty. As Gillian Brown has shown in *Domestic Individualism* and *The Consent of the Governed,* women writers as well known as Harriet Beecher Stowe were intimately engaged with the politics of citizenship as practiced within the framework of domestic life. "American individualism," Brown argues, "takes on its peculiarly 'individualistic' properties as domesticity inflects it with values of interiority, privacy, and psychology" (*Individualism* 1). This is achieved through the late-eighteenth- and early-nineteenth-century cultural construction of the home as a refuge from the turbulence of the marketplace where the individual citizen can develop those character traits essential to the formation of democratic values (3). The resulting emergence of the home as "at once the separate sphere of women and the correlative to, as well as the basis of, men's individuality" has been seen by Brown and other feminists as leading ultimately to the simultaneous advancement and delimitation of "individualism by identifying self-hood with the feminine" (4–5).

Political consent assumes particular importance within the domestic sphere once it is understood that, in Brown's words, "individual judgments and choices cannot occur in isolation, but always proceed in relation to existing conventions" (*Consent* 9). In language that might be applied directly to the preceding discussion of "The Soul selects her own Society – ," Brown points out that the liberal tradition descending from John Locke "registers the connection between personal and political spheres." Citizenship arises through "the citizen's continuous labor of crediting and discrediting ideas" (8), a labor predicated on belief in a permeable mind susceptible to external influences that threaten liberty of thought. The act of throwing off tyrannical "intruders in the mind" consequently affirms individual political authority as epistemologically enacted even while it implies the presence of a vulnerable and hence feminine self (111). Brown's argument that literature actively engaged with female political consent through representations of female experience that repeatedly demonstrate the dangers imposed by social pressures might also be applied to Dickinson: "The portrait of persons as shadowed by the conditions in which they are born, even when the conditions of rank and political inheritance are radically changing, attests to the role, rather than the rule, of standards in the life of the individual. This modern coupling of the individual to cultural currents and channels . . . immediately brings under scrutiny the predominant modes of influence—whether parents, teachers, governors, textbooks, icons, or novels. The now familiar attacks so regularly brought to bear on the perceived engines of individual formation arose with, not against, the liberal state" (179). As readers we should not be astonished to discover Dickinson poems that not only illuminate the dangers posed by familiar social precedents, but that also place us in the position of making up our minds about which if any of the behaviors projected onto the page are worthy of our consent.

That we as readers still find it difficult at times to acknowledge Dickinson's engagement with politics may in part be a reflection of the extent that American culture continues to be influenced by the equivocal political role assigned women in the philosophical tradition out of which nineteenth-century American democracy emerged. This is a point Linda Kerber forcefully establishes in *Women of the Republic* when she argues that Dickinson's era inherited an Enlightenment tradition within which "the nature of the relationship between women and the state remained largely unexamined" (15). "Only by implication did the most prominent male writers say anything of substance about the function and responsibilities of women in the monarchies they knew and in the ideal communities they invented." The lack of attention given to the female citizen's political role that Kerber describes appears rather strikingly in Locke's enormously influential *Two Treatises of Civil Government* in which he invests female political identity with an undecidability closely resembling that which I previously associated with perceptions of literary politics both inside and outside the academy. Political scholar Kate Nash makes the connection clear in "Liberalism and the Undecidability of 'Women'" when she writes that Locke "is highly inconsistent in his treatment of women, seeing them sometimes as the same as men, with the same capacities and the same relation to political society, while at other times he sees them as different from men, naturally subordinated to them and excluded from the public sphere of politics" (4). Such a position substantially reinforces Kerber's reference to the Enlightenment's failure to clarify the political authority of women while at the same time providing support for Brown's observation that Locke's writing "registers the connection between personal and political spheres" (*Consent* 9).

Nash makes her argument by comparing passages in Locke's *First Treatise,* where he argues that men and women are equal, with passages in the *Second Treatise,* where he argues that women are subordinate. In the *First Treatise,* for instance, Locke presents the Genesis story of Adam and Eve as illustrating God's granting dominion to male and female equally: "God says unto Adam and Eve, have dominion ... that these words were not spoken till Adam had his wife, must not she thereby be lady, as he lord of the world? ... for shall we say that God ever made a joint grant to two, and one only was to have the benefit of it?" (Locke 23). Yet in the *Second Treatise* Locke authorizes the male assumption of power when male and female wills conflict: "But the husband and wife, though they have but one common concern, yet having different understandings, will unavoidably sometimes have different wills too; it therefore being necessary, that the last determination, i.e. the rule, should be placed somewhere, it naturally falls to the man's share, as the abler and the stronger" (155). The consequence of Locke's inconsistency is the impossibility of achieving, in Nash's words, "a complete closure of the frontier between the two spheres" (4). Woman's role in the sphere of public politics, as defined by Locke, is thus both affirmed and compromised; woman's position effectively teeters between public and private functions, so that whether or not women are perceived as political depends on point of view and context. For a writer like Dickinson, who addresses the cultural concerns of her historical moment through poems that offer multiple points of view and shifting contexts, the perception that women are agents of political change necessarily contends with the perception that they are not.

Three Unreliable Speakers

"There is a flower that Bees prefer –" (Fr 642) can be read as evidence of Dickinson's concern with the proper exercise of female sovereignty that continued to vex American culture due to the cultural construction of domestic space and the continued influence of Locke and other Enlightenment thinkers. At first glance, the poem appears to conform to an entirely familiar and predictable riddle structure but turns out to challenge the stability of that form by supporting multiple interpretive possibilities, each offering a different political message.

> There is a flower that Bees prefer –
> And Butterflies – desire –
> To gain the Purple Democrat
> The Humming Bird – aspire –
>
> And Whatsoever Insect pass –
> A Honey bear away
> Proportioned to his several dearth
> And her – capacity –
>
> Her face be rounder than the Moon
> And ruddier than the Gown
> Of Orchis in the Pasture –
> Or Rhododendron – worn –
>
> She doth not wait for June –
> Before the World be Green –
> Her sturdy little Countenance
> Against the Wind – be seen –
>
> Contending with the Grass –
> Near Kinsman to Herself –
> For privilege of Sod and Sun –
> Sweet Litigants for Life –

And when the Hills be full –
And newer fashions blow –
Doth not retract a single spice
For pang of jealousy –

Her Public – be the Noon –
Her Providence – the Sun –
Her Progress – by the Bee – proclaimed –
In sovreign [*sic*] – Swerveless Tune –

The Bravest – of the Host –
Surrendering – the last –
Nor even of Defeat – aware –
When cancelled by the Frost –

On first encounter, the poem's riddle form engages the interior thought processes of speaker and reader in what appears to be a closed game. There are many Dickinson poems that operate this way; "It sifts from Leaden Sieves –" (Fr 291) and "I like to see it lap the Miles –" (Fr 383) are two of the best-known examples. However, just as solving the riddle emerges as one facet of a far more complicated poetic picture with these two poems, so it is with the "Purple Democrat." In the words of the literary scholar Cheryl Walker, the surface text conveys a "version of the self made acceptable to nineteenth-century patriarchal society" while the "deeper and less acceptable script points to a part of the self that has been violated, almost rubbed out but that speaks nevertheless" (Burden 31–32). Accordingly, the surface riddle affirms conventional American democratic practice: the female flower fearlessly confronts conventions, enjoys public affirmation and proceeds impervious to the threat of defeat or death.

The "deeper and less acceptable script" that Walker refers to emerges once the disjunctive power of the poem's thirty-eight dashes is combined with the sharp delineation of male and female perspectives that divides the poem into two 4-stanza groupings.[22] In the first three stanzas, the flower *passively* fulfills nineteenth-century female stereotypes: as the object of universal desire, as a nurturer who has provided for each according to capacity, and as comparable to traditional symbols of female beauty—the moon and other flowers. The seventh stanza then affirms these female accomplishments with the male bee's voice that here frames the purportedly democratic and independent female with male symbols of "Noon" and "Sun." These symbols together constitute the "Public" domain and "Providence" that circumscribe what is referred to ironically as the female's "Progress."[23] By contrast, the four opposing stanzas present an *active* female who rejects seasonal cycles, contends for legal property rights, disdains fashion, and battles on oblivious of defeat. The resulting symmetrical structure suggests both that the bee's sovereign proclamation of the flower's purple status celebrates conformity rather than independence and that the flower's independence is too remote from collective experience to effectively challenge patriarchal politics.[24]

One of the best ways to think about the role Dickinson's dashes play in opening fissures in the narrative unity of the poem comes through a comparison of the above 1998 variorum version of the poem with the version produced in the 1890 first edition. This first print publication of the poem visually and syntactically demonstrates an editorial effort to eliminate the disjunctive potential of the dash in order to reinforce the generic lyric expectation of a single, internally unified voice.

Purple Clover.

THERE is a flower that bees prefer,
And butterflies desire;
To gain the purple democrat
The hummingbirds aspire.

And whatsoever insect pass,
A honey bears away
Proportioned to his several dearth
And her capacity.

Her face is rounder than the moon,
And ruddier than the gown
Of orchis in the pasture,
Or rhododendron worn.

She doth not wait for June;
Before the world is green
Her sturdy little countenance
Against the wind is seen,

Contending with the grass,
Near kinsman to herself,
For privilege of sod and sun,
Sweet litigants for life.

And when the hills are full,
And newer fashions blow,
Doth not retract a single spice
For pang of jealousy.

Her public is the noon,
Her providence the sun,
Her progress by the bee proclaimed
In sovereign, swerveless tune.

The bravest of the host,
Sundering the last,
Not even of defeat aware
When cancelled by the frost.[25]

The most obvious differences between this version of the poem and the 1998 varorum have to do with the imposition of conventional print norms governing capitalization and punctuation. Normalization of capitalization and punctuation signifies an effort to make the poem more completely fulfill the riddle and lyric potential of Dickinson's language. The complete eradication of all dashes—Dickinson's only punctuation in the varorium poem and the manuscript holograph—dramatically increases the sense of syntactic continuity in a manner that magnifies the dominant single voice of lyric poetry while also sustaining focus on the subject of the riddle.

One intriguing feature of the manuscript poem that can be understood as counteracting such efforts to unify syntax and voice and which does not appear in either of the print versions presented here is Dickinson's location of the final stanza on the top of the next fascicle page (Dickinson, *MBED* 749). Dickinson's division of stanza four earlier in the poem (747–748), so that two units of two lines each split the fourth stanza across two pages, contrasts with the unbroken quatrain here, drawing attention to the isolation of this last stanza. Whereas the earlier division might have the effect of drawing reader attention to the shift from social conformity to unruliness that takes place in stanza four, the setting apart of the last stanza might give emphasis to the way it provides an ending very different from that conveyed in the preceding stanza. Even though Dickinson's decision with both stanzas may well have been dictated by space rather than rhetorical strategy, the serendipitous separation of the final stanza visually loosens the formal unity of the text in a manner consistent with the voicing possibilities I want to explore.

Sally Bushell's argument in support of what she describes as Dickinson's

1. "There is a flower that Bees prefer –" (J 380/Fr 642), *MBED* 747–749. By permission of the Houghton Library, Harvard University. *MS AM 1118.3 (94a)* © The President and Fellows of Harvard College.

Her sturdy little Countenance
Against the Wind - be seen -

Contending with the Grass -
Near Kinsman to Herself -
For privilege of Sod and Sun -
Sweet Litigants for Life -

And when the Hills be full -
And newer fashions blow -
Doth not retract a single
spice
For pang of jealousy -

Her Public - be the Noon -
Her Providence - the Sun -
Her Progress - by the Bee -
proclaimed -
In sovereign - Swerveless Tune -

The Bravery of the Host -
Surrendering - the Cause -
Nor even of Defeat - aware -
When Cancelled by the Frost -

———

A Secret told -
Ceases to be a Secret - then -
A Secret - kept -
That - can appal but One -

Better of it - continual
be afraid -
Than it -
And whom you told it
to - beside -

———

procedure of intending unintended meaning lends support to the approach I have in mind: "We cannot be sure whether unintended meaning occurs indirectly as an unconsidered consequence of, say, writing on a certain page of a certain size which may limit or constrict or shape that work, or whether such a shaping was actively envisaged and chosen by the writer from the start" (30). For readings sensitive to the disjunctive power of the dashes and the isolation of particular words signaled by capitalization, the separation of the final stanza underscores even further the arbitrary nature of efforts to impose closure on the form and content of the poem. As the preceding analysis of gendered divisions within the poem has indicated, there is a sense in which ending the poem with the voice of the male bee, which is the focus of the penultimate stanza, satisfactorily resolves the poem according to patriarchal political expectations. The presence of the isolated stanza, in combination with the dashes and the disruptive assertion of capitals, performs the contrary function of opening the poem to alternative voicing possibilities that significantly enhance the poem's questioning of patriarchal authority. Even if Dickinson's arrangement of her manuscript poem is coincidental, her unintended action fortuitously complements the variorum poem to release heterogeneous voices through a process Mikhail M. Bakhtin has described as "dramatic juxtaposition" and "counterposition" (*Problems* 28).

For the purpose of further clarifying the opposing models of female conduct that Dickinson built into this poem, I will visually divide the stanzas according to the passive/active, conforming/rebelling axis that I have described as constituting the primary source of tension and opposition in the poem:

Passive	Active
1.	4.
There is a flower that Bees prefer –	She doth not wait for June –
And Butterflies – desire –	Before the World be Green –
To gain the Purple Democrat	Her sturdy little Countenance
The Humming Bird – aspire –	Against the Wind – be seen –
2.	5.
And Whatsoever Insect pass –	Contending with the Grass –
A Honey bear away	Near Kinsman to Herself –
Proportioned to his several dearth	For privilege of Sod and Sun –
And her – capacity –	Sweet Litigants for Life –
3.	6.
Her face be rounder than the Moon	And when the Hills be full –
And ruddier than the Gown	And newer fashions blow –
Of Orchis in the Pasture –	Doth not retract a single spice
Or Rhododendron – worn –	For pang of jealousy –

7.

Her Public – be the Noon –
Her Providence – the Sun –
Her Progress – by the Bee – proclaimed –
In sovreign – Swerveless Tune –

8.

The Bravest – of the Host –
Surrendering – the last –
Nor even of Defeat – aware –
When cancelled by the Frost –

What this admittedly artificial rearrangement does is make even more visible the way Dickinson's poem yokes stunningly opposed options for female social conduct. Seeing the stanzas this way also makes more visually apparent the subtle differences in syllable count and rhyme scheme that can be understood as reinforcing central tensions. The first obvious alteration of the poem's metrics takes place at the beginning of stanza four, where the speaker's description of the female clover shifts attention from the passive to the active aspects of the flower's conduct. Up to this point, each stanza began with an eight- or nine-syllable line, but here the opening line is reduced to six syllables. This shift in the length of the opening line is then carried out for the rest of the poem, so that Dickinson's metrical design draws attention to a major change in the way that the speaker describes the clover. This shift in syllable count also represents the point in the poem where the general pattern of alternating six- and eight-syllable, or three- and four-foot lines characteristic of common meter ceases to inform Dickinson's metrical design. For this reason, Dickinson's visual division of stanza four in the manuscript version seems fortuitous, as doing so is yet another way that the arrangement of the poem draws attention to a significant change in the purple democrat's behavior.

The next major departure from an initial governing pattern takes place in stanza six, the third of three stanzas expressing the clover's nonconformity. In this case, the prevailing a-b-c-b rhyme scheme is violated by a stanza with no end-rhyme at all. Significantly, the lack of end-rhyme in this stanza is compensated for in the next when Dickinson provides two true rhymes and a slant rhyme (a-a-b-a). By this means, the prosody of the poem draws attention to the major shifts in the poem's presentation of the clover. The first of these marks her transition from passive to active, and the second marks the bee's effort to impose patriarchal order on what appears to be a growing list of the clover's departures from female social norms. The absence of end-rhyme in stanza six reflects the clover's increasing social intransigence by refusing to conform to the established rhyme pattern, and the excess of end-rhyme in stanza seven reflects the male bee's efforts to compensate by reestablishing the order threatened by the purple democrat.

My reading of the poem treats Dickinson's presentation of such pronounced oppositions as an examination of rival modes of behavior that invite reader scrutiny as a dramatic enactment of female sovereignty. In Martha Nell Smith's terms, I approach the poem as a "dialogic drama" (*Rowing* 53) in which tensions already established by the polarization of female social options are further aggravated by the degrees of potential disjunction added by the dashes and shifts in prosodic structure. Weighing the multitudinous possibilities for speaker inflection and tone that emerge as voicing options expand centrifugally further complicates reader efforts to determine what stance the speaker assumes in relation to the female social behavior that is the subject of the poem. In the interest of coherence, I will cease to focus on the expansion of voicing possibilities and confine my analysis to three of the most sharply drawn voices attributable to the speaker.

Joining the riddle function of the poem with the prosodic features just described, plus the internal divisions identified previously, allows for the identification of three primary speaker voices espousing three distinct political messages, in relation to which the reader would have to position him- or herself. The first is that of the gender-neutral riddle speaker who seeks the confirmation of Emersonian individualism provided by the bee's sovereign male voice. This speaker communicates a vision of public consent according to which the reader joins the bee in diffusing and thereby appropriating the lyric expression of rebellious female conduct, effectively reducing the purple democrat to an acceptable reflection of reader and bee: in resolving the poem as a riddle, reader, speaker, and bee all affirm the clover and perceive all parts of the poem as uniformly contributing to an overarching unity. A reading based on this voice concludes that the poem is a riddle about a clover that has a greater resistance to the approaching frost than do other grasses or flora. This voice presents the poem as characterized by sameness and is therefore politically neutral. The concluding stanza may for this reason be interpreted as affirming the Emersonian ideal of achieving "union . . . when all the uniters are absolutely isolated" (*Selections* 216). The purple democrat's status as "Bravest – of the Host" meshes perfectly with her absence of awareness that she is performing a public role, thus establishing that she is both isolated and contributing to union.

The second speaker voice expresses what might be thought of as the external male view that acknowledges as acceptable only those outward female traits that coincide with conventional patriarchal expectations. This voice also affirms the bee's assertion of male sovereignty but does so without the riddle form's demand for reader consent. As a consequence, the supposed elevation of the sovereign female emerges as a form of patriarchal containment within which female consent is superfluous. This voice introduces political content into the poem by both affirming passive female conduct and subordinating acts of female nonconformity, thereby acknowledging the conflicted status of the purple democrat even while silencing female resistance by means of the bee's proclamation. This speaker applauds the purple democrat as leading a "host" and therefore acting for the common good. What becomes clear through this voice is that the purple democrat's independence declared in stanzas four through six must be contained by patriarchal discourse before her independent action can be understood as contributing to the public good. As a consequence, this voice illuminates the role of social agency in making isolated actions beneficial to the public. Where Emerson would present unity as the natural outcome of individual genius expressing universal spirit,[26] here unity emerges as the product of social and political appropriation.

The third speaker voice is that of the female who witnesses the purple democrat's experience of being simultaneously alienated from the male foundations of political power and oblivious of the powerlessness entailed by that alienation. This speaker most emphatically registers the sovereignty trap described by Kathleen Jones when she acknowledges that the purple democrat's obsession with personal power seals her off from the experience of others as completely as she has been sealed off from patriarchal politics. Even though she has exerted her self-reliant individualism by breaking out of passive conformity and asserting her independence, she is in the end oblivious even of her defeat by the frost ("Nor even of Defeat – aware –"). This is the most overtly political of the speaker voices, as it magnifies female alienation and hence difference from the patriarchal status quo. Where the second voice magnified the containment of female difference within patriarchal sameness, this voice concentrates on the political erasure of the purple democrat ("cancelled by the Frost –"). Within such a reading, frost reinforces the chill of the purple democrat's isolation in addition to acknowledging the inevitable arrival of death. To have been "cancelled" suggests that the purple democrat's isolated action, no matter how brave, made no lasting impact. As a consequence, this reading stands in direct opposition to the Emersonian conviction that isolated action contributes to a more perfect union.

When all three voices are considered collectively, the poem's analysis of female political subjectivity emerges with considerable force. As Marietta Messmer has noted, the introduction of voices such as these, that each seek to impose monologic unity, can actually magnify the presence of alternative voices by exposing "a highly complex negotiation between subtle strategies of monologic control within gestures of dialogic polyvocality" (21). Accordingly, the simultaneous contemplation of the three voices I have identified sets in motion a politically laden drama within which political complacency and ideological appropriation emerge as the outcomes of choices that either negate female consent by subordinating it to male sovereignty or enact a form of independent sovereignty powerless to alter the patriarchal system it rejects. By presenting conflicting assessments of

the relationship between individualism and democracy, the poem, to use Bercovitch's words, turns "cultural symbology against the dominant culture" (360),
granting readers the opportunity to see beyond the contending social forces that
dictate the purple democrat's ineffective exercise of sovereignty. When readers
then imagine more positive alternatives, reading the poem itself becomes a literary enactment of democratic thought processes essential to the exercise of sovereignty. Nancy Ruttenburg describes this kind of reading as the conversion of
"negative traits into positive ones" that requires "reconceptualizing democracy as
a theater of verbal (symbolic) action, an experiential ground whose materializations, both historical and literary, would ultimately foster a recognizably democratic (polycentric) cultural semiotic" (15). To the extent that Dickinson's poem
succeeds in provoking this sort of imaginative formation of democratic social
space, the poem clearly moves beyond the private domain of an isolated author
or reader.

The next two poems I want to look at approach the problem of female sovereignty by exposing obstacles within the female imagination that prevent individual speakers from resisting social convention, even when they are drawn to
political action. These poems may be thought of as investigations into the incapacitating power of social norms that enter the thought process through gendered narratives of female heroism and economic self-definition. The speakers in
these two poems demonstrate a significant difficulty women confront who wish
to pursue Emersonian individualism but have no way of imaginatively engaging
a self not already determined by cultural expectations that effectively prevent the
spontaneous outpouring of genius so crucial to Emerson's model. Shira Wolosky
describes this dilemma when she writes, "the ideologies of selfhood that Whitman or Emerson might pursue are different for Dickinson simply because of her
gender" ("being in the body" 134). Citing Joyce Appleby, Wolosky notes that "liberal individualism in many of its strictures presumes 'the human personality to
be male.' For a woman within nineteenth-century culture, to achieve one's selfhood is also to subordinate it, as daughter and wife." An outcome of this cultural
subordination is "a general ambivalence to achievement" that emerges in these
particular Dickinson poems as the decisions of speakers to rationalize inaction
by elevating the desire for political sovereignty above the actual exercise of it. In
this way, the act of choice is deferred and democratic thought is epistemologically stymied.

Dickinson's poems point beyond this paralysis through the careful management of negative conduct by speakers whose inactions prompt readers to assess
their failures independently, thereby mimicking in the act of interpretation the
resistance to authority that speakers are incapable of and that is so crucial to
the expression of political sovereignty. For the purposes of this discussion, we

should bear in mind that "liberty" is closely allied to the "will," for, as political historian Harold Laski has observed, "sovereignty" is largely a "problem of representing wills" (66), the free expression of which constitutes liberty. The poem "Unto like Story – Trouble has enticed me –" (Fr 300) presents a female speaker who is powerfully attracted to direct participation in public politics but unable to harness her will and therefore prevented from exercising her sovereignty.

Unto like Story – Trouble has enticed me –
How Kinsmen fell –
Brothers and Sisters – who preferred the Glory –
And their young will
Bent to the Scaffold, or in Dungeons – chanted –
Till God's full time –
When they let go the ignominy – smiling –
And Shame went still –

Unto guessed Crests, my moaning fancy, leads me,
Worn fair
By Heads rejected – in the lower country –
Of honors there –
Such spirit makes her perpetual mention,
That I – grown bold –
Step martial – at my Crucifixion –
As Trumpets – rolled –

Feet, small as mine – have marched in Revolution
Firm to the Drum –
Hands – not so stout – hoisted them – in witness –
When Speech went numb –
Let me not shame their sublime deportments –
Drilled bright –
Beckoning – Etruscan invitation –
Toward Light –

Provoked by an unidentified but urgent sense of injustice ("Trouble has enticed me –"), this speaker imagines herself in the familiar heroic narrative ("like Story") of "Brothers and Sisters – who preferred the Glory – / And their young will / Bent to the Scaffold, or in Dungeons – chanted –." After having emphasized the importance of exercising "their young will" that is so crucial to the story the brothers and sisters appear in, the speaker is overwhelmed by the power of narrative precedent, surrenders her own will and appears incapable of action. The poem ends when the speaker, who has acknowledged that "Feet, small as mine – have marched in Revolution," distances herself from the story that now appears to require more from its characters than she can offer. Her last words wistfully imagine an unspecified future date when she might live up to the standards of her heroic predecessors: "Let me not shame their sublime deportments – / Drilled bright – / Beckoning – Etruscan invitation – / Toward Light – ." We are left to conclude that even though this speaker has encountered "Trouble" adequate to link her story to the heroic acts of others, she is unable to mobilize her will.

The deep irony of the poem is achieved through processes of analogy and metonymy that lead the speaker to substitute a preexisting story for her own and then judge herself unqualified to act as one of the characters. Ostensibly drawn to "like Story" as a means to address her own distinct "Trouble," the speaker finds that the process of identification with the story allows her to experience a dramatic resolution that is aesthetically pleasing but disconnected from the real events of her life that made the story attractive in the first place. She then stands back from that aesthetic experience and declares herself incapable of performing similarly in the world she shares with others. Trouble has indeed "enticed" her to the story; the word "enticed" suggesting a predisposition to resolve real-life problems through immersion in stereotypic romantic narratives. Such an inclination would help account for the speaker's disconcerting failure to seize liberty and instead fall under the sway of conjecture and fancy in the second stanza: "Unto guessed Crests, my moaning fancy, leads me." The manuscript version of the poem presents "lures" as a variant for "leads," emphasizing the enchanting, enthralling, perhaps even delirious power of the familiar heroic plot that follows. That the speaker's fancy is "moaning" contributes further to the seductive delirium that the speaker passes into as she identifies with the story. From this point to the conclusion of the stanza, the speaker imagines the rapid completion of a life characterized by martial certitude and a martyr's death: "I – grown bold – / Step martial – at my Crucifixion – ." The failure to act that is then detailed in the last stanza now becomes comprehensible as the result of the speaker's initial desire for political action having been blunted by a flight of fancy that confines desire for public action to the interior space of the isolated bourgeois imagination.

Mary Loeffelholz's analysis of the poem's political message provides a precedent for the conclusion I am offering here: "It might be possible, following Betsy Erkkila, to read this poem as laying claim to a privileged class individualism through identification with the language of aristocracy, but my own sense is that the poem acts out the hollowness and insecurity of any such self-fashioning" ("Invitations" 17).[27] The elevated achievements associated with the stock characters that populate predictable romantic plots are here presented as so far removed from actual experience that the speaker's inaction emerges as the product of a misdirected imagination.

By exposing the inadequacy of the speaker's political imagination, the poem asks readers to judge for themselves the extent that their own bourgeois inaction is predicated on similar forms of aesthetic detachment. Rather than accepting the speaker's behavior as consistent with social values or an epistemology that Dickinson espouses, this reading approaches the speaker as a model of episte-mological incapacitation whose ability to express the independence essential to personal liberty has been crippled by an imagination so constricted that she is incapable of envisioning a story of her own. Instead, she is mired in culturally acceptable stereotypes that proclaim the exceptional nature of female heroism, placing it beyond the speaker's reach.

The prosodic design of the poem underscores the speaker's struggle and ul-timate failure to discover a suitable method for imaginatively addressing what-ever the problem is that has motivated her initial desire for action. Unlike most Dickinson poems, this one yokes two of the standard quatrains consistent with ballad, common measure, and hymnody so that the poem is organized as three octets instead of six quatrains. It also extends the first and third lines of each quatrain (now the first, third, fifth, and seventh lines of the octet) from a norm of eight syllables to a norm of eleven syllables (in eight out of twelve instances) and shortens the second and fourth lines from a norm of six to a norm of four syl-lables (in nine of twelve instances). Violating the standard stanza pattern draws attention to the way each octet gathers one of the three main movements of the poem: (1) the speaker's contemplation of a story she considers similar to her own; (2) the speaker's immersion in a story that culminates in a glorious "Cru-cifixion"; and (3) the speaker's determination that she cannot realistically aspire to the heroic achievements she has contemplated ("Let me not shame their sub-lime deportments –").

Each individual stanza in its own way reinforces this three-part sequence. The octet that most fully maximizes the unity afforded by rhyme is the second, where end-rhyme locks each line in place: a-b-a-b-c-d-c-d. This makes sense, as it is in this stanza that the speaker is most fully immersed in the stereotypic plot of heroic martyrdom—she simply inserts herself within a preordained order. The rhyme here might be thought of as the structural signal that the speaker is engaged in an escapist activity that leads her away from her trouble rather than giving her a means to address it. The structure of the first stanza, however, be-trays the speaker's wish to discover a meaningful pattern to her life. It is com-posed of alternating eleven- and four-syllable lines that conclude with alternat-ing feminine and masculine endings. The iambic dimeter of the masculine lines

2. "Unto like Story – Trouble has enticed me –" (J 295/Fr 300), *MBED* 239–240. By permission of the Houghton Library, Harvard University. *MS AM 1118.3 (111)* © The President and Fellows of Harvard College.

As Trumpets rolled -

Feet - small as mine - had
marched in Revolution
Firm to the Drum -
Hands not so stout - hoisted
them - in witness -
When speech went numb -
Let me not shame their
sublime deportments -
Drilled bright -
Beckoning - Etruscan invitation
toward Light - to -

in this sense contends with the mix of iambs, trochees, and amphibrachs that appear in the feminine lines, mimicking the female speaker's wish to discover a mode of meaningful female expression in a world characterized by a fixed male order. This stanza's use of end-rhyme links lines two, four, and eight, setting up an a-b-a-b-c-d-e-b sequence that reveals a faltering of rhyme in the feminine lines of the second embedded quatrain. This faltering immediately follows the speaker's mention of "will" exercised by "Brothers and Sisters," drawing attention to the speaker's struggle to express her own will.

The structure of the third octet may be thought of as a synthesis of the first two, incorporating the end-rhyme of the second stanza in true rhymes that link four of the eight lines to create an a-b-c-b-d-e-f-e pattern that is stronger than stanza one but weaker than stanza two. The last stanza also incorporates both the four-syllable dimeter line of the first stanza and the two-syllable spondaic line introduced in the second stanza. This removal of unstressed syllables also coincides with a reduced syllable count in the third, fifth, and seventh lines of the last stanza, a reduction that first enters the poem in the seventh line of the second octet where the shortest feminine line in the poem concludes with the word "Crucifixion." That this word should mark the point where the line's iambic pattern suddenly shifts to an amphibrach that preserves the feminine line ending is particularly intriguing given the word's religious and historical significance. While naming the most heroic act in Christian history, the metrical positioning of the word underscores the near submergence of the feminine within a narrative of male-inspired triumph. The incorporation of pure rhyme in the four masculine lines of the last stanza then reinforces the speaker's failure to discover a form of feminine self-expression. The speaker's ultimate deferral of action correlates with her inability to imagine a universe not dominated by a masculine order that either excludes her or relegates her to a marginal role. Her timidity is thus enforced by an imaginative life that fuels feelings of inadequacy. She stands back from the world, incapable of exercising sovereignty, transfixed by incapacitating visions of the heroic few "Beckoning" her "Toward Light – ."

The speaker in "I play at Riches – to appease" (Fr 856) similarly contemplates but ultimately resists the powerful appeal of direct political engagement, only in this poem Dickinson goes even further in identifying the cultural forces that disable the female political imagination:

I play at Riches – to appease
The Clamoring for Gold –
It kept me from a Thief, I think,
For often, overbold

With Want, and Opportunity –
I could have done a Sin
And been myself that easy Thing
An independent Man –

But often as my lot displays
Too hungry to be borne
I deem Myself what I would be –
And novel Comforting

My Poverty and I derive –
We question if the Man –
Who own – Esteem the Opulence –
As we – Who never Can –

Should ever these exploring Hands
Chance Sovereign [sic] on a Mine –
Or in the long – uneven term
To win, become their turn –

How fitter they will be – for Want –
Enlightening so well –
I know not which, Desire, or Grant –
Be wholly beautiful –

Even though the mention of an "independent Man" in line eight points to the possibility that the speaker is male, an alternative and additional argument for a female speaker is supported by the poem's repeated identifications of culturally constructed attributes of maleness that are contemplated but never embodied. This is especially clear in the fourth stanza, where the plural "we," constituted by the speaker and "Poverty," distinguish their lot from that of the "Man" who possesses the power to "own." Here, more than anywhere else in the poem, the issue of ownership surfaces as the pivotal legal determinant that separates the speaker from the "independent Man" she describes at the end of the second stanza. Ownership and independence then combine with the reference to "Sovereign" hands that appears in the fifth stanza to establish the poem's focus on female exclusion from direct participation in public politics.[28] As with "Unto like Story," the poem ends with the speaker simultaneously affirming both her "Desire" and her inability to act on that desire.

What most distinguishes "I play at Riches" from "Unto like Story" is that in this later poem the speaker's power to imagine a future when she might become a player on the public stage is even more severely compromised by the force of cultural conformity that in this instance takes the form of her concern with spiritual well-being. The consistent use of alternating iambic tetrameter and trimeter lines throughout the poem points to a level of conformity that exceeds that conveyed in the earlier poem's much less patterned meter, suggesting that this speaker is more fully integrated within culturally normative, predictable modes of thinking. Where crucifixion posed too high a hurdle for the speaker in "Unto like Story," here the speaker is paralyzed by fear of damnation. Curiously, the poem concludes with hesitation—"I know not which"—suggesting that the speaker believes she possesses the power to break the pattern of sublimated desire so vividly expressed in the poem's opening lines: "I play at Riches – to appease / The Clamoring for Gold – ." The reasons for this hesitation are revealed early on, in the references to "Thief," "Sin," and "independent Man" that allude to the Genesis account of Eden, where Eve's taking of the forbidden fruit led to expulsion from the garden and the resulting dependence on independent labor. The logic linking Eden to independent sovereignty defines the speaker as a nineteenth-century American Eve for whom participation in public politics is the forbidden fruit.

Conversely, the speaker's reiterated desire for greater sovereignty implies that her dependent status is not completely satisfying. She does, after all, strive to appease a clamoring, a hunger, and her own "exploring Hands," all of which appear as persistent features of her experience. However, the most subversive element of the poem may be its demonstration that religious precedent shapes aesthetic taste in a manner that infringes on the exercise of free will. This is achieved when the expression of female liberty encapsulated in the speaker's final dilemma is shown to be a form of self-deception: if religion does in fact motivate the speaker's decision to sublimate her desire, then the final question about which is "wholly beautiful" has already been answered. The reader who perceives the speaker's entrapment within such contradictory logic is in the position of imagining a broader political aesthetic, one that denies the appropriative power of religious ideology and is capable of conceiving beauty in the sphere of public politics.

Detecting the poem's subversive awakening of the reader's independent political imagination is best accomplished through an analysis of structural elements linked directly to the female citizen's mistaken belief that she expresses individuality by not doing the "easy Thing." To begin with, it is helpful to see that—as with "Unto like Story"—the poem is organized in three parts, only with this poem each part is composed of three 2-stanza groupings, each of which situates the speaker in a different time frame. The first two stanzas focus primarily on the past, as in "It kept me"; the "But" that opens the third stanza shifts the focus from past to present; the "Should" that begins stanza five then introduces a subjunctive contemplation of the future that absorbs the final two stanzas. This coordination of past, present, and future, signified by "kept," "But," and "Should," conveys a superficial impression of individual progress, as if the appropriately unified lyric speaker were gathering strength in anticipation of a bold new step. Close examination of the three parts of the poem, however, especially consideration of the disjunctive power of the dashes, shows that beneath the speaker's conscious desire for personal liberty the voice of scriptural precedent exerts an incapacitating influence on her ability to translate conscious desire into social action.

In this poem, dashes serve primarily to magnify the many potential ruptures in the speaker's account that the surface logic of her language attempts to suture shut in classic lyric fashion. Examination of the dashes is useful, then, as a means of articulating an alternative, shadow narrative that stands in dialogic tension with the one the speaker struggles to affirm. The first example comes early, when a dash separates the speaker's admission that she "play[s] at Riches" from her assertion that play satisfactorily substitutes for actual possession. As a consequence, we begin to question whether the play does indeed "appease / The Clamoring for Gold – ." The next dash sustains the possibility that the speaker is indeed denying the facts of her experience by disjoining the playing at riches from the criminal behavior (becoming a thief) that the play is supposed to have prevented. When we then encounter the embedded Eden story ("I could have done a Sin"), we do so after already beginning to doubt the speaker's authority. Dickinson's line, "It kept me from a Thief, I think," now underscores the speaker's lack of conviction by placing commas on either side of "I think," making it possible to conclude that even the speaker is not entirely certain that she did not become a thief after all, or that she never seriously contemplated becoming a thief in the first place. If we interpret "play at Riches" as enacting the female citizen's domestic contribution to democratic consent, then the object of theft—the "Gold" mentioned in the second line—would be full political enfranchisement, the female equivalent of those rights accorded to the "independent Man" the speaker describes at the end of the second stanza. The speaker's uncertainty, then, conveys the amorphous interior experience of the female citizen, who is expected to provide a foundation for political decisions but not take direct action.

In this context, the speaker's succeeding claim that she "could have done a Sin / And been Myself that easy Thing / An independent Man –" comes across as a self-justifying rationalization. Her claim to distinguish her life of play as superior because it marks refusal of the "easy" option of direct action now appears highly suspect. In rather spectacular fashion, this speaker embodies the ethic of female sacrifice that Barbara Welter has shown to be a major influence on the way nineteenth-century American culture encouraged women to imagine themselves: "She would be another, better Eve, working in cooperation with the Redeemer. . . . The world would be reclaimed for God through her suffering, for 'God increased the cares and suffering of woman, that she might be sooner constrained to accept the terms of salvation'" (44). Welter's analysis clarifies the extent that expressions of female independence required a violation of gender expectations that would be anything but "easy." As Sandra M. Gilbert and Susan Gubar have made abundantly clear, the popular and elite press of Dickinson's day condemned as monstrous women who transgressed conventional female codes and thereby surrendered any claim to femininity: "assertiveness, aggressiveness— all characteristics of a male life of 'significant action'—are 'monstrous' in women and therefore unsuited to a gentle life of 'contemplative purity'" (28). In this context, the speaker's defense of herself leads the reader to consider what exactly it is that the speaker is so determined to deny that she gratefully displaces her own doubt with the received certainty of scriptural authority. Dickinson's presentation of manuscript variants that offer "might" as an alternative for "could" and "distant" as an alternative for "easy" magnify the uncertainty the speaker experiences as she struggles to sublimate her own unruly impulses.

The next two stanzas, where the speaker situates herself in a present founded on the scriptural precedent she has just affirmed, reveal that the contentment she so ostensibly proclaims rests on a circular logic she does her best to ignore. Her equivocal posture is signaled by the dash after "be" in the third line of stanza three, at which point it marks a break in the speaker's otherwise continuous narrative of escape from the "lot" she finds "Too hungry to be borne." Instead of completing the thought and stating what she imagines her lot would be if she were the "independent Man" mentioned at the end of stanza two, she abruptly shifts her focus to the more appropriately passive though qualified "novel Comforting" that comes from affirming the superiority of her conventional female role. The increased frequency of dashes in stanza four draws additional attention to the strained logic the speaker now employs to justify her inaction. When she reaffirms her superiority, stating, "We question if the Man – / Who own – Esteem the Opulence – / As we – ," her language is freighted with uncertainty. The final words, "Who never Can – ," suggest both the speaker's awareness of her own entrapment within a culture that denies women the right to "own" the property so essential to having a voice in public politics and her failure to truly imagine "the Opulence" of ownership. As a consequence, this two-stanza unit betrays the speaker's sublimation of the discomfort she feels when affirming her preference for an economic and political lot that denies her the political authority conferred on men.

The final stanzas relate the speaker's ultimate rationalization of female inaction by declaring that the longer she delays her assumption of full sovereignty the better able she will be to manage it when it is finally achieved. The entire construction of the speaker's future, that is the subject of these last two stanzas, reinforces both her passivity and her inability to imagine the future clearly. Even though her hands are described as "exploring" at the beginning of stanza five, the possibility of actually grasping sovereignty is presented as a matter of chance, once again establishing the speaker's failure to imagine a viable course of action. As if abashed by her own temerity at even considering such a future, the speaker in these and succeeding lines immediately translates the concrete and immediate objects of her desire into distant and safe abstractions. First she displaces her "I" with the synecdoche "Hands," then she replaces the present with an indefinite future—the "long - uneven term"—during which she may conceivably "win" political rights, but only after her hands have patiently awaited that moment when "To win, become their turn." The halting delivery signified by the dashes comports well with the quashed aspirations of the speaker who unconvincingly mouths the familiar narrative of female political deference so effectively outlined by Kerber (284–285). The speaker's declaration at the beginning of stanza six that her hands will "Fitter . . . be - for Want -" for this reason rings hollow.

When the "I" then returns in the concluding two lines, it does so as a signal that the speaker's struggle with desire has been suspended for the time being and that she is now reflecting on the significance of her actions. The absence of resolution so apparent in the speaker's closing admission, "I know not which, Desire, or Grant - / Be wholly beautiful - ," reveals that this state of temporary paralysis is one the speaker has inhabited before and that the collisions with patriarchal power just detailed have been part of a "play[ing] at Riches" that has repeatedly appeased the speaker's "Clamoring for Gold." When the manuscript at this point presents "Right" and "sight" as variants for "Grant," the poem acquires the additional status of echoing the history of female exclusion from American politics (*MBED* 936). Juxtaposing the assertiveness of legal right with the passivity of a grant, plus the displacement from public to private implied by the interiority of sight, suggestively compresses into three words the historical denial of female suffrage, the consequent subordination to male prerogative, and the aesthetic displacement of political desire, all issues with which this poem grapples. The final and most profound irony of this poem might for these reasons be its demonstration that the speaker's outward expression of female political passivity rests on inverted logic, whereby she perceives inaction in the present as the necessary precondition for an expansion of rights in the future. Readers aware of this irony are as a consequence liberated to imagine for themselves alternative forms

3. "I play at Riches – to appease –" (J 803/Fr 856), *MBED* 935–936. By permission of the Houghton Library, Harvard University. *MS AM 1118.3 (162a)* © The President and Fellows of Harvard College.

Who own - esteem the
Opulence.
As we - who never Can -

Should ever these ⁺blessing
hands
Chance Sovereign On a
Mine -
Or in the long - uneven
term
⁘ own, become ⁺their
turn -

⁺How fitter this will be
⁺for want -
Enlightening so well -
I know not which,
obtain. Or ⁺grant -
Be ⁺wholly beautiful -
⁺ right ⁺ distant ⁺ so much
Comporting ⁺ my ⁺'tis ⁺ by ⁺ Right -
sight ⁺ Chupot ⁺ utmost ⁺ I shall be -

of social action not bound by the ideological constraints that so effectively para-
lyze this speaker.

Social Class and the Poet's Politics

A clear assumption implied by the preceding discussion of sovereignty and consent in Dickinson's poems is that, important as class identity is, class should not
be viewed as either neutralizing or overly determining Dickinson's politics. On
the contrary, her potentially debilitating class status appears to have enabled her
to observe and comment on discrepancies in the democratic logic of her culture in ways that may have been less available to writers whose daily income depended on the commercial success of their published writing. This is not to suggest that Dickinson's work is free of the anxieties and prejudices that plague the
nineteenth-century American middle class; the point, rather, is that Dickinson's
material security afforded her a unique opportunity to reflect on the illogic of
her culture as experienced by a woman of her class. Bourdieu's account of artistic autonomy in "The Field of Cultural Production" usefully delineates the pre-
conditions for autonomous artistic production in language applicable to Dickinson's experience that helps account for her ability to engage with political issues
even though she did not involve herself in overt political action: "in the most
perfectly autonomous sector of the field of cultural production, where the only
audience aimed at is other producers . . . the economy of practices is based, as in
a generalized game of 'loser wins,' on a systemic inversion of the fundamental
principles of all ordinary economies: that of business (it excludes the pursuit of
profit and does not guarantee any sort of correspondence between investments
and monetary gains), that of power (it condemns honours and temporal greatness), and even that of institutionalized cultural authority (the absence of any
academic training or consecration may be considered a virtue)" (*Field* 39). In her
own way, Dickinson rather famously eschews profit, honors, and academic consecration. She never tried to sell a poem; she refused to publish when requested
to do so; and she received little if any training in the writing of poems. In fact,
her prose and poetry were often remarked as significantly flawed for her failure
to conform to the rules broadly thought of as characterizing the written expression of educated Americans. "All men say 'What' to me," she famously observed
in an August 1862 letter to Thomas Wentworth Higginson (*L* 415).

   While it might be argued that Dickinson benefited from a high level of academic training, one could certainly make an equal case that her academic background at Mount Holyoke Female Seminary, in particular, included pressures
to conform that she resisted throughout the course of her life. Even this singu-
larly privileged form of cultural "consecration" contributed to the consolida-

tion of artistic values that were at times directly opposed to conventional bourgeois practice. Most worth noticing, however, is the extent that in broad terms Dickinson's artistic life did overlap rather remarkably with Bourdieu's "autonomous sector." By means of her gift-based epistolary distribution of poems and her rejection of print publication, Dickinson distanced herself from "temporal greatness," while the conversations she conducted through her letters with other writers, such as Higginson, Helen Hunt Jackson, and Susan Huntington Gilbert Dickinson, provide evidence that she sought an audience of sympathetic artists. Her almost exclusive reliance on the dash, plus her dialogic display of multiple voices and speakers, make for a body of work that asks readers to become collaborators who jointly participate in the production of cultural meaning. Even the care with which she preserved her manuscript fascicles, sheets, and scraps may indicate her dedication to a future audience less conditioned by the poetic conventions of her day. Poems like "In Ebon Box, when years have flown" (Fr 180), "This is my letter to the World" (Fr 519), "The Bird must sing to earn the Crumb" (Fr 928), "Tell all the truth but tell it slant –" (Fr 1263), and many others contemplate a future readership.

There is, however, no denying that between the broad strokes of Dickinson's life that appear expressive of artistic autonomy, there yet remain many examples of the sort of slippage Erkkila has described in terms of Whig politics. Bourdieu readily admits that alliances between cultural producers and those who inhabit the "economically and culturally dominated positions within the field of class relations . . . are not exempt from misunderstandings and even bad faith" (*Field* 44). Important as it is, therefore, to reject the "reductionist vision which claims to explain the act of production and its product in terms of their conscious or unconscious external functions," such as class identity, the far more important interpretive principle is that the field of cultural production is always characterized by struggle that can contribute to political undecidability. In specific reference to the network of interpretive positions available in Dickinson's writing, Loeffelholz has recommended that "we see Dickinson's web as spun out between the poles of bourgeois and social art," remembering at all times that in the case of this particular artist, "autonomy is relative" ("'Plied'" 13). As with the "The Soul selects her own Society" and the "Purple Democrat" poems, the multiple readings Dickinson's poems so often support frequently stand in tension with one another.

This aspect of Dickinson's writing—her sometimes maddening penchant for contradicting herself—is often remarked on by critics precisely because what emerges through readings of multiple poems is not a sense of resolution but rather a positive desire to sustain struggle within and around the field of cultural production. Robert Weisbuch advises that as readers "we must become prohibitive in shutting down some of the mind's demands for certainty" ("Prisming" 197) because, in the final analysis, "the struggle is more valuable" (222). Accepting this element of struggle is crucial to negotiating both the undecidability of distinct poems and the many poems scattered across the Dickinson corpus that challenge or contradict one another, refusing either a complacent submission to orthodoxy or strict adherence to an activist political agenda. One of the more blatant examples of opposing stances appears when "The Soul should always stand ajar" (Fr 1017) is compared with "The Soul selects her own Society –" (Fr 409). As I have already noted, the speaker in the earlier poem remarks on a soul "Unmoved" by an "Emperor . . . kneeling / Opon her Mat," who "Choose[s] One," and then "close[s] the Valves of her attention – / Like Stone"; whereas the speaker in the later poem cautions the soul against keeping "the Heaven" waiting lest he "Depart, before the Host have slid / The Bolt unto the Door / To search for the accomplished Guest." Both of these poems stand in sharp contrast to "Of Bronze – and Blaze –" (Fr 319), "Strong Draughts of Their Refreshing Minds" (Fr 770), and "To earn it by disdaining it" (Fr 1445), all three poems that were examined previously as examples of private and public intersections.

Rather than interpreting such contradictions within Dickinson's corpus as evidence of vacillations within a master narrative that either denies or affirms communal self hood, these poems and the many like them may be understood more productively as part of a pervasive political aesthetic that traces the female citizen's struggle to embrace experience that defies containment within the binary logic of public and private. According to such a view, those poems that affirm the possibility of an isolated self stand at one pole within a spectrum of relationships with the external world countered at the other pole by poems that convey an inescapable sense of immersion in the public sphere. A poem like "To my quick ear the Leaves – conferred –" (Fr 912), where the speaker complains that "Creation seemed a mighty Crack – / To make me visible," would exemplify that pole where there appears no alternative to public exposure. The many poems that register details of struggle may be approached as charting a middle ground between self and other, where the impossibility of binary distinction is most forcibly asserted. One speaker tells us, for instance, that those "Who never lost, are unprepared / A Coronet to find!" (Fr 136B) then goes on to explain that achievement is predicated on the recognition that uncertainty, vulnerability, and doubt accompany struggle: "Legions" must be "overcome" and "*Colors* taken / On Revolution Day" if the self is to receive "the Royal scar" that will earn the approval of "Angels." Similarly, "To learn the Transport by the Pain –" (Fr 178B) describes a "sovreign Anguish" and the speaker of "A Plated Life – diversified" (Fr 864) states, "'tis when // A Value struggle – it exist – ."

What is important here is not just the particular experience conveyed within specific poems, though that is certainly important also; what matters more for an understanding of the way Dickinson's writing enters, skirts, or denies the domain of public politics is her collective consideration of both public action and the multiple impulses that motivate withdrawal into the most private recesses of the self. Dickinson's poems tell us that the personal and the political always stand in tension with each other. This is precisely what Wolosky recommends when she reminds readers that the "notion of poetry as a self-enclosed aesthetic realm" only begins "to emerge at the end of the nineteenth century. Within the course of the nineteenth century itself, such an enclosed poetic realm seems not to have been assumed. . . . Instead, poetry directly participated in and addressed the pressing issues facing the nation" (14). As a consequence, scholarly pronouncements, like the following by Paula Bernat Bennett, that present Dickinson as sealed off from history because she could "afford to write in a void and write the void into her poetry, cutting its links to the social world and to the material connections she shared with others" ("poet peers" 228) should be viewed as presenting only part of a more complex cultural picture that acknowledges struggle with social forces.

American Women Poets and the Politics of Dickinson's Poems

In light of Dickinson's ability to compose poems that persistently demonstrate the central role imagination plays in limiting or empowering female sovereignty, it should perhaps come as no surprise that among the first to acknowledge the political implications of Dickinson's writing have been women writers whose own imaginative work is openly political. One of the most important public events ever to affirm Dickinson's influence on the politics of other women writers came through the May 15, 1986, centennial tribute that took place in South Orange, New Jersey, where fifteen women poets—including Adrienne Rich, Gwendolyn Brooks, and Denise Levertov—dedicated an entire day to communicating their responses to Dickinson. At that gathering, Sharon Olds publicly declared, "I think she's political, intensely political" (12). Olds then dedicated a poem to Dickinson titled "He Comes for the Jewish Family, 1942." Responding to Dickinson with a poem so deeply rooted in the all-too-real horror of politically enforced racial injustice, Olds can be understood as fulfilling the political desire evident in many of Dickinson's speakers but ultimately frustrated by the cultural restrictions imposed on their imaginations. In this sense, Olds collaborates with Dickinson by taking heart from her precursor's honest expression of frustrated desire and seeking to embody that desire more completely in her own considerably more public utterance.

When Martha Nell Smith writes that the poets who participated in the New

Jersey celebration affirmed Dickinson's "connectedness," she does so with special emphasis on a "responsibility to others" that Olds and the rest reciprocate when they unite Dickinson's work with their own politically charged writing ("Introduction" 6). Smith draws on Gwendolyn Brooks's centennial comments to convey her own conviction that turning to Dickinson's words "will be a profoundly political act" precisely because doing so constitutes a form of political dissent: "It's a political act," Smith states, "to refuse to join what Gwendolyn Brooks calls the 'self crowned' editors 'in the seduced arena,' the 'harmony hushers,' those who determine the worth of words according to supply and demand and official sanction" (8). Separating Dickinson from institutional recognition and the economics of supply and demand further establishes Dickinson's position within Bourdieu's sphere of autonomous cultural production. In the remarks by Brooks that Smith drew from, Brooks deliberately brings Dickinson into the present moment as a voice urging political activism. "I'm sure that Dickinson would have felt this way," Brooks states, "if she had lived into this most challenging time" (7). Frances Payne Adler reiterates the sentiment expressed variously by Brooks, Olds, and the thirteen other poets when she titles her talk "Toward a Poetry that Matters: Emily Dickinson as Activist/Activator." And Toi Derricote voices what may well have been a common interest of all participants when she announced her wish that "we could meet, break into groups, and everybody talk about politics, poetry, and Emily Dickinson" (2). Following these words, Derricote quoted Dickinson lines that directly address the poet's engagement with the larger world: "I took my Power in my Hand – / And went against the World –" (Fr 660). That poem's closing admission that "Myself / Was all the one that fell" speaks to the unfinished business of female political engagement, on whatever scale and to whatever extent possible.

At another gathering that also took place in 1986, this one at a junior high school in Santa Barbara, Chicana writer Sandra Cisneros spoke of Dickinson as a motivating force in her own life as a writer. In her lecture to the students, Cisneros told of her "favorite American poet, Emily Dickinson . . . who in her later life never even strayed beyond the house and its gardens, but who wrote in her lifetime 1,775 poems" ("Notes" 74–75). These poems, Cisneros explained, provided "inspiration and hope all the years in high school and the first two in college when I was too busy being in love to write" (75). Cisneros's comments are particularly intriguing as they represent an explicitly democratic transmission of Dickinson's work to a new generation of readers who will hereafter turn to Dickinson's words with the knowledge that an openly political minority writer recommended that they do so.

Equally intriguing is the fact that Cisneros, a writer whom John Carlos Rowe has grouped with Leslie Marmon Silko, Louise Erdrich, Helena Viramontes, and

Le Ly Hayslip as contributing to "the most remarkable 'renaissance' in American literary history" (252), should have based a chapter of her immensely popular book *The House on Mango Street* on Dickinson's poem "Four Trees – opon [*sic*] a solitary Acre –" (Fr 778). How, precisely, does this poem, surely one of the least obviously political of any Dickinson poem, inform a work that Rowe describes as literature that can contribute "significantly . . . to the practical politics of the rights movements by women and minorities that continue to shape American social and cultural reality" (252)? Fortunately, Geoffrey Sanborn provides an answer to this question that further clarifies the way even Dickinson's most abstract celebrations of private subjectivity can powerfully evoke imaginative perceptions of democratic social space.

Looking most closely at the first stanza of Dickinson's poem, Sanborn emphasizes the importance Dickinson attributes to the fact that the "Four Trees . . . Maintain." He then presents Cisneros as translating the tree's power to maintain into a "strength" her protagonist, Esperanza, associates with "keeping" (*House* 74–75). "They send ferocious roots beneath the ground," Esperanza tells us, while also growing upward, where they "bite the sky with violent teeth and never quit their anger." "This," Esperanza concludes, "is how they keep." Sanborn argues that the "keeping" attributed to the trees represents the artistic concept of "intransitiveness" that Cisneros draws from "Dickinson's emphasis on the subversiveness of intransitive existence and Dickinson's association of that subversiveness with the stubborn materiality of writing" (1340). The private resistance enacted through intransitiveness introduces what Sanborn describes as a socially subversive "heretical space" that is both private and dependent on the perception of " 'lack at the very heart of [social] structures' " (1336). When Dickinson and Cisneros invoke this heretical space through their use of intransitiveness, they perform the political act of restoring "contingency to privacy" and identifying "privacy as the pre-condition of new collective formulations" (1343). Sanborn focuses on this last literary gesture, the one that invests privacy with social significance, as offering readers a universally accessible private space for the creation of democratic alternatives to conventional social practice. Cisneros discovered political potential in Dickinson's minimalist poem precisely because the poem is about the establishment of sovereignty through resistance to cultural forces that constrain the will.

One of the most impressive accomplishments of this and other Dickinson's poems is their power to reach beyond their place and moment of origin to awaken the desire for more effective expressions of political action in readers of other racial, ethnic, and economic communities. When Cisneros concludes *The House on Mango Street* by having Esperanza declare that she has "gone away to come back" (110), she does so with the aim of establishing that Esperanza's turn to privacy is part of a larger plan that includes her community. Esperanza will come back, she states, "For the ones I left behind. For the ones who cannot out." Like Dickinson's, Esperanza's exploration of her own isolated subjectivity is conducted with a sense of responsibility to others, to those who cannot yet speak for themselves. Sanborn emphasizes precisely this point when he recommends that we revise our view of Dickinson's politics: "Instead of viewing Dickinson as someone whose self-gratifying isolation is essentially at odds with democratic sociality," he writes, "we should view her as someone whose 'exposure of our passionate and limitless desire to be the ideal' makes possible 'its continual deconstruction and displacement'" (1345; Kaja Silverman qtd. by Sanborn). Such language clearly resonates with the frustrated desire for political participation expressed by many of Dickinson's female speakers, whose struggles to realize incompletely conceived political ideals drives home the shortcomings of a culture that proclaims democratic values but cripples the political imagination of half its members.

When it comes to the political reach of her work, Dickinson's class identity should for this reason not be seen as an obstacle that necessarily limits her appeal; instead, class should be understood as crucial to framing her writing within a particular historical community out of which she emerges as one model of resistance that can be transferred to readers in other communities precisely because it is *one* model, not *the* model. The particular appeal of her work as a political writer lies in her ability to provoke imaginative responses in readers like Olds, Derricote, and Cisneros who inhabit very different racial, social, economic, and historical circumstances. Sanborn's analysis of Dickinson's "'continual deconstruction and displacement'" (1345) of the ideal can as a consequence be understood as central to Dickinson's poetic placement of readers in the "theater of verbal (symbolic) action" that fosters the "recognizably democratic (polycentric) cultural semiotic" described by Ruttenburg (15). By sorting through the conflicting voices that complicate and often displace the surface narratives of Dickinson's speakers, readers transfer Dickinson's resistance to the ideological constraints of her historical moment to the precise circumstances of their own lives.

An important element of Dickinson's appeal is therefore Dickinson's own historical orientation, grounded in her perspective as a white, middle-class American woman. In a significant passage that appears in Cisneros's "Notes to a Young(er) Writer," Cisneros relates her discovery of Dickinson's privileged socioeconomic status, paying special attention to Dickinson's relationship with her family's domestic laborer, Margaret Maher. "Maybe Emily Dickinson's Irish housekeeper had to sacrifice her life," Cisneros wonders, "so that Emily could live hers locked upstairs in the corner bedroom writing her 1,775 poems" (75). Sanborn treats this discovery by Cisneros as compromising Dickinson's usefulness as a model of political revolt, asserting that these facts reveal Dickinson's "restrictive understanding of who might carry out that revolt" (1341). I depart from Sanborn's analysis at this point, arguing instead that Cisneros's perception of socioeconomic difference in fact contributes to the political relevance Dickinson has for her, as the discovery of difference clarifies the extent that the resistance Dickinson models has not yet been situated in the community Cisneros inhabits. In this sense, Cisneros's perception that Dickinson's circumstance is similar to but still different from hers liberates Cisneros to adopt Dickinson for her own purposes. The same cultural specificity that disqualifies Dickinson from assuming elevated, universal standing as a voice for all women, makes her work available to writers like Cisneros who serve the interests of their particular communities by adopting the voices of equals.

That the historical record now shows Dickinson's influence on political writers like Cisneros, Olds, and Brooks does indeed strengthen the case that Dickinson can herself be read as a political writer. This achievement goes a long way toward satisfying Rowe's requirement that "the politics of American literature . . . be revaluated in terms [of] . . . the discursive communities such literature helps constitute" (14). Facts alone are not likely to dispel uncertainties about the politics of Dickinson's writing, however. The range of voices so central to the presentation of choice in the poems means that conservative readings are always supportable and every bit as inevitable as readings that draw attention to the ways Dickinson challenges the political ideology of her day. One unavoidable outcome of Dickinson's class-inflected politics is that her writing will always bear the conservative imprint of white middle-class New England womanhood, even while urging an expanded exercise of democratic sovereignty. Readers will quite naturally struggle with the question of political undecidability as they balance the evidence of class privilege with evidence of political resistance. The crucial point to bear in mind, then, is that in Dickinson's writing we discover a site of consistent but imperfect political resistance, a site that can tell us as much about our own political beliefs as about hers. If she is expected to speak for all readers, she may finally speak for none; but if viewed as one among many voices in an unfolding drama of democratic sociality, Dickinson's effort becomes representative by virtue of those very features that are so often limiting and, ultimately, so distinctly human.

2

Democratic Rhetoric and the Gymnastic Self

Central to Dickinson's relationship with readers and her elevation of individual sovereignty is the rhetorical stance she consistently strikes in her poetry. In this chapter, I look at Dickinson's characteristic representation of what I refer to as the gymnastic self that emerges through her writing as the verbal expression of democratic personality. In the development of this self, Dickinson draws on widespread nineteenth-century rhetorical practices that scholars today have identified as distinctively democratic in their aims. Through her juggling of verbal registers that mix colloquial vocabularies with various specialized discourses and polysyllabic Latinate terms, Dickinson resembles writers like Ralph Waldo Emerson and Walt Whitman who also sought to promote democratic modes of thought and action. What distinguishes Dickinson from Emerson and Whitman is her refusal to acknowledge history as the material expression of divine order. Like many other women writers of her day, Dickinson refused to view historical processes that had consistently excluded women from positions of public authority as providing adequate precedent for female self-expression in a democratic age. Rather than constructing poems that make use of speakers who effectively guide readers by modeling or prescribing virtuous conduct, the way that Emerson and Whitman do, Dickinson and other women poets magnify the inadequacies of choices made either by the speakers themselves or by those the speakers observe. In this way, Dickinson and many other women writers ask their readers to resist historical precedent and imagine forms of female action that will change the course of history. What distinguishes Dickinson from other female poets is her close focus on the disruptive thought processes that make possible any subjective departure from comfortable patterns of conformity. For Dickinson, more than any of her contemporaries, the assertion of a sovereign self is always a rhetorically staged balancing act that weighs the ease of conduct within the sameness of the status quo against the uncertainties associated with the difference of unprecedented thought and action.

In an 1881 letter to Elizabeth Holland, Dickinson describes herself as leading a "Gymnastic Destiny" and closes with a riddle about a bird that sings "as firm in the centre of Dissolution, as in it's [*sic*] Father's nest –" (*L* 687). "Phenix [*sic*], or the Robin?" she asks, then figuratively walks away from her reader, ending her letter with the statement, "While I leave you to guess, I will take Mother her Tea –" (*L* 688). The verbal play so deftly displayed here effectively communicates the relationship with readers Dickinson repeatedly establishes in both poems and letters. Put simply, Dickinson asks that readers join her in the performance of a gymnastic self. The linguistic balancing act that unites the paired opposites, "Dissolution" and "Father's nest," with "Phenix" and "Robin" also unites Dickinson the dutiful daughter and verbal trickster with Elizabeth Holland, the participant in a harmless parlor game and arbiter of existential conundrums. Such deliberate conflations of cosmic and domestic, grand and commonplace, do indeed complement the clash of monarchical and democratic terms explored in the previous chapter; the difference is that in her rhetorical juggling of verbal registers Dickinson appears to have adopted a practice less dictated by unconscious class allegiances and more clearly consistent with widespread nineteenth-century efforts to create a linguistic body capable of accommodating the fluid personality demanded by democratic citizenship.[1]

Along with her implicit declaration that she herself possesses a fluid, multifarious self, Dickinson's posing of the closing riddle for Holland represents one instance of what I want to explore as a characteristic rhetorical demand that readers invest daily patterns of thought with unruly gymnastics. Doing so performs the dual function of ensuring that choices about self-expression remain a conscious feature of everyday life while also magnifying the value of subjective experience as crucial to the resistance upon which democratic sovereignty depends. Emerson does this as well, as when he chronicles his own entrapment in familiar experience and inscribes the word "whim" on his lintel so that he will leave space in his life for spontaneity (*Selections,* "Self-Reliance" 150) or declares that the "one thing we seek with insatiable desire is to forget ourselves, to be surprised out of our propriety" ("Circles" 178). Whitman similarly admits to the dangers of being seduced by localized patterns of thought and feeling; one familiar example is his demonstration in section twenty-eight of "Song of Myself" that sensual, emotional and intellectual impulses can tyrannize the self (ll. 619–641), another occurs in section thirty-seven where death and suffering draw consciousness into a narrowing spiral of loss (ll. 945–958), prompting his "I" to conclude in section thirty-eight that "I have been stunn'd" and "discover myself on the verge of a usual mistake" (ll. 960, 962). All three writers encourage their readers to retain a sense of self incommensurate with the concrete exigencies of the immediate historical moment in order that the self not cede control to predictable patterns of behavior. By this means, all three present readers with distinct versions of the sort of personality called for in a liberal democracy where citizenship emerges as a continuous balancing of the private and public features of the individual self.

As Kenneth Cmiel has pointed out in *Democratic Eloquence: The Fight over Popular Speech in Nineteenth-Century America,* American culture was deeply invested in the role played by language in the formation of democratic personality: "The nineteenth-century debate over language was a fight over what kind of personality was needed to sustain a healthy democracy" (14). Precisely what form this personality might take and how such a form materialized in literary America has excited much critical and theoretical discussion that bears directly on Dickinson's status within the community of contemporary democratic writers. Cmiel makes the argument, for instance, that the spread of democratic rhetoric received its greatest impetus through the emergence of what he refers to as " 'middling styles' " or a " 'middling rhetoric' " that "encouraged people to shift back and forth across linguistic registers, [in] a process that confused social perception" (17). Alexis de Tocqueville acknowledges the particular problem this linguistic variability posed for educated Englishmen who complained "that the Americans often mix their styles in an odd way, sometimes putting words together which, in the mother tongue, are carefully kept apart" (478). The outcome was, in Cmiel's words, "new thinking about language [that] more closely connected to what contemporary sociologists call 'role theory' than to any classical sense of a 'unified soul' " (14).[2] Dickinson's hybrid embrace of phoenix and robin, together with the ironically disclosed false dichotomy posed by her concluding riddle, fits the pattern Cmiel outlines: Dickinson is clearly interested in expanding rather than restricting the self's role-playing potential.[3]

The tensions generated through such an unstable and hence gymnastic hybridity extend also to a range of idioms descending from distinct religious, republican, monarchical, scientific, philosophical, and literary traditions, to name just a few. Christopher Looby has argued that the "very vagueness and undecidability of the hybrid rhetoric . . . made it a magnificent instrument" (228), not because it obscured tensions, but rather because "the contradictory nature of such a rhetoric . . . underwrote whatever energy and effect the rhetoric had, precisely because of the tension built into it. The violent conflation of the two idioms with their partially discrepant implications guaranteed an inner instability" that "made subjective reorientations possible" (229). Tocqueville explains that this linguistic process can "often make both the old and the new signification ambiguous" (479). He then describes the particular challenge posed by writers who present readers with the rhetorical instability Looby has in mind: "writers hardly ever appear to stick to a single thought," he complains, "but always seem to envisage a group of ideas, leaving the reader to guess which is intended" (480). Dickinson's inclusion of a riddle in her letter to Holland as the appropriate format for contemplating multiple simultaneous identities signals her welcome of this destabilization; she playfully requests that Elizabeth "guess" who she is, despite years of prior acquaintance.

A central difference between Dickinson's approach and that of both Emerson and Whitman is that Dickinson magnifies the need for choices that readers must make without actually enacting those choices for her readers and by that means producing verbal models of exemplary selves. As Margaret Dickie has pointed out, Emerson "saw himself as a representative self and wrote as a man at the center of his age" (15). Emerson's eponymous Merlin, for instance, performs as an ideal poet who may be defined by his past actions: "Merlin's blows are strokes of fate, / Chiming with the forest tone" and through his work, the poem tells us, we see "Extremes of nature reconciled" (*Selections* 448). Whitman's democratic speaker in "Song of Myself" likewise embodies the ideal liberal posture when he describes himself as "Both in and out of the game and watching and wondering at it" (1. 79). Dickinson does point to the need to risk entry into history, as in "We lose – because we win –" (Fr 28), where gamblers choose to toss the dice and thus enter social life fully alert to the odds of losing, but she does not present a consolidated self that successfully triumphs over forces that threaten dissolution.

Instead, like many of her female literary precursors and contemporaries, Dickinson leaves it up to her readers to imagine for themselves the forms such triumph might take. In Dickie's words, "Because she was a woman and a poet, [Dickinson] was freer than [Emerson] from the conviction that she was representative and also from the necessity to be so" (15). Elizabeth Oakes-Smith epitomizes the female writer's practice of hinting at forms of experience not embodied on the page when her speaker in "The Poet" exhorts an unidentified future poet to lift her voice and bridge the chasm separating private sorrow from public joy. "Sing, sing—Poet, sing!" the speaker urges, believing that by exercising her talent the poet's "Lays of sorrowing," provoked by "the thorn beneath thy breast," will transform in the public air, becoming "Lays that wake a mighty gladness, / Spite of all their mournful sadness" (Walker, *Poets* 75). Virginia Jackson accurately describes the aspect of Oakes-Smith's poem that I want to focus on when she states that by moving between "a received literary identity and the antithetical experience it lifts into metaphor" (225) the poem provides "a view, as it were, behind the wings of poetic production" (226). Dickinson similarly draws readers into the poet's anticipation of democratic poetic achievement when her

speaker in "This was a Poet –" (Fr 446) explains that the poet "Distills amazing
sense / From Ordinary Meanings" yet leaves it to the reader to imagine what the
ordinary meanings are and what amazing sense might emerge out of them. Alice
Fulton encapsulates this significant feature of Dickinson's writing: "Her poems
prolong the intoxicating moment before choice when all options are potentially
ours" (152–153).

In her poems, as in letters like the one to Elizabeth Holland, Dickinson seeks
to keep her reader's imagination fresh by rhetorically invoking an incompletely
articulated otherness—the diverse self of the letter and the poet pointed to in
the poem—that insists on an immediacy produced by the reader's imaginative
engagement with the choices Dickinson presents. By this means Dickinson in-
tensifies the letter reader's physical sensations of an actual visit by the person
who penned the letter and increases the poem reader's sense of personal discovery. Dickinson's comment to Holland about disappearing for a moment in
order to serve her mother tea further reinforces the letter's metonymic construction, just as the poem's poetic anticipation of the ideal poet metonymically in-
vokes the reader's ideal. William Merrill Decker has described the "metonymic
turn" of Dickinson's letters in a manner that might also provide insight into the
poems (161), especially if Decker's comments are read in the context of Marietta
Messmer's argument that the letters are "generic acts of transgression" that collapse artificial boundaries separating letters from poems while also bridging the
gap between private and public utterance (48).[4] Decker proposes that Dickinson's construction of "the letter . . . as type or relic of the writer" is a central con-
ceit that runs through much of Dickinson's correspondence (161). As a consequence, letters for Dickinson approximate bodily encounters, imposing demands
on readers similar to those that attend actual face-to-face encounters.

In this context, the apparent dilemma Dickinson poses for readers like
Elizabeth Holland bears a striking resemblance to the identity confusion Nancy
Ruttenburg has associated with the emergence of democratic personality in
Puritan New England: "In place of the comparatively solid knowledge gleaned
from the infallible marks of reputation, long acquaintance, and church member-
ship, cultural authorities found themselves struggling to understand what modern society terms personality: an individuality which, lacking a transcendent
referent, reveals itself in and as a series of representations, each of which might
plausibly support the claim to constitute the truth about the self" (82).[5] If we
read Dickinson within this cultural context, it makes sense that she would refuse to provide Thomas Wentworth Higginson the stabilizing pictorial likeness
he requested in the early months of their friendship (L 411), giving him instead
the discontinuous self of her letters and poems; the retiring writer quieter than
"the Mouse, that dents your Galleries" and the assertive master poet who declares

"I have no Tribunal" are notable examples that appear in one 1862 letter (*L* 409). Neither should we think strange Dickinson's 1871 observation to Louise Norcross that "riddles are healthful food" (*L* 488).

The rhetorical concern with democratic personality so evident in the letters surfaces with equal force in Dickinson's poems, where the gymnastic inclusion of widely varied linguistic registers and idioms takes place without the stabilizing context provided by a date, a place, or a specific correspondent, thus making discovery of the speaker's identity even more dependent on linguistic performance.[6] One of Dickinson's earliest poems, "Sic transit gloria mundi" (Fr 2), amply demonstrates the embrace of private and public functions that characterizes the letters in general, while also showing that Dickinson adopted this democratic rhetorical practice for her own poetic purposes from an early stage in her writing life. Following the opening Latin phrase, Dickinson's speaker rapidly dances from elevated to vulgar diction and from high-minded aspirations to the most mundane of diurnal details. Hence the highbrow connotations evoked by the polysyllabic Latin terms of the first line are undermined by the mock Elizabethan mostly single-syllable terminology that makes up the paraphrase in the second: " 'How doth the busy bee.' " The poem then moves from the irreverent schoolgirl Latin of the second stanza's "Oh veni vidi vici! / Oh caput cap-a-pie!" to a celebration of popular culture in the third stanzas's hurrahs for Peter Parley and Daniel Boone. The seventh stanza's stately cadences further advance the poem's rhetorical aims by satirically coupling the discourse of selfless civic duty with a Saxonized expression of fastidious self-centeredness:

Unto the Legislature
My country bids me go,
I'll take my India rubbers
In case the wind should blow.

The aim served by this speaker's rhetorical juggling is that of humorously loosening the hold any linguistic register may have on the development of a flexible and responsive democratic self. As Looby has indicated, a "violent conflation" of idioms like that utilized here destabilizes subjectivity, making possible the sort of gymnastic reorientation Dickinson advocates (229).

The preceding are merely a few of the many Dickinson poems and letters that reveal her participation in political debates that implicitly informed the rhetorical readers and composition guides to which she was exposed during her formal education. The four main texts that scholars have linked to Dickinson's education provide the backdrop for Dickinson's own rhetorical strategies, and demonstrate that Dickinson formulated her position through engagement with arguments that informed the literary culture of her day. In *Emily Dickinson's Textbooks,* Carlton Lowenberg identifies Samuel P. Newman's 1839 *A Practical System of Rhetoric . . .* , Richard Green Parker's 1844 *Aids to English Composition . . .* , Ebenezer Porter's 1841 *The Rhetorical Reader . . .* , and Richard Whately's 1834 *Elements of Rhetoric . . .* as Dickinson's primary sources of formal training in rhetoric. A quick overview of the philosophical positions that characterize just three of these works supports the notion that Dickinson would have developed her own rhetorical approach with the understanding that her stylistic choices carried political weight.[7] The varied approaches communicated in these works lend strength to Cmiel's contention that nineteenth-century grammars and rhetorics expressed the "contradictory cultural pressures" detectable in the culture at large: "The popular grammars and dictionaries of the early nineteenth century appeared to be part of an educational movement that not only perpetuated and diffused refined cultural forms but *also* undermined the rule of the refined" (56). The range of opinions and the disparity in approach that surface in the texts Dickinson studied suggest that the emphasis on choice that is so central to her writing may have derived at least in part from the choices she herself had to make when sorting through contending authoritative resources as a girl.

The most well known and the most authoritarian of the rhetorical guides Dickinson used is Ebenezer Porter's *Rhetorical Reader,* the text Edith Wylder drew upon in establishing her theory that Dickinson's "dashes" perform as elocutionary marks. Dickinson would probably have encountered this text at the Amherst Academy, where it was listed in the school catalogues covering the years Dickinson attended. In the opening pages of this text, Porter identifies his audience in a manner leaving little doubt that for him a systematic study of rhetoric contributes to civic order by stabilizing patriarchal class and gender distinctions: "Every intelligent father," he declares, "who would have his son or daughter qualified to hold a respectable rank in well-bred society, will regard [rhetorical polish] as the very first of polite accomplishments" (2). His approach to teaching similarly expresses his top-down philosophy. In his preface he repeatedly assures the reader that his system is designed to curb native habits (vi) and establish in their place a thoroughly integrated set of rules so seamlessly internalized as to "govern . . . practice spontaneously, and without reflection" (18). Moreover, Porter's declamation exercises require that the student enter "as far as possible the *spirit of the* author; then *transcribe* [the piece] in a fair hand; then *mark with pencil,* the inflections, emphasis, &c. required on different words;-then *read it rhetorically to his Teacher,* changing his pencil marks as the case may require; and then commit it to memory *perfectly*" (vii). The persistent micromanagement of reading conveyed by these words suggests that for Porter sound rhetoric and hence civil order is an outgrowth of stable and predictable identity.

Richard Whately's *Elements of Rhetoric* contrasts sharply with Porter's primarily through its deliberate grounding in democratic principles and its condemnation of elocutionary systems. Dickinson most likely encountered this book in her family library where it appeared "inscribed with her father's name and the year 1839" (Lindberg-Seyersted, *Punctuation* 24). In his introduction, Whately justifies rhetorical study as the means to unite all segments of society. He writes that "the nature of the government in the ancient democratical States caused a demand for public speakers, and for such speakers as should be able to gain influence not only with educated persons . . . , but with a promiscuous multitude" (Whately 11). A particular problem democratic America posed for skilled practitioners of rhetoric is what Whately describes as the public distrust of rhetorical display: "Such is the distrust excited by any suspicion of Rhetorical artifice, that every speaker or writer who is anxious to carry his point, endeavors to disown or to keep out of sight any superiority of skill; and wishes to be considered as relying rather on the strength of his cause, and the soundness of his views, than on his ingenuity and expertness as an advocate" (12–13). Whately's rejection of elocutionary systems that "study analytically the emphases, tones, pauses, degrees of loudness, &c." (260), derives from his belief that such systems inevitably reveal their artifice. He concludes, "Whoever therefore learns, and endeavors to apply in practice, any artificial rules of Elocution, so as to deliberately modulate his voice conformably to the principles he has adopted . . . will hardly ever fail to betray his intention; which always gives offense when perceived" (261). Brita Lindberg-Seyerstad argues in *Emily Dickinson's Punctuation* that the "Dickinson we know from the letters and the poems: original, independent, reckless, must have listened willingly to this condemnation of artificiality, and if she had earlier been drilled in another school [Porter's], she very likely disregarded its teachings in favor of Whately's recommendations of a truly natural style of elocution" (25). Whately's interest in the democratic origins of American rhetoric complements his concern with a heterogeneous public and a respect for natural forms of expression that dramatically distinguishes him from Porter. For Whately, conformity to fixed rhetorical rules contributes to distrust and a reduction in the free exchange of ideas crucial to democratic citizenship.

The third text, Richard Green Parker's *Aids to English Composition*, shares Whately's resistance to rules, but goes even further in urging that grammar and rhetoric meet the pragmatic demands of a changing American public. Richard Sewall has argued in his biography of Dickinson that it is "more likely that [she] followed such liberal advice as [Parker's] rather than so confining a system as Porter's" (349 n. 9). He then proposes that she would have been particularly attracted by the following passage from Parker's opening paragraph: "Genius cannot be fettered, and an original and thinking mind, replete with its own exuberance, will often burst out in spontaneous gushings, and open to itself new channels, through which the treasures of thought will flow in rich and rapid currents" (Parker 3).

Parker's respect for innovation as a tool essential to the outward expression of genius is consistent with his overall conviction that rhetorical form be subservient to the language user's inner nature, and not the other way around. Sewall points out that Parker's comments on the flexibility of the dash and capitalization would have appealed to Dickinson. In describing the dash, Parker observes that when used "by modern writers, it is employed as a substitute for almost all the other marks; being used sometimes for a comma, semicolon, colon, or period; sometimes for a question or an exclamation" (41). His remarks on capital letters are similarly suggestive of Dickinson's usage: "Any words when remarkably emphatical, or when they are the principal subject of the composition, may begin with capitals" (35). Even if Dickinson did not draw directly from Parker in developing her own approach to rhetorical flexibility, it is important to recognize that her linguistic practice represents an application of published guidelines that carried with them a distinct awareness of the relationship between democracy and literary stylistics.

Viewing Parker's discussion in the context of the Porter and Whately rhetorics makes it abundantly evident that Dickinson's education contained contradictions that she had to come to terms with independently. Her conflation of linguistic registers, her active solicitation of reader participation, and her investigation of democratic subjectivity suggest her responsiveness to Whately. Similarly, her frequent disregard of formal conventions, her flexible dashes, and her use of capital letters indicate sympathy with Parker. What she gains from Porter is harder to assess purely on the evidence provided by her literary corpus. I would argue, though, that Porter clarified the way a strict adherence to linguistic rules supports what Dickinson would view as a negative vision of civic order, one characterized by patriarchal authority, rigid class distinctions and unified identity. Her more liberal view of civic order would be consistent with a broad Whig tendency to adopt middling rhetoric that Cmiel describes as having become so pervasive that even "Whigs of the highest culture went 'down to the people' in the 1840 campaign" (61). Such a view would almost certainly have registered in the staunchly Whig Dickinson home. In that case, the "Gymnastic Destiny" Dickinson traces through her poems and letters may even have been influenced by family discussion as well as the debates carried out in the textbooks she encountered in school.

Examples of poems that juxtapose, mix, and blend verbal registers can be found throughout the Dickinson corpus. In "A little East of Jordan" (Fr 145B), the patriarch Jacob is described as a "Gymnast" who wrestles an angel without knowing it. Direct mixing of earthly and divine elements is reinforced by common-place and elevated idioms, as when the angel requests a pause for "Breakfast" and Jacob's discovery of his adversary's divinity is revealed in elevated poetic language that incorporates sacred scripture: "Light swung the silver fleeces / 'Peniel' Hills beyond, / And the bewildered Gymnast / Found he had worsted God!"[8] The speaker of "Many a phrase has the English language –" (Fr 333) cele-brates the versatility of English by uniting specialized geographic metaphors and technical linguistic terminology with popular descriptions of nature. En-glish, the poem explains, is enormously flexible: "Murmuring, like old Caspian Choirs, / When the Tide's a'lull –" and "Saying itself in new inflection – / Like a Whippowil – ." Dickinson similarly intermingles common and refined language in "What Soft – Cherubic Creatures –" (Fr 675), where she describes the "Dimity Convictions" of "Gentlewomen" as "A Horror so refined" that these women are "Ashamed" of the oxymoronic "common – Glory" revealed in the "Fisherman's – Degree" assumed by "Deity." In like manner, the speaker of "By my Window have I for Scenery" (Fr 849) imbues the ordinary with extraordinary features by inserting a specialized phrase in her question about the tree outside her window: "Was the Pine at my Window a 'Fellow / Of the Royal' Infinity?" The contradic-tory evaluations of a female life described in "She rose as high as His Occasion" (Fr 1019) are captured in language that juxtaposes the anonymous "Dust" of an undistinguished existence with a linguistically coded honorific burial signified by "Westminster," where a presumably significant literary achievement is me-morialized. Lastly, a child's innocent observation that forms the first line of "I held it so tight that I lost it" (Fr 1659) is translated by the last line into a com-ment on literary genre: "Of many a vaster Capture," we are informed, "That is the Elegy – ." In these and the many other poems that regularly employ a diver-sity of idioms and specialized vocabularies, Dickinson requires her readers to ex-perience the extraordinary elasticity that characterizes the epistemological het-erogeneity of the democratic self.

Emerson, Whitman, and Contemporary Women Poets

Dickinson was far from unique in drawing attention to the flexibility of the democratic self, and it is important to appreciate how much her rhetorical prac-tice was part of a broad cultural interest in promoting democratic values. Emer-son and Whitman, as well as many nineteenth-century women writers, also present language as a way of instilling in readers an awareness of democratic versatility. Emerson famously calls for a poet who can artistically celebrate the raw material of American life when in "The Poet" he deploys a magnificent mix of political and social referents to describe such a genius viewing America with "tyrannous eye" and discerning "in the barbarism and materialism of the times, another carnival of the same gods whose picture he so much admires in Homer" (*Selections* 238). He gives verse expression to this democratic aim in "Merlin" where his bard "Must smite the chords rudely and hard" (447) and "mount to paradise / By the stairway of surprise" (448). The outcome of such art may be discerned under the heading "Art" in "Mottoes," where Emerson presents a "drudge in dusty frock" who is enabled by art to "Spy behind the city clock / Retinues of airy kings" (461). Whitman enumerates in considerably more personal language what the average American, like Emerson's drudge, is capable of embracing. "Of every hue and caste am I," he writes in section sixteen of "Song of Myself," "of every rank and religion, / A farmer, mechanic, artist, gentleman, sailor, quaker" (11. 345–347). Whitman even more dramatically juxtaposes contrary linguistic registers a few lines later where the descriptive specificity of "The moth and the fish eggs" that "are in their place" is immediately conjoined with the highly abstract language of "The palpable . . . and the impalpable," each of which is also "in its place" (11. 352, 354). Lydia Sigourney accomplishes a similar yoking of the concrete particular with the voluminously abstract when in "To a Shred of Linen" her speaker addresses "A defunct pillow-case" that is then imaginatively transformed into a "fair page" of linen paper upon which "Wisdom and truth, their hallow'd lineaments / Trace for posterity" (Walker, *Poets* 22, 23). Lucy Larcom in like manner proclaims the fluid imagination of the democratic self when in "Weaving" she asks her readers to consider that the factory girl who "All day . . . stands before her loom" is "entangled in her dreams" just as Alfred Lord Tennyson's "fair weaver of Shalott" was, "Who left her mystic mirror's gleams / To gaze on light Sir Lancelot" (228). As these examples demonstrate, the mixing of verbal registers in Dickinson's poems can be read as her own incorporation of a rhetorical practice that had broad currency in her day.

Positioning Dickinson's democratic rhetoric in the context of Emerson, Whitman, and contemporary women writers is important not only because doing so demonstrates shared political interests but also more importantly because it draws attention to the extent that Dickinson joins other writers in producing poetry that aimed to influence the political awareness of readers. For this reason Emerson calls poets "liberating gods" (*Selections*, "The Poet" 236). "They are free," he declares, "and they make free." Whitman, especially, expresses his determination that poetry act as a bridge to readers who will enter a joint project of imagining the shape and form of democratic life. He makes this clear in the second section of "Song of Myself" when he informs his readers, "You shall not look through my eyes either, not take things from me, / You shall listen to all sides and filter them from your self" (11. 36–37). In this same spirit he can ask future readers the following questions in "Crossing Brooklyn Ferry": "What I promis'd without mentioning it, have you not accepted? / What the study could not teach—what the preaching could not accomplish is accomplish'd, is it not?" (ll. 99–100). What Emerson and Whitman ask is that readers give their own shape to the personality whose lineaments each author has limned as exhaustively as he can.

For these two male writers, democratic society is realized through each individual's embodiment of choices that contribute to a continuous historical unfolding rooted in the distant past. This is one aspect of what Emerson described in "The Transcendentalist" as the "optative mood," or the belief that the spiritual, artistic, and social upheaval of the moment "cannot pass away without leaving its mark" (*Selections*, 198). Dickinson's approach is far more elusive, reflecting a deep distrust in the capacity of previously codified, known history to accommodate the new democratic self she calls for in her writing. Where Emerson can figuratively construct the collective present as if it were positioned on stairs "which we seem to have ascended" ("Experience" 254) and Whitman can place his "I" on "an apex of the apices of stairs" ("Song" 1. 1149), Dickinson issues a cautionary note. She repeatedly advises readers by means of speakers keenly aware that truth illuminates the deceptions perpetuated by history and that this discovery can be deeply unsettling. "Tell all the truth but tell it slant –" (Fr 1263) one speaker urges, "Too bright for our infirm Delight / The Truth's superb surprise . . . / The Truth must dazzle gradually / Or every man be blind – ." Rather than trusting in the ultimate union of poetic truth and history, Dickinson's language calls for a personality courageous enough to promote changes that will shock those whose vision of the future is founded on past precedent. Once again, we see that for Dickinson resistance to the status quo is crucial to the emergence of democratic sovereignty. Where Emerson and Whitman model a yielding to cosmic forces that carry the self forward on a progressive historical tide,[9] Dickinson opposes such a proposition, situating the democratic self in an ateleological process of making choices not founded on a self-evident universal truth or ideal cosmic order.[10]

Like many other nineteenth-century women writers, Dickinson consistently expresses distrust for historically established models of selfhood. Her practice is to illuminate the options available to readers and leave decisions about concrete historical action up to them. Such a procedure is common among nineteenth-century women writers who, in Alicia Ostriker's words, "had to state [their] self-definitions in code, disguising passion as piety, rebellion as obedience" (*Stealing* 6). Elizabeth Petrino reinforces Ostriker's observation, adding that this strategy enabled women writers to address national issues: "Nineteenth-century American female poets chose to use a rhetoric of secrets, silence, and deferral rather than overt expression to bypass the era's norms of expression and involve the reader actively in issues of national importance" (208). The unavoidable outcome of this concealment is the literary request that readers in effect pierce beneath the surface of the text to locate alternative meanings. Readers who admit both the underlying meaning and the need for a deceptive surface text gain insight into the management of a subjectivity that is capable of simultaneously inhabiting multiple spheres of action. This poetry promotes both the fluidity encouraged through rhetorical variation and the ability to imagine a self equally capable of subversive and conventional thought. Unlike male writers who habitually took it for granted that individual self-definition was intimately linked to the historical embodiment of democratic values, even those women writers who actively promoted democratic citizenship frequently incorporated in their writing the distinct possibility that women could choose to form selves distantly removed from public politics. For women like Dickinson, the crucial first step in the direction of public influence was the development of a habit of thought whereby individual choices automatically included the consideration of political implications.

This is not to say that male writers like Emerson and Whitman were free of political anxieties. It is to say that much of the political uncertainty easily detectable in Emerson's writing reflects a fear of moving too quickly from a positive weighing of alternatives to the far more risky act of historical implementation that reduces the range of choices available to conscious thought. Thus in *Nature* Emerson can advocate a "gymnastics of the understanding" integral to the spiritual apprehension of "profounder laws" (*Prose* 40) that lie behind the surface fluctuations of experience while urging a reluctance to take action in "The Transcendentalist": "Unless the action is necessary, unless it is adequate, I do not wish to perform it" (101). Accordingly, Emerson can state in "Experience," "I accept the clangor and jangle of contrary tendencies," asserting finally, "Between these extremes is the equator of life, of thought, of spirit, of poetry,—a narrow belt" (204). The poet speaker in "The Sphinx" echoes these sentiments:

'Eterne alternation
   Now follows, now flies;
And under pain, pleasure,—
   Under pleasure pain lies.
Love works at the center,
   Heart-heaving always;
Forth speed the strong pulses
   To the borders of day.' (431)

As a negative corollary to the fluid responsiveness here presented as the achievement of a self attuned to cosmic pulsations, Emerson presents the foreclosure of choice threatened by the iron grip of historical contingency. This is made clear in

"The Transcendentalist" where even the most enlightened of persons admits that immersion in the moment dramatically constricts awareness of individual potential: "in the space of an hour, probably, I was let down from this height; I was at my old tricks, the selfish member of a selfish society" (*Prose* 102). This complete exhaustion of personal options is further reflected in this person's inability to imagine a future where union with the universe remains a possibility. "When shall I die," he asks, "and be relieved of the responsibility of seeing an Universe I do not use?" Here Emerson plainly expresses the basis for his belief that the actions that best serve the interest of the individual and the community come through periods of isolation, during which the individual sufficiently strengthens the capacity for heightened perception that alone provides assurance that historical action will indeed unify the individual act with the collective good.

What is most frustrating about Emerson's politics is the apparent contradiction between his confidence in historical progress and his reluctance to take direct action in the present. The obvious solution to this frustration is to recognize that Emerson's idealism enables him to expand the historical frame for individual action to so vast an extent that confidence in the inescapable political significance of the individual is sustainable even though the ultimate outcome of the individual's actions may only be evident in the distant future. As a consequence, he can in *Nature* bemoan the "retrospective" (*Prose* 27) tendency of his age and claim in "Experience" that even "Under the oldest moldiest conventions a man of native force prospers just as well as in the newest world" (204). These seemingly opposing views of history can be explained by the difference between actions determined by immediate causes and those directed by what Emerson describes in *Nature* as "thoughts of the Supreme Being" (47). That Emerson sees humans as gymnastically slipping in and out of balance with the divine order is made clear in "Experience," where he describes the "consciousness in each man" as "a sliding scale, which identifies him now with the First Cause, and now with the flesh of his body" (208). For Emerson, "the dignity of any deed" is determined not by what has been "done or forborne," but by the "sentiment from which it sprung" (208). History that focuses narrowly on the actions of individuals is unworthy of emulation because "the individual is always mistaken" (207), while history that points to the deeper cause working *through* individuals is of great value precisely because it inspires a further unfolding of individual genius. Paradoxically, then, for Emerson the strongest evidence that a fully realized democratic personality is achievable comes through the experiences of individuals whose deepest inspiration defies containment in language. "The baffled intellect," he notes, "must still kneel before this cause, which refuses to be named,—ineffable cause, which every fine genius has essayed to represent by some emphatic symbol" (208). The all-important political perception conveyed by Emerson's idealist vision is that unity, or the realization of democratic sociality, is best promoted through symbolic actions that form the basis of usable history.

Emerson further complicates his conception of politics in the present by removing significant action from the center of public life and situating the promise of a future ideal democracy in the isolated conduct of individuals whose actions shadow forth the ultimate unity of the individual with the first cause. Beginning with the perception that "Our virtue totters and trips, does not yet walk firmly" (Emerson, *Prose*, "The Transcendentalist" 103), Emerson argues that even those whose lives most closely approximate the requirements of usable history remain on the periphery of social life, exerting limited but significant influence on the future both by direct engagement and tactical removals: "But the thoughts which these few hermits strove to proclaim by silence, as well as by speech, not only by what they did, but by what they forebear to do, shall abide in beauty and strength, to reorganize themselves in nature, to invest themselves anew in other, perhaps higher endowed and happier mixed clay than ours, in fuller union with the surrounding system" (104). The point to be grasped here is that ultimate union is inevitable, so that the obscure acts of isolated individuals acquire a kind of retroactive significance by contributing to that future culmination.

Sacvan Bercovitch acknowledges the centrality of this link when he writes that for Emerson, "Individualism . . . implies the reciprocity between self-interest and the general good" (333). T. Gregory Garvey is even more direct when he states that through his writing Emerson "apprises individuals of sources of personal power through which they can create model selves and thereby provoke reform in their societies" (xii). Commenting specifically on the political force of individual character, Emerson affirms in "Politics" that true character has yet to reveal itself: "As a political power, as the rightful lord who is to tumble all rulers from their chairs, its presence is hardly yet suspected" (*Prose* 219). And Emerson makes it clear that the future merging of isolation with union applies equally to the poet: "He is isolated among his contemporaries, by truth and by his art, but with this consolation in his pursuits, that they will all draw men sooner or later" (184). What this means is that Emerson can confidently proclaim the political import of individual action by pointing to forms of conduct that pass beyond the reach of language but nonetheless invest language with political meaning.

Scholars critical of Emerson's politics raise questions about the political efficacy of a democratic vision that bases so much on a future culmination and consequently diminishes the demand for direct public action in the present moment. John Carlos Rowe epitomizes this critical posture when he accuses Emerson of promoting a false politics of "aesthetic dissent" whereby "rigorous reflection on the process of thought and representation constitutes in itself a critique of social reality" (1). The problem for Rowe rests precisely with what he sees as the restricted efficacy of self-avowedly political writing that remains distantly removed from immediate collective action. This difficulty is captured in a poem like "Merlin," where we are told that "The rhyme of the poet / Modulates the king's affairs" (*Prose* 450), but are given no concrete application to specific historical circumstances, either in Merlin's age or Emerson's.

Even a poem like "Each and All" can be read for political content according to the Emersonian scheme because, in a manner consistent with the title, the speaker concludes by affirming the fusion of self and deity, thereby providing a model of the ideal self, even though the poem sustains only the most tenuous of relationships with the human community. The narrative structure is indeed designed to embrace persons outside the poem by conflating external society with the reader described as "thee from the hill-top looking down" (432), but what transpires is the speaker's passage out of language into ineffable unity, so that the reader is left with a vague outline of individual behavior that exemplifies highest spiritual achievement but excludes the reader from the culminating event. Emerson's speaker proceeds by illustrating the epigrammatic observation that "Nothing is good or fair alone" with multiple specific examples from his own life. Engaging familiar rhetorical fluidity, Emerson translates "delicate shells" (433) into "sea-borne treasures" that become "unsightly, noisome things" and he describes a "graceful maid" whose "gay enchantment was undone" so that she becomes "A gentle wife, but fairy none." On the strength of insight gathered through these experiences, the speaker then discovers an "eternal sky, / Full of light and deity" and ends the poem by stating, "Beauty through my senses stole; / I yielded myself to the perfect whole." Here language points beyond itself, exemplifying that form of transcendence most productive of political character, but does so without establishing a direct connection with the historical particulars of the reader. We are left to conclude that for Emerson political force accumulates power over a great expanse of time, so that those like Rowe who place a premium on immediate application discover no clear evidence of significant political content.

Whitman's presentation of a gymnastic democratic self in many ways presents an immediate populist alternative to the slow force of Emerson's political vision. The anxiety that registers most vividly in Whitman's approach to history results not from the fear of losing perspective through his own precipitous entry into the democratic moment, but rather from his concern that due to his own inadequacies he will remain isolated and locked out of history despite his efforts to link arms with his fellows and enter the promiscuous ebb and flow of democratic sociality. As he famously states in the 1855 preface to *Leaves of Grass,* "The proof of a poet is that his country absorbs him as affectionately as he has absorbed it" (*Leaves* 636). His early elaboration of the task he has set for himself makes clear his wish to bring about Emerson's culmination in the immediate present: "The direct trial of him who would be the greatest poet is today. If he does not flood himself with the immediate age as with vast oceanic tides . . . and if he does not attract his own land body and soul to himself and hang on its neck with incomparable love and plunge his semitic muscle into its merits and demerits . . . and if he be not the age transfigured. . . . and if to him is not opened the eternity which gives similitude to all periods and locations and processes [. . .] and makes the present spot the passage from what was to what shall be, [. . .] let him merge with the general run and wait his development" (633–634).

The title of Whitman's great omnibus, *Leaves of Grass,* suggests his determination to make Emerson's enlightened hermit a central figure on the public stage by elevating one of the most common features of America's floral landscape and thereby showing that in democratic culture the average is indeed divine. Thus at the end of "Song of Myself" the speaker who has previously declared himself "an acme of things accomplished" (1. 1148) can calmly "bequeath" himself "to grow from the grass I love" (1. 1339). Or in the final lines of "Crossing Brooklyn Ferry" Whitman's "I" can affirm the apotheosis of the average American when he claims for himself and future readers the divine halo that symbolically fuses past and present in the speaker's spiritualized body: "Diverge, fine spokes of light," he exults, "from the shape of my head or any one's head in sunlit water" (1. 116). Like Emerson, Whitman does not hesitate to present an emerging democratic self on the printed page; but unlike Emerson's, Whitman's self persistently informs the reader that democratic personality is immediately available to all persons in all walks of life. Ruttenburg puts the matter succinctly when she writes that with the completion of *Leaves of Grass,* "Whitman claimed to be the poet of 'Democracy' insofar as he had poetically annulled the gap between being and representation, self and other, silence and speech, and in so doing had put an end to the critical practice of attempting 'to create an American literature by prescription'" (295). For Whitman, the democratic self that Emerson envisions in the distant future is available now; his job as poet is to flood the present with the experience of that self.

Nowhere is Whitman's wish to be a part of present history more vividly expressed than in his rhetorical efforts to embody the vital heterogeneity that for him is at the core of democratic sociality. "Political democracy," Whitman observes in "Democratic Vistas," "as it exists and practically works in America, with all its threatening evils, supplies a training school for making first-class men. It is life's gymnasium, not of good only, but of all" (*Walt Whitman* 952). That the gymnasium here alluded to applies to books and the experience of reading is made clear later in the essay: "Books are to be call'd for, and supplied, on the assumption that the process of reading is not a half sleep, but, in the highest sense, an exercise, a gymnast's struggle; that the reader is to do something for himself, must be on the alert, must himself or herself construct indeed the poem, argument, history, metaphysical essay—the text furnishing the hints, the clue, the start or frame-work. Not the book needs so much to be the complete thing, but the reader of the book does. That were to make a nation of supple, athletic minds, well-train'd, intuitive, used to depend on themselves, and not a few coteries of writers" (992–993). Whitman has of course built into *Leaves of Grass* numerous examples of the ways a democratic text engages with readers. None are more pronounced than the appeals to readers that take place in the closing sections of "Song of Myself." In section forty-seven, for instance, Whitman bridges the divide separating speaker from reader as he has done many times, in this instance using parentheses to suggest an intimate aside or seeming whisper in the reader's ear: "(It is you talking just as much as myself, I act as the tongue of you, / Tied in your mouth, in mine it begins to be loosen'd.)" (11. 1248–1249). The desired reader role is further defined in section fifty-one where the speaker explicitly requests that the reader exchange roles with him: "Listener up there! what have you to confide to me? / Look in my face while I snuff the sidle of evening, / (Talk honestly, no one else hears you, and I stay only a minute longer)" (11. 1321–1323). What must be emphasized here is that Whitman's text contains no particle of doubt concerning the speaker's or the reader's ability to speak for each other. Whitman's self, like Emerson's, assumes a universality that is not apparent in Dickinson's writing and frequently absent in the writing of her female contemporaries.

Women Writers and the Problem of History

A central reason for the reluctance of nineteenth-century American women writers to describe selves that successfully embody democratic personality is their awareness that women have not yet acquired the direct experience of public life essential to imagining positive solutions to the dilemmas posed by their political circumstances. In this context, Ostriker's observation that the "typical poem . . . usually contains little action" and "much aspiration" makes perfect sense (*Stealing* 32). Of the many women writers who have specifically addressed the need for women to gain experience in the public sphere, none make the case more directly than Judith Sargent Murray and Margaret Fuller. Both of these women go to great lengths to provide a historical context demonstrating the female capacity for public action. Murray cites the case of Portia (27), Artemisia (28), "Christina, queen of Sweden" (29), and many other publicly active women in her 1790s essay "Observations on Female Abilities"; while Fuller, in her 1844 work *Woman in the Nineteenth Century*, chronicles the achievements of such luminaries as Joan of

Arc (25), Sappho, Semiramis, "Elizabeth of England," and "Catherine of Russia" (26) as precedents for contemporary achievements by women the likes of George Sand (44), Angelina Grimke (67), and Lydia Maria Child (87). But as Sandra M. Gilbert and Susan Gubar have made admirably clear, efforts like these that are so openly dedicated to establishing a justification for female participation in the public sphere reflect a substantial anxiety felt by many women who perceived their own desire for public action to be at odds with official history. Nina Baym characterizes women's place in history at this time as reflecting a major transition in the way American culture viewed the balance of male and female political power: "Because men were endowed with greater physical strength than women, they had dominated the past; as the dominion of physical force contracted, so would the reign of men, and women—the weaker sex—would increasingly enter history decisively and directly" (*American Women Writers* 214). For Murray and Fuller, the problem of creating a place for women in present history would be partially solved by calling attention to the public acts of past women as evidence that women could responsibly assume a greater role in public politics once granted the opportunity.[11]

However, these writers also faced the challenge of demonstrating that women could make valuable contributions to the historical process currently unfolding, as only by establishing the present importance of women could the acts of past women be seen as contributing to *official* history and not be perceived as an inferior alternative. Murray announced her approach to this particular problem in her 1790 essay "On the Equality of the Sexes," in which she makes the case that if women and men are granted the same opportunities in life, they will demonstrate like abilities. This is the point of the poem that begins the essay, where Murray writes of men: "They rob us of the power t'improve, / And then declare we only trifles love" (4). In the essay proper, Murray spells out the need to provide equal education to both sexes: "And if we are allowed an equality of acquirement, let serious studies equally employ our minds, and we will bid our souls arise to equal strength. We will meet upon even ground, the despot man; we will rush with alacrity to the combat, and, crowned by success, we shall then answer the exalted expectations which are formed" (10).

Fuller presents a similarly robust vision of the future participation of women in history, but replaces Murray's language of combat with the language of mutual benefit. Writing as Murray does, for all women, Fuller significantly explains that time must be allowed to elapse after the removal of artificial limits so that women can grow into the expanded sphere that will then be theirs to occupy: "We would have every arbitrary barrier thrown down. We would have every path laid open to woman as freely as to man. Were this done and a slight temporary fermentation allowed to subside, we should see crystallizations more pure and of more various beauty. We believe the divine energy would pervade nature to a degree unknown in the history of former ages, and that no discordant collision, but a ravishing harmony of the spheres would ensue" (20). Fuller expresses the need for a period of adjustment that was implied by Murray's emphasis on education but to a degree obscured by her figurative rushing to combat. What both Murray and Fuller point to is the absence of equal opportunity that has prevented women from developing abilities that must now be granted free expression, with the understanding that the resulting changes will take place in a public arena shared by the sexes.

For Dickinson and many of her female contemporaries, the poetic focus became that of ushering female readers through the transitional phase implied by Murray's requirement for education and signified by Fuller as the time needed for a "temporary fermentation." One of many Dickinson poems that speak to this concern is "She could not live upon the Past" (Fr 1535). As one of the few poems by Dickinson that has no form of punctuation, not even a dash, the poem stands out by virtue of its relative lack of grammatical directives. Also noteworthy is the fact that this absence of syntactic framing complements the subject's lack of historical orientation, as if to say that the "She" of the opening line, like the "we" of Murray and Fuller, has yet to define her role in the historical environment she now imagines herself inhabiting:

> She could not live upon the Past
> The Present did not know her
> And so she sought this sweet at last
> And nature gently owned her
> The mother that has not a Knell
> For either Duke or Robin

In addition to providing a "Duke or Robin" that parallel in important ways the phoenix or robin of the letter to Elizabeth Holland, the poem also performs as a riddle that turns on the unidentified "sweet" of line three. One answer to this riddle is that the sweet the female subject now seeks is her own role in history. After having decided that the "Past" offered no foundation for life and that she is not acknowledged in the "Present," this female turns to nature and there discovers the freedom to imagine an unrestricted future. Once "owned" by nature and not confined by the artificial or "un-natural" death "Knell" of past precedent, she is free to contemplate a gymnastic self equally capable of attaining the regal status of "Duke" or the commonplace status of "Robin." In this instance, "nature" is not treated as an extension of past history but rather as a yet-to-be disclosed "mother" who expands the scope of female historical potential.

This reading's analysis of the poem as representing political subjectivity on the threshold of public history receives potentially significant reinforcement from the fact that the holograph manuscript was written "on a fragment of a subscription form, preprinted for the 1880s" (Franklin, *Poems* 1342) and therefore materially linked to a form designed to unite the private self to the outside world. In Melanie Hubbard's words, Dickinson's practice of writing late poems on documents like the subscription form "was to make her compositions literally 'of their milieu,' both by appropriating the print environment of her time and by theorizing thought's specific and material appearing" (27).[12] This particular poem specifically rejects the idea of joining a "preprinted" or preordained larger world and may for this reason be read as a repudiation of the "natural" self catered to by the subscription form. Dickinson's appropriation of scraps and her use of printed materials in the creation of her own scene of writing is a matter I will return to in my fifth chapter where I explore more fully the political implications of Dickinson's late manuscripts.

"She could not live upon the Past" is typical of many poems by Dickinson and other women poets who address the problem posed by a history that does not yet accommodate the full range of female potential but rarely describe the historically situated exemplary self so frequently conveyed in works by Emerson and Whitman. Instead, the tendency among many nineteenth-century women poets is to stress the need for women to imagine unprecedented historical acts through poems that confront the inadequacy of known history. Dickinson offers a good example of this sort of poem in "A Deed knocks first at Thought" (Fr 1294). The primary function of the poem is to make plain the need to translate thought into action:

> A Deed knocks first at Thought
> And then – it knocks at Will –
> That is the manufacturing spot
> And Will at Home and well
>
> It then goes out an Act
> Or is entombed so still
> That only to the Ear of God
> It's [*sic*] Doom is audible –

The opening words, "A Deed," signal the poem's concern with establishing the way interior thought is inextricably bound to external acts. Dickinson's insertion of the word "manufacturing" in line three magnifies this point by further exposing the artificial separation of private and public that is central to the poem's larger message. In suggesting that "manufacturing" can take place internally,

the poem rhetorically connects the isolation of interior thought with labor performed in the external marketplace.[13] Once this is established, the conditional
character of the fourth line—"And Will at Home and well"—points to the fact
that *if* the will is "well," which is to say "healthy," thought will progress naturally and behave in the manner described in line five: "It then goes out an Act."
The alternative, or unnatural conduct of an unwell will, is the subject of the
final three lines, where thought that is not translated into action is described as
condemned to both tomb and doom if it remains "audible" "only to the Ear of
God." Playing a role in history is as a consequence presented as the natural result
of healthy behavior, while confining thought to an isolated interior space is presented as a violation of the same vision of nature referred to by the speaker in
"She could not live upon the Past" (Fr 1535).

Most surprising, perhaps, is the poem's condemnation of communication that
is confined to God. This challenge to private spiritual communion with deity
would have had special resonance for nineteenth-century women who were encouraged to maintain the private space of the home as a spiritual refuge from the
secular corruption of the public world. The message that complete development
of the self requires action that takes place out of the home would for this reason
have spoken with particular force to women readers conditioned to view nature
as having biologically predisposed women to locate self-fulfillment in the home.
At no point does Dickinson spell out the precise historical form an alternative
female nature might assume, but she does structure the poem in such a way that
her readers must at least imagine the possibility of some form of action outside
of the home.

The open call for an entry into history that Dickinson issues in her poem is
consistent with the urge for action that many other nineteenth-century American women poets built into their poems. A good example is Alice Cary's "Contradiction," a poem in which the speaker explicitly challenges the reader to consider
the extent that her own will has failed to influence the course of her life. In this
five-stanza poem, Cary dedicates three stanzas to detailing the pastoral scenes the
speaker most loves in life. The first stanza begins with a description of "the deep
quiet—all buried in leaves" and the third with "Flocks packed in the hollows—
the droning of bees" (Walker, *Women Poets* 183). The fourth stanza, however, signals an abrupt change in the direction of thought as the speaker confronts the
discrepancy between her interior desire and the outward form her life has actually taken:

Yet, strange contradiction! I live in the sound
    Of a sea-girdled city—'t is thus that it fell,
And years, oh, how many! Have gone since I bound
    A sheaf for the harvest, or drank at a well.

The succeeding stanza concludes the poem by directing the female reader's attention to scenes from her own life that may or may not be consistent with her own interior desires:

> And if, kindly reader, one moment you wait
>> To measure the poor little niche that you fill,
> I think you will own it is custom or fate
>> That has made you the creature you are, not your will.

One important component of this final stanza is the requirement that the reader set aside "one moment" to "measure the poor little niche that you fill" (184), a requirement that by its existence admits the tendency of readers *not* to pause and consider the contradictory features of their own experience. This disruptive request for self-reflexive thought in effect lays the foundation for future assertions of sovereignty that must begin with resistance and culminate in action predicated on a mobilized will. In this instance, Cary's speaker tells the reader not only that her "niche" is "poor" and "little," but that she inhabits it because she has not sufficiently activated her will to avoid becoming an unnatural "creature" of "custom or fate." Cheryl Walker is amply justified in describing these lines as "a critique of popular notions of individualism" (*Women Poets* 169); a critique that I would also describe as a goad to women readers who risk having their lives dictated by custom. Like Dickinson, Cary forcefully proclaims the importance of translating thought into action while not specifying the precise form the reader's action should take. In this way, both writers place readers in the position of imagining discrepancies between the futures they may have once considered natural and the direction their lives have actually taken.

Lydia Huntley Sigourney employs a strategy of misdirection in "The Suttee" as a method of provoking female readers to similar reflections on the potentially unnatural influence exerted by cultural expectations, in this instance such influence is embodied by the institution of marriage.[14] As with the Dickinson and Cary poems, this poem refuses to prescribe a specific course of action, only in this case marriage and the legal and religious institutions that support it are subject to a degree of scrutiny that makes it difficult for readers not to consider parallels with American culture.[15] In this particular instance, the poem's histrionic staging of strange and horrifying customs attributed to an exoticized and distantly removed culture enable the poem to perform as a naïve representation of cultural otherness at the same time that it obliquely critiques an institution very much at the heart of American domesticity. As Ostriker has noted, poems like this one provide striking instances of authors "pretending not to know, not to feel, what they do know and feel" (*Stealing* 33).[16] Taking as its subject the Hindu

suttee, or practice of ritually burning the widow on her deceased husband's funeral pyre, the poem gives special attention to the ways in which the cultural
rite stands at odds with nature. Initially, the youthful widow is roused from her
passive "consent to the dread doom" by the cry of "her wailing babe" (Bennett,
Women Poets 5), to which her soul responds more "tremulous[ly]" than "the Mi-
mosa in its shrinking fold // From . . . rude pressure." The infant is then placed
on what Sigourney describes as his mother's "yearning breast," thereby driving
home the point that the course of nature is at odds with this cultural practice. To
magnify the point even further, Sigourney demonizes the crowd gathered around
the pyre, by referring to their determination to remove the child and start the
fire as like "that Spirit malign / Who twined his serpent length mid Eden's bow-
ers" (6). When the child is torn from her arms, the widow, now described as a
"victim," attempts to leap from the pyre only to be restrained by "a rough cord
[that] / Compress'd her slender limbs, and bound her fast / Down to her loath-
some partner." Finally, the fire is ignited and the widow utters her "dire death-
shriek . . . amid the wild, demoniac shout / Of priest and people."

Two messages conveyed through Sigourney's presentation of marriage de-
serve particular attention. The first of these is her interest in exposing the extent
that patriarchal culture distorts nature. Sigourney places men in the foreground
of the poem when she opens with the "chanting of infuriate priests" (5) and directs reader attention back to males when the final lines convey the interior experience of "the men who stood / Near the red pile and heard the fearful cry" (6).
The poem's many previous assertions of the unnatural character of the suttee
are in this way clearly affiliated with the expression of male power. To the extent
that this poem functions as an explicit critique of patriarchy, it is more openly
subversive than either the Dickinson or the Cary poems, where social convention
was also presented as unnatural but men were not so clearly isolated as the agents
of female entrapment. As if in response to the aggressive critique advanced in
her poem, Sigourney uses her final lines to extend a figurative palm leaf to the
male world. By describing the way male observers of this horrific event "oft amid
their nightly dream would start," Sigourney implies that even in the sleeping male
mind nature persistently exerts a remedial influence, albeit a relatively ineffective
one. The second message of the poem stands in counterpoint to the first by projecting a foretaste of potential female power. This takes place when the widow
speaks with a "voice of high command" and attempts "to leap / Among the astonished throng." Sigourney's point here is that once woman is awakened to the
crisis that defines her social condition, nature will act through her and she will
behave with an authority bound to astonish the masses. The problem is that the
widow has discovered her power too late, and she perishes on the pyre.

When both messages are considered together, the underlying meaning solidifies: female consent to patriarchal practice has led to a crisis that calls for imme-diate action. This message certainly conforms to what Nina Baym has described as the "self-conscious poetic practice" characteristic of Sigourney's elegies that is designed to counter "a male model of romantic egotism or a female stereo-type of withdrawn narcissism" ("Reinventing" 154). Add to this Mary Loeffel-holz's proposal that the schoolroom functioned as the central social model for "Sigourney's characteristic literary genres . . . inseparable from their matrix of republican ideas" (*School* 36), and it becomes even clearer that Sigourney set out to educate her female readers in the need for political action. The poem even sug-gests that men are on some level aware of the injustices too often perpetrated on women by marriage and may perhaps express sympathy once they are presented clear evidence of woman's true nature. Like Dickinson and Cary, Sigourney il-luminates the importance of women taking action in the present without pro-viding a clear model of the form that action should take. Despite the fact that Sigourney has in this poem narrowed the field of female political action to the institution of marriage, she has left it up to her readers to see beneath the exotic surface of her text and imagine for themselves the ways a Hindu widow's expe-rience might apply to their own.

One last poem by a Dickinson contemporary will further demonstrate the ingenuity of American women writers who with great frequency sought to pro-vide female readers texts that would give them experience exercising their natural capacity to think independently about their proper role in history. Helen Hunt Jackson's "Found Frozen" achieves this end through a speaker who reflects on the death of a woman whose actual life stands in sharp contrast to the official public record. The poem appears in sonnet form and in a manner consistent with the sonnet tradition serves as a testimonial to the speaker's love for the departed woman. An outstanding feature of this poem is the speaker's insistence that the hardship suffered by the departed was inflicted by persons who sincerely loved her to the best of their abilities; consequently, the speaker does not assert that she *loved* the woman more than others, but that she *understood* her more com-pletely and therefore witnessed a range of experience that escaped the grasp of the others. As her memorial to the real life of the deceased, the speaker opens with her own imaginative reconstruction of the dead woman's life. The hard-ship of the deceased woman's life forms the subject of these lines, reflecting the speaker's determination to privilege accuracy and sound knowledge over decla-rations of affection or personal triumph. When these lines are followed by ref-erence to a very different public epitaph, we detect the speaker's sense of futility in her realization that the life she tries to memorialize will be overshadowed by what she describes as the "common record."[17]

She died, as many travellers [*sic*] have died,
O'ertaken on an Alpine road by night;
Numbed and bewildered by the falling snow,
Striving, in spite of falling pulse, and limbs
Which faltered and grew feeble at each step,
To toil up the icy steep, and bear
Patient and faithful to the last, the load
Which, in the sunny morn seemed light!
                                                        And yet
'T was in the place she called her home, she died;
And they who loved her with the all of love
Their wintry natures had to give, stood by
And wept some tears, and wrote above her grave
Some common record which they thought was true;
But I, who loved her first, and last, and best,—*I* knew.
(Walker, *American Women Poets,* 287)

One distressing aspect of this poem is the possibility that the speaker "who loved her first, and last, and best" is the dead woman's mother. As the person who first saw her enter life, the mother would of course be in a position to speak comprehensively about the life now past. That the speaker uses the language of winter landscapes, exhaustion, and self-deception to describe this life suggests the challenge that looking real life in the face would pose for any bereaved person, much less the mother.

Like "The Suttee" and "Contradiction," this poem emphasizes female victimization by giving special attention to the dead woman's mistaken consent to a course of life that turned out differently than she had expected: her "sunny morn" became "Numbed and bewildered . . . Striving." Were it the case that the speaker is the mother, the poem would register numerous failures of history; not only the notable failure of "they who loved her," but also the failure of the mother/speaker either to inform her daughter adequately or influence what "they" wrote, plus the likely failure of those who knew the speaker to provide an accurate future account of her life.[18] Interestingly, the readers of the poem would have to be included in this last category. As a consequence, the poem suggests that like the speaker readers, too, have failed to assume the natural role of friend or family by not intervening in a life blighted at least in part by false expectations. The speaker's representation of the deceased life in terms of harsh natural scenery signifies her recognition that the "nature" she inhabited could have taken a different form. Clearly, part of this poem's logic in promoting reader efforts to imagine a more complete historical account of female experience is to implicate readers in the continued failure of history to depict women's lives accurately. By presenting a speaker who was intimate with the dead woman and may even have been her mother, the poem asks readers to begin the difficult task of imagining the ways they may have been complicit in the historical exclusion of their own female friends and family members. In this way Jackson achieves the sort of urgency so pronounced in the Sigourney poem, while also asking readers to apply the speaker's thought processes to their own lives the way that she, Dickinson, and Cary each did in their poems.

Dickinson's Subjective Reorientations

As the above analysis indicates, Dickinson's approach to history and the promotion of democratic personality may be seen as incorporating the refusal to model exemplary selves visible in the work of many contemporary female poets, while also steering away from Emerson's long-term vision and Whitman's fusing of reader and author in a present culmination, both of which presuppose that known history is the unfolding of a divine order. Like other women poets, Dickinson presents readers with both a sense of urgency and the need to develop a political habit of thought consistent with an undisclosed female nature; unlike Emerson and Whitman, then, she does not embrace history with the confidence borne out of a thoroughgoing idealism. For her, democratic personality emerges through the translation of thought into action that can only take place through independent choice and the imaginative contemplation of a self without historical precedent. "We lose – because we win –" (Fr 28), a familiar Dickinson speaker reminds us; those who enter history are "Gamblers" who "Toss their dice again!" Dickinson never points to a cosmic order that will establish the sort of ideal union of self and community envisioned by Emerson and embodied by Whitman. This absence of ontological structure invests Dickinson's poetry with a profound sense of immediacy at the same time that it clarifies the risks attendant on departures from past precedent. What distinguishes Dickinson's approach to history from that of other women writers is the extent that she magnifies the role of epistemological reorientation, so that readers become aware of the fact that they are making choices for which they themselves must assume responsibility and for which the outcome is not at all certain. Where other men and women writers call for readers to imagine positive political change, Dickinson remains cognizant of the appeal exerted by the status quo. Even when making the case that healthy action takes place outside the home, Dickinson acknowledges the home as the locus for thought and the effort required to exceed its bounds.

The fluid, gymnastic self of her poetry and letters always balances the phoenix of re-birth with the robin of predictability.

Sensitivity to the difficulties subjective reorientation poses for her readers is testified to by the many poems that provide instruction in democratic conduct. As the speaker of "My Cocoon tightens – Colors tease –" (Fr 1107) demonstrates, the defiance of social codes can be serious business that demands both an inkling of expanded potentiality and the willingness to persist in the face of repeated missteps. Having stated that "A dim capacity for Wings / Demeans the Dress I wear – ," the speaker then declares her belief in a "power of Butterfly" that she will ultimately secure through her own "Aptitude to fly." The final stanza expresses her acceptance of the uncertainty that comes with the gymnast's refusal to adopt established rhetorical patterns:

> So I must baffle at the Hint
> And cipher at the Sign
> And make much blunder, if at last
> I take the clue divine –

Dickinson applies a like strategy in "A little East of Jordan" (Fr 145), where she presents Jacob as a paradigmatic "Gymnast" who requests a blessing from the angel he has defeated, thereby adroitly conflating triumph with submission and winning God's compliance. In this instance, Dickinson demonstrates that while rhetorical gymnastics can contribute to democratic leveling on a cosmic scale, there is no settled outcome consistent with binary resolution; instead, Dickinson describes Jacob as a "bewildered Gymnast" whose glimpse of God's face has indeed yielded " 'Peniel' Hills" but locates those hills in the "beyond." As in "My Cocoon tightens," Dickinson shows that the bewildering self-transformation associated in that poem with "Butterfly" power is the corollary of positive personal growth. As if to clarify the ease with which Jacob's accomplishment is universally available but obscured by class-marked linguistic codes, the speaker of "Color – Caste – Denomination –" (Fr 836) declares, "These – are Time's Affair." "Death's large – Democratic fingers" ultimately reveal that whether the "Chrysalis [be] Blonde – or Umber," all are "Equal Butterfly." Dickinson's point here appears simple: democratic personality announces itself as a perpetual emergence from the encrusted rhetoric of the historical moment. Such an emergence requires the assertion of a sovereign self willing to resist prevailing political conventions, like those that prohibit women from serious experimentation with literary rhetoric or urge the view that race signifies spiritual difference.

Here it is worth reemphasizing the point that the centrifugal force of Dickinson's at-times radical departures from linguistic and social convention are frequently accompanied by centripetal affirmations of conservative impulses. Remaining responsive to the full scope of Dickinson's rhetorical accomplishment for this reason requires equal sensitivity to her recognition that the desire to escape doubt and seek instead the certainty of binary resolution is a constant source of tension crucial to the expression of a democratic personality. To retain what Dickinson referred to in the cocoon poem as an "Aptitude to fly," readers and speakers must maintain a precarious balance between linguistic and social poles. Dickinson makes this point with some force through the speaker of "To hear an Oriole sing" (Fr 402):

> To hear an Oriole sing
> May be a common thing –
> Or only a divine.
>
> It is not of the Bird
> Who sings the same, unheard,
> As unto Crowd –
>
> The Fashion of the Ear
> Attireth that it hear
> In Dun, or fair –
>
> So whether it be Rune –
> Or whether it be none
> Is of within.
>
> The "Tune is in the Tree –"
> The Skeptic – showeth me –
> "No Sir! In Thee!"

While this speaker rather blatantly gives voice to the rhetorical couplings that contribute to Dickinson's presentation of democratic self hood, her desire for binary resolution prevents her development of a polymorphous democratic subjectivity.

In this instance, Dickinson provides three clues that illuminate the speaker's fixed sense of identity: one metrical, one syntactic, and one grammatical. The first arises from the fact that the only six-syllable third line in all five tercets occurs at the end of the first stanza; the rest of the stanzas contain four-syllable third lines. In the first stanza, though, the qualifier "only" interjects a note of exclusivity, providing the two additional syllables while simultaneously establishing the opposition separating "common" from "divine." The final lines in all the other stanzas confirm sharp lines of opposition, signaling a progressive hardening in the speaker's elitist views.

Dickinson's syntactic clue comes through dashes that challenge syntactic closure and magnify the speaker's struggle to remove uncertainty. This is especially pronounced in the final stanza, where three dashes appear, drawing attention to the speaker's efforts to stitch together disparate observations. The two exclamation marks that surface in the concluding line can for this reason be read as emphatic efforts to impose certainty. This terminates a series of destabilizing dashes that run throughout the poem, beginning with the dash after "thing" at the end of line two that precedes the conjunction "Or" that begins line three, as if to increase the speaker's uncertainty in distinguishing the common from the divine. In the second and third stanzas dashes appear after final words, suggesting that the speaker's imposition of syntactic order defers uncertainty but does not eliminate it. The "So" that begins the fourth stanza launches the process of closure that the period at the stanza's end confirms, representing the speaker's efforts to deny the disjunctive power of the dash that once again precedes the conjunction "or," as it did in the first stanza. At this point the speaker has made up her mind to assert her will despite any contrary impulses or perceptions. However, the three dashes in the final stanza visually and syntactically imply that the speaker has merely refused to acknowledge uncertainties that nonetheless persist. For this reason, the final stanza confirms the speaker's determination to impose exclusivity despite her own internal resistance to doing so.

Dickinson's grammatical clue now appears in her careful placement of quotation marks in combination with the two exclamation marks in the final stanza. The quotation marks signal distinct voices, the first declaring "The 'Tune is in the Tree'" and the other "'No Sir! In Thee!'" When combined with the two exclamation marks that conclude the poem, the effect is that of silencing the first voice. Collectively, these grammatical signals point to the speaker's participation in an escalating argument, the intensity of which is in part fueled by her own unacknowledged doubts. By designating an external other—"The Skeptic"—the speaker consolidates her own opposing position, thereby denying herself the gymnastic alternative of straddling boundaries that would enable a democratic embrace of the other. The consequence is our discernment of this speaker's preference for a nondemocratic, unified selfhood. In this particular instance, the imposition of a rigidly unified self is directly linked to the speaker's claim that the appreciation of beauty ("To hear an Oriole sing") is the result of acquired attributes ("The Fashion of the Ear") that define the speaker as inhabiting a status above that of the "Crowd" mentioned in the second stanza. These features support the conclusion that aristocratic self-regard is both isolated from nature and dishonest.

Dickinson's willingness to present readers with speakers who deny or in other ways fail to achieve democratic personality constitutes one of the unique features of her political writing. And nowhere is this more clearly demonstrated than in her poems that explore the possibility of democratic liberty. To suggest, as I do here, that Dickinson's poetic representations of liberty display a range of approaches to liberty that are not consistent with any systematic philosophical stance, including whatever the biographical Dickinson's personal philosophy may have been, is to diverge rather dramatically from Karen Sanchez-Eppler's important study *Touching Liberty: Abolition, Feminism, and the Politics of the Body*. In that work, Sanchez-Eppler takes the following excerpt from a Dickinson letter to Joseph Lyman as a starting point for her chapter on Dickinson: "So I concluded that space & time are things of the body & have little or nothing to do with ourselves" (Sewall, *Letters* 71).[19] Sanchez-Eppler then matches this language to that of key poems to propose that for Dickinson liberty is an interior experience: "Dickinson claims freedom for herself by forfeiting any engagement with the nation and, even more radically, by forfeiting her own body" (105).[20] I arrive at a very different understanding of liberty by taking into account Dickinson's practice of presenting readers with choices rather than modeling exemplary attitudes. In this instance, I would juxtapose the "mid to late sixties [or] early seventies" (Sewall, *Letters* 68) letter to Lyman with the one Dickinson wrote in 1885 to Mabel Loomis Todd, in which she presents an altogether different view of nationhood and embodiment: "'Sweet Land of Liberty,'" she writes, "is a superfluous Carol till it concern ourselves – then it outrealms the Birds" (*L* 882). Dickinson then signs the letter, "America." In both the letter proper and her signature, Dickinson declares that the language of liberty attached to America through the song lyric becomes real only when the singer appreciates the blessings of liberty on a personal basis. When she signs the letter "America," Dickinson conflates nation and self in a manner consistent with this logic: she is indeed a singer who embodies liberty by singing from within the "Land of Liberty" to a correspondent who is out of the country (Todd was in Europe). On the strength of this reading, I would extend Sanchez-Eppler's observation that Dickinson represents "national issues and public divisions as nonsocial—lodged within the interiority of the self" (130) by adding that Dickinson *also* presents liberty as social action that unites the interior self with the external world. In these two letters, as elsewhere, Dickinson demonstrates the sort of fluid and gymnastic self that requires readers to confront undecidability and make up their own minds.

Before looking at poems that specifically address the individual management of liberty, I want to examine the way Dickinson poems like "A Deed knocks first at Thought" (Fr 1294) provide a context for thinking about what liberty is and how it is achieved. In "A Deed knocks," the basic elements of liberty are presented as part of a circular sequence that begins with a deed, or completed act, that previously passed through the thought, will, and action that becomes a deed once completed. The freedom to translate what is willed into action is presented politically as the assertion of individual sovereignty that is the essence of liberty. These basic elements of liberty are further defined in "To be alive – is Power –" (Fr 876B), where the speaker argues that even though life itself is power, "to be alive – and will! – " is even better, as to will is to be "able as a God." In what might be thought of as a classic expression of democratic sovereignty, this speaker goes on to state that through the exercise of will we become "The Maker – of Ourselves," which is the most one can expect in our state of "Finitude." Here the clear implication is that liberty is the highest expression of personal power and that this crucial expression is situated in the finite, rather than the spiritual, world. Based on what these two poems tell us, liberty may be thought of as cyclical and finite; that is, liberty implies the freedom to enter the finite world of human history through the exercise of will that links past deeds to future actions. Given this definition of liberty, it is clear that one thread of Dickinson's writing presents individual power as achieved through participation in the domain of history and politics.

With this understanding of liberty firmly in mind, we can look at "What if I say I shall not wait!" (Fr 305) as a misguided perception of liberty that functions as a cautionary tale to be understood in conjunction with the above poems, as well as poems like "The Soul has Bandaged moments –" (Fr 360), a poem probably written at about the same time but which provides a far more balanced view of liberty. What immediately stands out in "What if I say I shall not wait!" is the speaker's belief that liberty may be achievable in the afterlife:

What if I say I shall not wait!
What if I burst the fleshly Gate –
And pass Escaped – to thee!

What if I file this mortal – off –
See where it hurt me – That's enough –
And wade in Liberty!

They cannot take me – any more!
Dungeons can call – and Guns implore –
Unmeaning – now – to me –

As laughter – was – an hour ago –
Or Laces – or a Travelling [*sic*] Show –
Or who died – yesterday!

One possible interpretation of the poem is that proposed by Sanchez-Eppler, who writes, "the poem suggests that death and bodilessness achieve liberty only by sloughing off the limits that constitute meaning" (124). I would qualify this analysis by adding that the poem itself makes the speaker's thought process available for reader scrutiny. Rather than promoting the view that liberty is achieved through escape from the body, the poem instead urges a reconsideration of such a view by, in Sanchez-Eppler's words, exposing "the delusion of ecstatic reunion promised in the first stanza" (125). Instead of viewing this speaker as representing *Dickinson's* view that "liberty issues from fleshlessness" (124), I propose interpreting the poem as an examination of the *speaker's* view that takes place as one of many examinations of liberty that Dickinson explores through a range of speakers.

The distance from the speaker that I recommend here depends on the initial recognition that even though the poem opens with the speaker's conventional declaration that she desires to "burst the fleshly Gate," the poem's focus is not on the next life at all. On the contrary, the speaker dedicates herself to detailing what she anticipates escaping *from* rather than any new relationship she expects to enter. As a consequence, the poem winds up expressing the speaker's contradictory desire to shed the pain of mortality and "wade" in "Liberty" at the same time that she describes liberty as dependent on mortal experience. In stanza three, for instance, the speaker imagines herself beyond the grasp of "Dungeons," "Guns," and "They," as if motivated by the wish to prove the impotence of worldly martial and legal powers.[21] Stanza four then represents the speaker's effort to imagine experience liberated from those forces, only at this point the speaker appears to hesitate on the verge of recognizing that the dead hold no more meaning in the world of the living than do "laughter" an hour old, momentary fashion ("Laces"), or the fading memory of a "Travelling Show." The poem's terminating ejaculation—"Or who died - yesterday!"—suggests either that the speaker has discovered the absurdity of her impulse to end her life or that she has confirmed that impulse; the interpretation could go either way.

Dickinson's combination of exclamation marks and dashes syntactically and grammatically conveys the speaker's naïveté in seeking to resolve the problems of history though action directed to a spiritual future. On the one hand, exclamation points magnify her willingness to assert herself, to take a clear stand against the injustices of mortal life: she will achieve union with the dead and strike a blow against worldly power all in one definitive act. On the other hand, dashes magnify the uncertainty implied by the subjunctive "What if" phrasing that appears three times in the first four lines of the poem. The resulting mismatch between the desire to act and the contemplated course of action reveals the speaker's confusion of spiritual and historical logic. Readers aware that liberty requires acts based on the imagination of a historical future will recognize the speaker's confusion and reject the choice she imagines, despite any sympathy they might feel for her position. If such readers also conclude that the speaker has hesitated in her resolve to take her life, they would be in the position of adding more "What ifs" to the speaker's list, thus introducing historical options into the speaker's thought process in a collaborative effort to imagine a logically consistent expression of female liberty.

In "The Soul has Bandaged moments – ," Dickinson provides an elevated overview of the self's passage in and out of liberty, demonstrating that the experience of defining the self through historical action forms part of a larger cycle characterized by alternating phases of pain and joy, isolation and union, entrapment and freedom. Unlike the speaker of "What if I say I shall not wait!" who desires definitive action, this speaker recognizes that while the great drama of human experience does indeed include extremes, the future is constituted by forms of repetition that do not support grand climaxes. As a consequence, even though this poem also includes imagery of imprisonment and escape, the emphasis falls on the soul's power to endure and thus imagine the joys as well as the sorrows that together define the fluid democratic self. Of particular interest is this poem's use of the male bee to substantiate the female soul's experience of liberty, as if to say that the two experiences are fundamentally equivalent but the female experience is so new that it must be verified with reference to the long-established male precedent:

The Soul has Bandaged moments –
When too appalled to stir –
She feels some ghastly Fright come up
And stop to look at her –

Salute her, with long fingers –
Caress her freezing hair –
Sip, Goblin, from the very lips
The Lover – hovered – o'er –
Unworthy, that a thought so mean
Accost a Theme – so – fair –

The soul has moments of escape –
When bursting all the doors –
She dances like a Bomb, abroad,
And swings opon the Hours,

As do the Bee – delirious borne –
Long Dungeoned from his Rose –

Touch Liberty – then know no more –
But Noon, and Paradise –

The Soul's retaken moments –
When, Felon led along,
With shackles on the plumed feet,
And staples, in the song,

The Horror welcomes her, again,
These, are not brayed of Tongue –

Particularly worthy of note is the female soul's initial act of "bursting all the doors" in order to escape domestic privacy and achieve the potency of a "Bomb" in the domain of "Hours," or public history. Such an act stands in sharp contrast to the inclination of the speaker in "What if I say I shall not wait!" who imagines bursting "the fleshly Gate," an act that would remove the speaker from history and eliminate the possibility of liberty. Where in that poem the contemplated act would remove the speaker from the human community altogether, in this poem the speaker's behavior is immediately associated with that of a male bee, driving home the point that action in the public sphere is as natural for females as it is for males. The sexes differ in their expression of liberty only in terms of where the action originates. For the bee, action originates outside the female sphere—he is "Dungeoned *from* his Rose" (my italics)—so that he begins in the public world that is socially positioned as the polar opposite of the female soul's point of origin. As a result, the poem communicates the strong impression that male and female are equally drawn to the sphere culture has artificially assigned the other. This doesn't mean that the poem recommends an exchange of socially assigned gender roles, but rather that the social gendering of the spheres artificially inhibits the expression of a natural impulse common to both sexes. Given the social code that prohibits female participation in the public sphere, it is not surprising that the female soul who dares to rend the social fabric enforcing domestic confinement will take public form as a potentially destructive "Bomb."

One of the most impressive features of this poem is the way that all its component parts coordinate to increase the reader's awareness of democratic fluidity and the movement of the self through time, despite contrary assertions of stasis. By this means, the poem promotes the view that the self is always in motion, always passing from one experiential phase to another, even when life seems to have stalled. This is an important issue, as the assertion of perpetual movement allows for the emergence of a gymnastic self that flourishes through its passage in and out of isolation. As a consequence, the poem urges the view that women are not by nature locked into domestic privacy any more than men are. Significantly, the poem's concern with movement through time is established by means of a third-person narrator whose distance from the events described adds a degree of objectivity that is reinforced by the poem's division into three distinct and seemingly disconnected two-stanza sections, each of which opens by identifying "moments" as the primary unit of time: "Bandaged moments," "moments of escape," and "retaken moments." The self detailed in each of these phases demonstrates the democratic soul's ability to assume multiple roles as it passes from being bandaged and accosted by a "Goblin" to a female "Bomb," whose experience mirrors that of a male bee, to being led in shackles and welcomed by a "Horror."

To increase both the sense of movement and awareness of the soul's role-playing potential, each phase also contains information illustrative of the soul's movement out of or into a significantly different stage of experience, so that, distinctive as each phase is, each phase also conveys a sense of transition to or from another phase. Thus in the first section the soul is introduced as "Bandaged," suggesting the recovery of temporarily diminished strength, then it is described as "too appalled to stir" and therefore temporarily static but also possessing lips a "Lover – hovered – o'er" at some moment prior to her encounter with the goblin who sips from her lips now. Similarly, in the second section the soul's "bursting all the doors" is itself an image of transition from one role to another, as is the reference to "retaken moments" in section three, where the welcome "The Horror" offers "again" simultaneously points to past and future experiences not included in the poem. What the poem does not provide is a clear declaration of the way each of the three phases relates to the others; instead, the poem directs attention to myriad intervening roles, each of which contributes to the collective sense that no single phase of experience is as isolated as it at first appears. As a consequence, the boundary separating private and public realms is significantly eroded at the same time that no effort is made to provide an underlying logic that would anchor all phases of the self within a coherent natural order. As Margaret Dickie has pointed out, such repetition "precludes the organization of events in a causal series," leaving open the question as to whether or not "repetitive routine gestures . . . imitate a deadened inner life or may themselves be the originator of that life" (28). The result is a poem that allies itself with core democratic values by asking the reader to contemplate both the hollow self determined by ceaseless Sisyphean repetition and the potent female self that renews life by perpetually bursting into history.

Dickinson's refusal here and elsewhere to anchor female liberty in specific action inserts a fundamental gap between thought and action that she leaves it to her readers to bridge. Unlike the Emersonian speaker whose experience resolves all questions as to the possibility of action leading to ultimate spiritual union, Dickinson challenges her readers to imagine a self capable of liberty before even raising the possibility of expressing liberty through historical action. In this way Dickinson preserves a mysterious sense of nature in order to allow the free expression of female liberty rather than risk making nature available for the erection of restrictive social codes of the sort perpetuated in patriarchal culture. For Dickinson, democracy finds its richest expression and its most compelling justification through the potential it affords all its members for the realization of a fluid democratic self. She departs from Emerson by not imagining a future where the isolated self contributes to a seamless union of social and spiritual orders. And she departs from Whitman in her insistence that the immediate achievement of democratic selfhood take place through unprecedented actions that do not lead to an increased recognition of self in other. Like many of the women writers of her era, Dickinson sought to provoke new ways of imagining an American future, a future that would over time introduce into public history a more accurate understanding of the real experience of actual women. But for the moment, her objective was to promote the democratic habit of thought that would enable women to imagine futures capable of accommodating a gymnastic self. To that end, her poems rhetorically expand the range of female experience and destabilize the view that nature is either known or knowable.

3
Dickinson's Uses of Spiritualism
The "Nature" of Democratic Belief

Through her use of spiritualist concepts and terminology, Dickinson continues the gymnastic juggling of verbal registers that I examined in the previous chapter as an expression of democratic rhetoric. Spiritualism's intimate association with democratic principles, particularly its capacity to empower female speech in public settings, made the language of spiritualism especially attractive as an additional tool for instilling the democratic habit of thought that I see as central to Dickinson's poetics. What I most want to explore in this chapter is the unique opportunity spiritualism offered Dickinson to question cultural assumptions about nature that made possible the appropriation of the natural world as the ontological foundation for social roles and religious belief. Spiritualism's primary concern with a limitless supernatural realm that eclipsed the natural world available to mortal perception made spiritualism an enormously attractive vehicle for a writer interested in opening readers' eyes to their unconscious acceptance of false assumptions about nature. Through her use of spiritualist discourse to reveal the limits of conventional definitions of nature, Dickinson encourages her readers to approach thought and action as provisional, as based on partial knowledge and therefore subject to revision and incapable of fully embodying either nature or the self. By insisting on the provisional, incommensurate character of self-expression, Dickinson promotes a view of language as disembodied and at all times requiring the active participation of users if it is to represent accurately an ever-changing understanding of the external world and the position of the individual within that world. In this sense, spiritualism enables Dickinson to define the democratic self even further by pointing to the process of linguistic regeneration necessary for language to escape entrapment in the past.

Within the context of spiritualist discourse current during Dickinson's adult life, the possibility of communication with inhabitants of the spirit world was a broadly accepted fact. Throughout America in the second half of the nineteenth century, the boundary separating the natural world from the invisible domain of the supernatural was bridged on a regular basis by spiritualist mediums who provided visible and audible proof of a natural universe that vastly exceeded mortal comprehension. Scholarly estimates as to the total number of spiritualist adherents in Dickinson's day vary, though central features of spiritualist belief and practice would have been known by most Americans. Bret E. Carroll points to the difficulty of distinguishing between Americans dedicated to the full range of principles held by the most articulate advocates of spiritualism and those who subscribed only to core tenets, such as belief in communication with spirits of the departed. Carroll asserts that despite difficulties in arriving at accurate numbers, there existed "a truly popular religious interest in the spirit world among antebellum Americans" (14). In her examination of spiritualism as a historical phenomenon extending from midcentury into the 1890s, Ann Braude cautions, "While Spiritualists often organized on a local level, they staunchly opposed national organization or anything that would make a census of the group possible" (25). This lack of a clear census has resulted in "estimates of the number of Spiritualists by contemporary observers [that] ranged from a few hundred thousand to eleven million (out of a total population of twenty-five million)." Within American culture, spiritualism was most frequently practiced by "Americans of English Protestant descent" in the North but also "found a natural resonance with African religious beliefs introduced by the slave population in the South" (28). Spiritualism's appeal to people in all regions of the country regardless of socioeconomic, ethnic, and racial identity is one of the most striking features of this religious movement.

The spiritualist message, that conventional notions of nature were actually imperfect attempts to perceive the infinite, complemented Dickinson's own awareness of "nature" as a cultural creation used to prescribe forms of social conduct.[1] Though certainly not a spiritualist herself, Dickinson very clearly found ways to appropriate for her own rhetorical and artistic purposes the distinctly democratic language and paradigms of this significant cultural discourse. Words from the spiritualist vocabulary—like "apparition," "spectre," "ghost," "spirit," and "phantom"—invest Dickinson's speakers with the medium's authority to challenge spiritual and social norms, while the spectacle of the female medium, whose "natural" privacy paradoxically sanctioned her public presence, provides a precedent for the extreme seclusion that has similarly made Dickinson's life a source of public fascination. By appropriating spiritualist language, Dickinson confirmed both the spiritual dimension of her own democratic aesthetic and the democratic dimension of her spiritual aesthetic.

Previous scholarly investigations of Dickinson's affiliation with spiritualism have not identified the link between Dickinson's appropriation of spiritualism and her advocacy of democratic personality. Barton Levi St. Armand's multiple studies of spiritualist influences in Dickinson's work have affirmed the influence of the medium in shaping Dickinson's literary persona by situating her efforts in the context of Romantic transcendentalism and the idealized vision of nature so important to that tradition.[2] Yet within his analysis the veil that both protects the medium and insulates the mystery of the spirit from worldly eyes is also presented as allowing access to nature defined as unchanging and hierarchic, a realm of idealized spiritual order.[3] Benjamin Lease, on the other hand, has concluded that Dickinson "would never find it possible to fix her fortune in absolute Nature—or in any other Absolute" (*Readings* 129). Lease emphasizes Dickinson's attraction to spiritualism's rejection of "gloomy orthodox Christian pronouncements" about the afterlife (76) and its merging of natural with supernatural (101, 115–120), but he restricts his analysis to the specific artistic effects achieved through Dickinson's having conducted her personal "religious quest . . . in the climate of a burgeoning spiritualist movement that left its mark on her mind and art" (102).[4] Different as their positions are in some crucial respects, both St. Armand and Lease assume that Dickinson subscribed to one of two orthodox views of nature—the transcendental Romantic or the spiritualist.

What Dickinson's life and poetry actually suggest, however, is that she sought to expose the contradictions implicit in the cultural demand for a clear definition of nature. In word and deed, she addresses herself to the tensions that both bond and distinguish the natural and the supernatural. Her aim, finally, is not to offer a new definition of nature but to propose the impossibility of arriving at any definition of nature that is not also a retroactive justification for the social deployment of cultural power. Dickinson therefore adopts spiritualist discourse as part of a poetics designed to alert readers to their role as independent democratic citizens. Recognizing that Dickinson incorporates spiritualist materials in this manner is yet one more witness to the fact that she was not a recluse dedicated to a hermetic lyric tradition, but rather an astute reader of culture who strategically incorporated current discourse in order to bend its language to her own political purposes.

The Political Dimension of Spiritualist Belief

That Dickinson would draw on spiritualism as a way of combining religion with politics is not at all surprising given the extent that spiritualism was popularly associated with democratic principles. As Stephen Prothero has observed, "What commended spiritualism to everyday folks was its democratic bent" (
Initially a religious movement that sought to democratize access to lead

roles by elevating the "natural wisdom of unlettered folk," spiritualism quickly established strong links with nineteenth-century reform efforts. However, as Prothero has significantly noted, "Spiritualists distinguished themselves from other nineteenth-century reform movements by affirming that spirits of the dead can and do communicate, through the agency of mediums, with the living" (198). Thus the movement that "had its obscure birth at Hydesville, in upstate New York," when "thirteen-year-old Margaret Fox and her twelve-year-old sister Kate" first contacted the spirit world on "the night of March 31, 1848" (Kerr 4), grew to embrace religious believers who sought empirical proof of life beyond the grave, reformers dedicated to elevating the underclasses, and activists seeking political guidance from the inhabitants of a superior spiritual plane. Mediums across America donned the clairvoyant's veil, conducted séances, translated the knocks or "rappings" of spirit visitants, and spoke from trance states to large gatherings as part of a popular religious movement that was distinctly democratic in orientation.

The cross-section of public figures identified with spiritualism was comprehensive, including people Dickinson knew well, in addition to writers and political figures known to all Americans. Most notably, perhaps, this group included first lady Mary Todd Lincoln, who communicated "with her dead son, Willie, and brought mediums to the White House" (Braude 27). After Lincoln's assassination, the first lady distributed a *carte de visite* on which appeared a spirit photograph taken by the spiritualist photographer William Howard Mumler that revealed the ghost of the late president standing behind his widow with his hands on her shoulders (Chéroux et al. 23, 26). It is highly likely that Dickinson knew of Higginson's enthusiastic defense of spiritualism in "The Results of Spiritualism, A Discourse, Delivered at Dodsworth Hall, Sunday, March 6, 1859."[5] Popular writers identified with spiritualism included poets Elizabeth Oakes-Smith (St. Armand, "Women," 5) and William Cullen Bryant and novelists James Fenimore Cooper, Harriet Beecher Stowe, Lydia Maria Child, and Henry James (Prothero 199). The political activists and educators William Lloyd Garrison, George Ripley, Sarah and Angelina Grimke, Amy Post, Susan B. Anthony, Elizabeth Cady Stanton, and Frances Willard were also associated with spiritualism. R. Laurence Moore effectively summarizes the enormous popularity of the movement: "scarcely another cultural phenomenon affected as many people or stimulated as much interest as did spiritualism in the ten years before the Civil War and, for that matter, through the subsequent decades of the nineteenth century" (4). Such broad participation from every literary and political walk leaves little doubt that Dickinson would have been aware of the main features of spiritualist belief.

Evidence that the spiritualist presence had penetrated Dickinson's more immediate neighborhood is provided by Daniel Lombardo in *A Hedge Away: The*

Other Side of Emily Dickinson's Amherst, his portrait of daily life in Dickinson's hometown. According to Lombardo, at least as early as 1849 spiritualist influences were being reflected in the conduct of Amherst citizens. In the summer of that year, Amherst College students conducted "an imaginary séance in the tower of Amherst College" (83). This event entered the news because of the public attention students attracted through their efforts to rename Mount Toby in nearby Sunderland. When the Sunderland town meeting soundly rejected the proposed name change, the students held the séance to summon the spirits of the previous graduating class to unify ongoing support for their effort to rename the mountain (84). Even though this was a largely comic episode, it does establish that in 1849 attributes of spiritualism were already a part of popular consciousness in Amherst. Later in Dickinson's lifetime, Montague, a rural community only a few miles north of Amherst, became a regional center for spiritualist gatherings. "By 1874, the New England Spiritualists Camp Meeting Association met yearly at Lake Pleasant in Montague, not far from Amherst" (Lombardo 174); reports of these Lake Pleasant gatherings were carried in the local newspapers that Dickinson would have read.

Quite possibly, the most universally identifiable spiritualist contribution to American culture took the form of the female medium.[6] Female trance speakers, especially, attracted public attention by speaking from elevated platforms and regularly addressing large gatherings of several hundred persons while in a trance state. Séance mediums may have been more numerous, but their presence was less sensational for the simple reason that their audiences were customarily limited to those few who could fit around a dining-room table. All types of mediums were located in all parts of the country and could be found in every major city.[7] One of the most fascinating aspects of the female spiritualist medium as a cultural phenomenon was the ease with which the same nineteenth-century construction of female biology that was used to determine female frailty and passivity could also define women as the ideal transmitters of spirit messages. Due to an ironic twist of cultural logic that might well have delighted Dickinson, the same understanding of nature that was used to justify female exclusion from the public sphere was employed by spiritualism to enable unfettered female access to the entire range of public discourse conventionally viewed as off-limits. This peculiar route to the public sphere is a matter of special concern to Braude, who observes that "Spiritualism made the delicate constitution and the nervous excitability commonly attributed to femininity a virtue and lauded it as a qualification for religious leadership" (83). Thus "mediumship allowed women to discard limitations on women's role without questioning accepted ideas about women's nature." Women's "natural" disposition in this sense enabled them simultaneously to affirm and deny their status as women by providing a justification for the biologically improvident act of entering the marketplace of public discourse. As mediums, women could transmit the wisdom of American political icons, like George Washington, Benjamin Franklin, and Thomas Jefferson, applying it directly to events taking place in contemporary America.[8]

The power of the female medium was predicated on the belief that women who entered the matrix of spiritualist discourse acquired authority by virtue of their ability to transmit voices, an ability they possessed because at those times they were both present and not present bodily. Consequently, they could be made available to the public eye because in their capacity as receptive female vessels they paradoxically ceased to be women. A higher nature transformed the culturally constructed "natural woman" into a being whose defiance of social codes was deemed acceptable by the public.[9] In terms of Dickinson's concern with nature and social expectation, mediumship provided a rare instance when the permeation of the natural by the supernatural threatened the stability of cultural codes enforcing female silence, but was nonetheless countenanced by the public. Read in the context of this wrinkle in cultural logic, Dickinson's 1863 observation "that the 'Supernatural,' was only the Natural, disclosed," makes perfect sense as an application of spiritualist discourse, especially when located in a letter to Higginson that explores death and the possibility of immediate spiritual revelation (*L* 424).

The presence of spiritualism in general, and the medium in particular, drew public attention to a pronounced discrepancy in the cultural appropriation of nature, whereby recourse to nature could be used to explain both the public prominence of women and their seclusion in the home. This historical circumstance made the concept of nature itself available for critique as an arbitrary cultural creation rather than a self-evident truth. Pierre Bourdieu explains that when this kind of critique takes place, "the social world loses its character as a natural phenomenon" and "the question of the natural or conventional character (phusei or nomo) of social facts can be raised" (*Outline* 169). That is, when the critique "brings the undiscussed into discussion, the unformulated into formulation," the process of deliberate analysis "break[s] the immediate fit between the subjective structures and the objective structures," destroying self-evidence and thereby making the social system available for reevaluation. The speaker of Dickinson's poem "There is no Silence in the Earth – so silent" (Fr 1004) hints at such a reevaluation when she discloses that certain silences conceal truths "Which uttered, would discourage Nature / And haunt the World – ." This contradictory incorporation of the same "natural" norm destabilizes or spectralizes fundamental facts, diminishing their solidity and raising the possibility that they are transitory cultural fabrications rather than direct expressions of a timeless natural order. Dickinson gives voice to this perception in "Facts by our side are never sudden" (Fr 1530), where the speaker states with some alarm that when facts "look around," as if aware that they can change, "they scare us like a spectre / Protruding from the Ground - ." As a consequence of nineteenth-century America's association of mediumship with unorthodox expressions of nature, references to mediumship, especially when reinforced by other spiritualist allusions, rhetorically invest the speakers of Dickinson's poems with the medium's power to imagine future selves incommensurate with the limited version of nature used to justify social codes.

The Medium's View of Nature

A surprising number of Dickinson's poems incorporate the language and mechanics of spiritualism for the express purpose of urging readers to envision their lives as taking place on a far grander scale than that prescribed by cultural convention. In "A solemn thing - it was - I said -" (Fr 307), for instance, the speaker imagines herself performing the medium's role of linking this world with eternity, but adds the twist of being able to view this world from the vantage of a spirit inhabitant of the infinite.[10]

A solemn thing - it was - I said -
A Woman - white - to be -
And wear - if God should count me fit -
Her blameless mystery -

A timid thing - to drop a life
Into the mystic well -
Too plummetless - that it come back -[11]
Eternity - until -

I pondered how the bliss would look -
And would it feel as big -
When I could take it in my hand -
As hovering - seen - through fog -

And then - the size of this "small" life -
The Sages - call it small -
Swelled - like Horizons - in my breast -
And I sneered - softly - "small"!

The poem's opening two stanzas establish the speaker's status as a medium by proclaiming her feminine passivity and helplessness: she can wear the white only "if God should count me fit" and then, if fit, her life will "drop . . . / Into the mystic well – ." The final two stanzas begin by presenting the speaker's contemplation of the infinite and then consider the way mortal life would appear when framed by such magnitude. "I pondered how the bliss would look – ," she states when imagining her approach to eternity, wondering if "it" would "feel as big – / When I could take it in my hand – / As hovering – seen – through fog – ." Once positioned in eternity, the speaker casts her gaze back to her previous life, disdainfully dismissing the restrictive scope of that life as enforced by "Sages": "And I sneered – softly – 'small'!" By shifting perspectives in this manner, Dickinson democratically inverts the speaker's role, elevating the conventionally diminutive in a manner that parallels the female medium's shift from the margins of culture to a position of authority. The fascicle holograph of this poem reinforces the identification of the speaker with a spirit medium by providing the variant "hallowed" for "timid" in line five and "purple" for "mystic" in line six (*MBED* 289). The linking of timidity and hallowedness can be read as giving additional emphasis to the passivity of the medium, while the balancing of "purple" and "mystic" underscores the act of spiritual union that makes possible the speaker's enhanced authority. The fascicle poem also provides the word "glimmering" as either an addition to or a variant for "hovering" in line twelve, adding a ghostly visibility to the hovering spirit presence.[12]

Dickinson turns this representation of the spiritualist medium to her own democratic purposes by presenting the speaker as actually viewing her own life from the perspective of the infinite, drawing on the practice Eliza Richards has identified as an "overdubbing [of] the spirit visitor's voice" characteristic of "spiritualist poetry" (122). According to Richards, "The dead and the living exchange places: the spectral voice of the medium haunts the literal voice of the visiting spirit. Participants in the exchange—mediums, seance attendants, readers of published spirit verse—simultaneously imagined the living in the position of the phantom dead and the dead resurrected and embodied in linguistic form" (122). Dickinson's version of this equation departs from the norm by not including reference to the "phantom dead"; instead, she emphasizes the speaker's consciousness and what she learns as a result of having assumed the perspective ordinarily attributed to the channeled spirit. This magnification of the medium's role in the transmission of spirit knowledge enables Dickinson to focus reader attention on the medium's contribution to the information received from the spirit world. Doing so positions Dickinson in the company of "poet-mediums" Richards describes as having "made claims for both the originality of receptivity and the individuality of spirit-medium" (120). Richards makes the case that for these mediums, meaning was conceived of as "the product of a transaction between two or more souls" that made the question of origin uncertain. Mediums, Richardson argues, become like authors who give a particular shape to ideas but do not claim to be their originators. This question about authorial originality is of particular importance in Dickinson's approach to poetry and a matter I explore further in chapter 5.

What interests me most in Richards's formulation is her articulation of a spiritualist aesthetic of authorship that closely resembles Dickinson's in its privileging the collective dissemination of shared meaning over the "system of possessive individualism valuing private ownership of intellectual property" (140). Richards summarizes this difference according to each group's understanding of plagiarism: "A logic of scarcity governs the individualistic aesthetic: the theft depletes the owner's work and the plagiarizer's work is derivative. A logic of surplus, on the other hand, governs the spiritualist aesthetic: supernatural power grows and multiplies when it is shared" (140). Dickinson's concern with the function of the medium and the creation of poems that engage readers in the shared creation of meaning downplays the importance of actual contact with a spirit authority, choosing rather to concentrate attention on the joint creation of meaning that takes place when readers join authors in collectively seeing beyond the limits of social norms by imagining how they appear when seen from the vantage of the infinite. In other words, Dickinson's speaker, who assumes the spirit's authority for herself, points to what many Americans may have already begun to suspect: that news of the supernatural supposedly conveyed by otherworldly spirits may in reality be an extraordinary example of self-hypnosis or ventriloquism knowingly or unknowingly performed by the medium. Readers aware of their collaborative role in the shaping of meaning can as a consequence see themselves reflected in the actions of the medium and likewise assume personal authority for imagining expressions of meaning not governed by socially codified versions of nature. Without explicitly affirming or denying the existence of an independent spirit world, Dickinson encourages her readers to engage imaginatively with the infinite and reject the limitations imposed by the sages of social convention. Read from this perspective, Dickinson's poems that examine the medium's experience can be understood as retroactively spelling out the implications for female participation in public life established by the historical precedent of the spiritualist medium.

Whether appropriating the role of the medium or incorporating the discourse of ghosts and apparitions, Dickinson's spiritualist poems consistently push readers to situate present life in the context of eternity for the purpose of loosening

A solemn thing – it was –
I said –
A Woman – white – to be –
And wear – if God should
count me fit –
Her blameless mystery –
        hallowed
A timid thing – to drop
a life   purple
Into the mystic well –
too plummetless – that it
come back – return
Eternity – until –

I pondered how the bliss would
look –
And would it feel as big –
When I could take it in
my hand –
As hovering – seen – through
fog – glimmering

4. "A solemn thing – it was – I said –" (J 271/Fr 307) *MBED* 289–290. By permission of the Houghton Library, Harvard University. *MS AM 1118.3 (71a)* © The President and Fellows of Harvard College.

And then - the size of this
"Small" life -
The Sages - call it small -
Swelled - like Horizons - in my
vest -
And I sneered - softly - "small"!

_____

I breathed enough to take
the Trick -
And now, removed from Air -
I simulate the Breath, so well -
That One, to be quite sure -

The Lungs are stirless - must
descend
Among the Cunning Cells -
And touch the Pantomime -
himself,
How + numb the Bellows feels!
    + Cool -

_____

the hold of transient social norms. The late poem, "The Life that tied too tight escapes" (Fr 1555), effectively represents this central function:

> The Life that tied too tight escapes
> Will ever after run
> With a prudential look behind
> And spectres of the Rein –
> The Horse that scents the living Grass
> And sees the Pastures smile
> Will be retaken with a shot
> If he is caught at all –[13]

Dickinson's reference to "spectres of the Rein" in the fourth line expresses the way the restrictive force of social authority that previously "tied" the life "too tight" acquires a ghostly insubstantiality when displaced by the larger vision of "living Grass." The speaker's prior role in life is not simply transcended and discarded; rather, the liberated life "Will ever after run / With a prudential look behind." Antecedent constraints still haunt the newly escaped life; they simply become less substantial. In this sense, the poem serves to dematerialize cultural codes without erasing them, so that readers are introduced to a world within which liberty is equated with resistance and not transcendence. The speaker of "One Blessing had I than the rest" (Fr 767) likewise uses spiritualist language in her grudging acceptance of such endless resistance. Having experienced "A perfect – paralyzing Bliss," that translates "Want – or Cold" to "Phantasms," the speaker ceases to question the necessity of dwelling in such a ghostly realm: "Why bliss so scantily disburse – / Why Paradise defer – / Why Floods be served to Us–in Bowls – / I speculate no more – ."[14] For Dickinson, the supernatural invests daily life with a ghostly insubstantiality that discourages complacency by pointing to a more capacious but incompletely realized spiritual reality. By giving particular emphasis to the expanded experiential range of her speakers, Dickinson focuses on spiritual growth as an ongoing historical process rather than union with the absolute that takes place outside of time.

Leading spiritualists in their own practice provided a useful precedent for Dickinson's insistence that the spiritualist understanding of nature take form as the historical redefinition of social norms. Andrew Jackson Davis, one of the most visible exponents of spiritualism in nineteenth-century America, announced the spiritualist position with characteristic verve when he wrote in his 1853 *The Harmonial Man; or, Thoughts for the Age* that "man's rights can be secured, not by making new laws but by repealing those, already in effect, which are found to militate against, and positively conflict with, the natural rights, liberties, and sovereignty of the individual" (20). "Man is just awakening, from his long sleep of ages, to a vigorous perception of his natural and spiritual powers," Davis declared, "and in proportion as his mind becomes illuminated by the Principles of Universal Nature, even so will he more and more realize the beauties and blessings of that Liberty which is Truth and Harmony" (18). O. G. Warren further spelled out the political direction of the movement in an 1855 essay in the spiritualist journal *Sacred Circle* where he claimed, "in Spiritualism you see the engine that shall revolutionize and democratize religion" (8). The medium and spiritualist chronicler Emma Hardinge again underlined the democratizing aims of spiritualism in her 1870 *Modern American Spiritualism: A Twenty Years' Record:* "Spiritualism, with a large majority of its American adherents, is a religion, separate in all respects from any existing sect, because it bases its affirmations purely on the demonstrations of fact, science, and natural law, and admits no creed or denominational boundary" (11). As these three writers' use of political language suggests, spiritualism's view of nature gave rise to the kind of antiestablishment rhetoric evident in the radical democracy of many reform efforts of the day. Braude cogently summarizes this distinctive feature of spiritualism: "while most religious groups viewed the existing order of gender, race, and class relations as ordained by God, ardent Spiritualists appeared not only in the women's rights movement but throughout the most radical movements of the nineteenth century" (3). What this tells us is that one important basis for the radical social and political orientation of spiritualism lay in the movement's view of nature and the belief following from this view that human institutions and the identities they fostered could never be more than partial or imperfect approximations of a primary spiritual reality.[15]

For this reason the twin concepts of "natural" and "supernatural" acquired a particular prominence within the spiritualist cosmology. As Bret Carroll has observed, for spiritualists "the two realms were so closely connected that distinctions between 'natural' and 'supernatural' misleadingly obscured the unity of 'Nature' (with a capital 'N')" (26).[16] With its focus on an alternative version of authority provided by the "supernatural," and on the power of those on the margins of society, spiritualism provided an important nineteenth-century cultural locus for the mobilization of what Nancy Ruttenburg has described as the "democratic personality [which] arises as a dramatic refusal to conform to collectively imposed and institutionally sustained norms of identity" (11). In Ruttenburg's formulation, this refusal to conform is "legitimated not with a reference to some notion of the 'natural' . . . but rather to the supernatural, through whose transcendent authority the anomalous is made representative and the marginal is made to be universal." Dickinson enacts a parallel refusal in a poem that rescues witchcraft from the margins: "Witchcraft was hung, in History," her speaker declares, "But History and I / Find all the Witchcraft that we need / Around us, Every Day –" (Fr 1612). Rather than rejecting history altogether, Dickinson privileges conduct deemed unnatural by the official record as a way of illuminating an alternative account of human events immediately applicable to the present moment.[17]

The Spiritualist Presence in the Poet's Life

Dickinson's familiarity with spiritualist practices and terminology can be traced to a relatively early stage in her correspondence, when references to spiritualist methods correspond to youthful efforts at establishing personal authority. Writing to her friend Jane Humphrey in January 1850, Dickinson muses over the possibility that Jane might write to her with a "spirit pen" (L 81).[18] This playful reference to supernatural communication suggests both an early acquaintance with mediumship and a predilection to use the language of spiritualism at a time when she vigorously challenged religious orthodoxy.[19] Certainly, by 1850 Dickinson felt an abundance of personal and historical motivation for welcoming an alternative avenue for self-expression. In 1848, when the Fox sisters entered the American scene and triggered the spiritualist movement, the Second Great Awakening was continuing its sweep through the Connecticut Valley, Dickinson was turning eighteen, and she was in the process of completing her year at Mt. Holyoke Female Seminary, where she had excelled as a student but refused to accept Christ as her personal savior.[20] Eighteen forty-eight was also the year of the Seneca Falls Women's Rights Convention where the "Declaration of Sentiments and Resolutions" opened with a clear challenge to any application of Blackstone that used the "law of Nature" (4) to legislate sexual inequality.[21] While certainly not a suffragist, Dickinson was awakening to the oppressive cultural appropriation of nature strenuously objected to by women's rights advocates who actively sought the expansion of female political authority by directly challenging the gendered "law of Nature" that justified the legal restriction of female sovereignty.

Questions about nature and spirituality may well have become particularly acute in April 1850 when Dickinson's father and Susan Gilbert joined Dickinson's mother and her sister, Lavinia, in proclaiming their acceptance of Christian revivalist doctrine. In sharp contrast to these public acts of conformity, Dickinson represented herself in a letter to Jane as very much alone: "Christ is calling everyone here," she wrote, "and I am standing alone in rebellion" (L 94). Barely a month after this letter, Dickinson described herself to Abiah Root as "one of the lingering *bad* ones" who resists Christian conversion and hangs on the margins, searching for an alternative means to interpret the changes she witnesses around her: "I slink away," she writes, "and pause, and ponder, and ponder, and pause, and do work without knowing why – not surely for this brief world, and more sure it is not for Heaven – and I ask what this message *means*" (*L* 98–99). The resistance to conformity and the continuous questioning that these lines convey situates Dickinson—even at this early stage of life—within a set of possibilities for female self-definition that has strong links to spiritualism, in particular the role of the female medium who, like Dickinson, receives mysterious "messages." Dickinson famously projects this aspect of her persona in the June 1864 letter to Higginson in which she states, "The only News I know / Is Bulletins all day / From Immortality" (*L* 431).[22] The speaker of Dickinson's poem "I sued the News – yet feared – the News" (Fr 1391) similarly adopts the medium's relationship to such "News," explicitly linking her reception of this news to knowledge of eternity: " 'The House not made with Hands' it was – / Thrown open wide – to me – ."

Considered in the context of spiritualism, several of the most enigmatic features of Dickinson's life raise the possibility that she drew on America's fascination with the medium's privacy as a means to enhance her own limited public presence. In 1849, for instance, Dickinson not only communicated the growing interest in independence from church and family that would receive fuller expression in 1850, but also introduced into her letters her adolescent practice of inserting "dashes" as her primary form of punctuation.[23] As a linguistic version of the spectral insubstantiality symbolized by the medium's veil, the dashes that continue in the letters and later surface in the poems consistently disrupt her syntax, inserting varying degrees of disjunction that effectively obscure public scrutiny of the writer's interior experience.[24] At the same time, however, the very dashes that appear to conceal the private self also define and project that self by enhancing the eccentric and oracular quality of Dickinson's experiments with prose and poetry. The increasingly reclusive character of Dickinson's daily life can also be seen as an additional veil that further magnified her privacy; yet, at the same time that she donned that veil, she was mailing hundreds of poems through her correspondence and by that means publicly proclaiming her vocation as a poet. Even Dickinson's final letter to Louise and Francis Norcross can be seen as expressing the female medium's paradoxical union of inaccessible privacy and public display by drawing on the title of Hugh Conway's popular novel *Called Back*. Dickinson's words, "Little Cousins, / Called back" (*L* 906), point to the extreme privacy of a journey beyond the veil while simultaneously identifying her experience with a novel in which the central scene depends on a clairvoyant revelation that effectively pierces that veil (Conway 92). In the novel, the narrator unlocks one of the primary mysteries of his life by using his wife's mediumistic powers to view a murder that took place years previously, the details of which had filled him with doubt and uncertainty. His vision grants him the certainty he desires but does not dispel his doubt that others will credit his experience. He affirms that he "related what happened," but admits "if my bare word is insufficient to win credence, I must be content on this one point to be disbelieved" (Conway 94). Dickinson may have been suggesting to her cousins that her experience of death would similarly unlock persistent mysteries in a manner satisfactory to her but do so in a manner inaccessible to them.

Looking at Dickinson's life through the lens of spiritualism, while also considering America's interest in the public presence of the private medium, suggests that her frequently noted withdrawal into privacy may have indeed performed the opposite function of attracting the notice of a particular public. As Michael Warner's study of the difference between "*the* public" and "*a* public" makes clear, *the* public acquires authority by means of multiple "self-organized" minor publics, each of which "organizes itself independently of state institutions" (68). Without the existence of these multiple publics, "the public could not be sovereign with respect to the state." From this point of view, individual sovereignty derives from participation in varied publics that lie outside formal framework of "preexisting institutions such as the church," thus instilling in a democratic citizenry an abiding interest in the discovery of new publics outside the institutional domain sanctioned by *the* public. Braude argues that in the context of nineteenth-century America this interest in alternative publics emerged as an inverse dynamic that took place on a national scale through the emergence of the female public medium, an emergence that finally reveals a contradiction within the fabric of American culture's construction of female privacy.

Similarly, in *Cultures of Letters* Richard Brodhead outlines how authors seized on the public's fascination with the private person, especially the private woman, to emphasize their own privacy as a technique of self-promotion. While it seems clear that Dickinson's lifelong interrogation of cultural meanings was a significant factor in her choosing the reclusive life that St. Armand has compared to the "veil of the medium" ("Ladies" 18–21), it is also clear that spiritualism held positive artistic benefits that may have appealed to Dickinson's more public aspirations on a number of levels. Brodhead affirms this possibility when he observes that the image of the popular female medium, particularly in the hands of accomplished promoters like P. T. Barnum, "is most essentially an image of woman as public performer" (51). In making his argument, Brodhead emphasizes the way nineteenth-century domesticity created a public appetite for veiled women by equating the natural with the private, thereby stimulating a desire to examine visually that which the canons of good taste withheld: "we might say that the Veiled Lady registers the creation of a newly publicized world of popular entertainment taking place simultaneously with the creation of a newly privatized world of woman's domestic life" (53). The calculus Brodhead traces, whereby public interest is intensified through the assertion of inaccessibility, may offer an additional strand of cultural logic that helps explain why Dickinson so carefully preserved hundreds of poem manuscripts while conducting a life shrouded by a veil of extreme privacy. According to this logic, Dickinson perceived that her natural timidity could ensure a public interest in the literary productions of her private life if she used it as part of a carefully managed public persona.[25] Her brother Austin's comments about her deliberate posing in letters and her theatrical appearance before Higginson in 1870, plus the many eccentric displays that led Mabel Loomis Todd to describe her in 1881 as "the Myth" may well figure as part of a strategy designed to generate interest in details of her privately created literary corpus.[26]

When viewed in the context of public fascination with spiritualism and the way spiritualism combined with the peculiarities of Dickinson's private life, it now seems almost predictable that early critical responses to Dickinson's posthumous publication would identify spiritualist qualities in her work. In his November 16, 1890, review in the *Springfield Republican*, Charles Goodrich Whiting noted that Dickinson "seemed to have at times the spiritual insight that was accredited to the Pythian priestess" (Buckingham 16). Nathan Haskell Doyle begins his December 1890 review in the *Book Buyer* by similarly affirming an oracular quality: "Speaking of Delphic utterances, such may be found in the poems of Emily Dickinson" (44). Arlo Bates expresses his initial response to Dickinson in the first sentence of a February 1891 review in *Book Buyer:* "From the supernatural to the poems of the late Emily Dickinson is only a step" (110). Lilian Whiting's September 26, 1891, review in the *Brooklyn Standard-Union* touches directly on the poetry's link with the medium's clairvoyance: "Miss Dickinson's poems have a fairly startling insight and vividness, as if with the vision of a clairvoyant she united the vivisective powers of the scientist" (176). To some degree, then—at least in the minds of these readers—the content and style of Dickinson's writing projected characteristics associated in the public mind with the female spiritualist medium. The fact that Dickinson's poems appeared posthumously, as the voice of a poet now departed, may have additionally magnified this association and in a small way contributed to the unanticipated popularity of the first editions of her poems.

The Disembodied Self

Behind the staging of the private self that may or may not have been deliberate, lies the firm conviction so frequently asserted in the poems that nature and the behavior of individual human beings founded on nature could never be commensurate. Nature provides no comprehensible foundation for the erection of an enduring individual or social identity. The poems repeatedly tell us that the best way to cope with the mismatch between spiritual fluidity and the seemingly fixed codes of culture was to promote a habit of agile thought that manifested itself whenever possible in contradictory outward expressions of self, like those of the female medium. In this sense, Dickinson was much more interested in what the presence of the medium said about the culture she inhabited than in any specific message the medium might actually communicate about that culture or the world beyond. Dickinson could never be more than half a reformer, never a utopian social idealist; her task was that of questioning authority and directing attention to the unruliness of the spirit, not establishing a new and improved foundation for perpetuating social authority. Some of Dickinson's most sweeping challenges to institutionalized forms of authority are for this reason located in poems that quietly but insistently interrogate the character and content of spiritual perception.

Many of these poems show that Dickinson joined the spiritualists in urging a democratization of spiritual experience through individual responsiveness to a spiritual reality incommensurate with the versions of nature used to underwrite social codes. The speaker of "Nature affects to be sedate" (Fr 1176), for instance, presents nature as greatly exceeding the powers of human perception:

> Nature affects to be sedate
> Opon [sic] Occasion, grand
> But let our observation shut[27]
> Her practises [sic] extend
> To Necromancy and the Trades
> Remote to understand
> Behold our spacious Citizen
> Unto a Juggler turned –

The speaker's acknowledgment that nature's "practises extend . . . Remote to understand" is democratically inflected through her reference to "Necromancy and the Trades," an association that unites the occult with the marketplace, indicating that nature does not respect the distinctions humanity attaches to these different categories. Not surprisingly, the attentive "Citizen" who seeks to ground thought in a coherent vision of nature is "Unto a Juggler turned."

This need to epistemologically juggle new input flowing from a dynamic and continually unfolding apprehension of nature is even more emphatically asserted in a short poem about the sorrows and joys that come from both letting go of and rediscovering "Earthly" embodiments of nature:

> The worthlessness of Earthly things
> The Ditty is that Nature Sings –
> And then – enforces their delight
> Till Synods are inordinate – (Fr 1400B)

This speaker's identification of nature's song as a "Ditty" capable of signifying both "worthlessness" and a delight that surpasses the power of "Synods" gymnastically unites the grand and the commonplace.[28] In doing so, the speaker also traces the path of thought that democratically situates the simple and the grandiloquent as extremes that characterize the experiences of all people.

One of Dickinson's most accomplished incorporations of spiritualist discourse in expressing the juggler's dexterity is "Of nearness to her sundered Things" (Fr 337). The speaker in this poem states that "The Soul has special times" when "The Shapes we buried, dwell about, / Familiar, in the Rooms" and "Bright Knots of Apparitions / Salute us, with their wings – ." These moments are so striking that the perceiver reverses the customary terms of loss and mourning, coming to see mortal life from the perspective of the now-infinite departed: "As we – it were – that perished – / . . . / And 'twas they, and not ourself / That mourned – ." Like the speaker in "A solemn thing – it was – I said –" (Fr 307), this speaker also assumes the medium's role of conveying the departed spirit's view of mortal life. In this poem, though, the reader's collaboration with the speaker is given particular emphasis through the use of the first-person plural "we." Doing so implies that the medium's experience is available to all people while also urging readers to consider the potential benefits that follow from the capacity to view present life from the perspective of the infinite. In this particular case, assuming the spirit's perspective requires that the reader imagine what it is about mortal life that might lead a departed spirit to mourn its loss. If this challenge to the imagination is taken seriously, the reader must reverse the poles of conventional Christian thought by imagining mortal life as offering benefits that become apparent to the departed. When this occurs, the reader joins the speaker in collaboration with the spirit presence, jointly creating the "ghostly subjectivity" that Eliza Richards associates with "a bi-directional system of communication, one that forges new meaning in the transaction between individuals, shaping cultural modes of interpretation in the process" (123, 148).

Dramatic shifts in spiritual awareness provoked by encounters with the supernatural that impinge on and reshape daily life, as these do, correspond closely to the "'nimble believing'" that James McIntosh defines as key to Dickinson's religious experience: "believing for intense moments in a spiritual life without permanently subscribing to any received system of belief is a key experience, and obsessive subject, and a stimulus to expression for Dickinson" (1). Spiritualism in Dickinson's writing might be understood as an aspect of nimble believing that pays particular attention to the role nature plays in establishing the sort of independent spiritual life that Ruttenburg has come to understand as a feature of democratic personality. Speaking specifically of Dickinson's treatment of nature, McIntosh affirms that "she habitually plays with what she perceives or imagines—dramatizing changing perspectives toward her experience of nature—and thus practices nimble believing in nature's presence" (146). The speaker of "I sued the News - yet feared - the News" (Fr 1391) represents such nimbleness by proclaiming both the attraction and the dread that accompany the discovery "That such a Realm could be - ." Dickinson repeatedly infuses her poems with unsettling discoveries of this kind to discipline her readers in the art of nimble belief appropriate to a constantly changing spiritual reality. Thus the speaker of "'Tis whiter than an Indian Pipe -" (Fr 1513) struggles to describe a spirit presence she is apparently observing: "'Tis dimmer than a Lace - ," she muses, "No stature has it, like a Fog / When you approach the place - ." At last, the speaker admits the indefinable character of spirit life by concluding, "This limitless Hyperbole / Each one of us shall be - / 'Tis Drama - if Hypothesis / It be not Tragedy - ." Framing such choices in language evocative of, if not drawing directly on, spiritualist practice would almost certainly have borne democratic implications at the time Dickinson was writing.

Two of Dickinson's letters to Higginson in which she challenges conventional distinctions between natural and supernatural suggest that she knowingly incorporated the radical democratic position espoused by midcentury American spiritualists. Dickinson's previously mentioned 1863 statement that "the 'Supernatural,' [is] only the Natural, disclosed" (L 424) parallels the spiritualist conviction that human institutions and the cultural constructs that support them, including the taming, codification, and domestication of nature, could never be more than partial or imperfect approximations of a primary spiritual reality. Indeed, a core precept of spiritualism was the conviction that human nature was perfectible, but achieving perfection was a protracted affair; imperfections implicit in all forms of social and cultural organization necessarily obscured apprehension of a more pervasive spiritual reality, so that disclosing the supernatural within the natural was necessarily a gradual process that extended far beyond mortal life.[29] Dickinson's 1876 observation that "Nature is a Haunted House - but Art - a House that tries to be haunted" (L 554) suggests that this wilder, haunted "nature" served for her as a model for the kind of art that loosens the hold socially predicated notions of "the Natural" have on our perception of spiritual experience.[30] Dickinson's aesthetic may for these reasons be thought of as sharing with spiritualism the principle that nature had to be rediscovered continually if the spiritual power obscured by conventional constructions of it were to become part of individual experience.

The short poem "It was not Saint – it was too large –" (Fr 1052) exemplifies Dickinson's practice of juxtaposing nature and religion as a way of provoking readers to think for themselves about the actual composition of spiritual experience. In this poem, the speaker attempts to label her perception in a manner consistent with conventional categories, but winds up using the term "spiritual" to indicate a kind of noncategorical alternative:

It was not Saint – it was too large –
Nor Snow – it was too small –
It only held itself aloof
Like something spiritual –

The imagery that opens the poem draws on orthodox Christian precedent ("Saint") and a familiar natural phenomenon ("Snow") to situate the discussion in customary discourses. This combination of saint and snow brings together the awe of visionary manifestation and the visual insubstantiality of a snow cloud to create the sensation of a ghostly spirit presence. The final two lines, however, deny the explanation seemingly invited by this riddle-like formulation, and instead offer the end-terms, "aloof" and "spiritual." Readers are left with a sense of the "spiritual" as a quality of experience that unites the supernatural of conventional religion with a common natural image to evoke a sense of otherness that inheres in familiar experience but refuses to be contained by it. Dickinson's use of spiritualist terminology in this instance is indicative of her broader practice of using spiritualist references to thwart closural processes that diminish subjective responsiveness and threaten the possibility of democratic independence. Geoffrey Sanborn's observation that though "Dickinson does not participate in Marxian or postcolonial discourses, she does model a practice that is the precondition of those discourses" effectively describes the ongoing resistance to culturally sanctioned forms of closure that Dickinson achieves here through her inclusion of spiritualist themes (1345).

Returning mystery to the experience of the self in nature and art, both positions Dickinson expressed to Higginson in her letters about nature as the supernatural revealed and art as a house that tries to be haunted, may be the most significant of the many uses she makes of spiritualist language in her poems. No Dickinson poem better illustrates her efforts to use nature and art to reveal an incommensurate self than "What mystery pervades a well!" (Fr 1433):

What mystery pervades a well!
The water lives so far –
A neighbor from another world
Residing in a jar

Whose limit none has ever seen,
But just his lid of glass –
Like looking every time you please
In an abyss's face!

The Grass does not appear afraid,
I often wonder he
Can stand so close and look so bold
At what is awe to me.

Related somehow they must be,
The sedge stands next the sea
Where he is floorless
And does no timidity betray –

But nature is a stranger yet;
The ones that cite her most
Have never passed her haunted house,
Nor simplified her ghost.

To pity those that know her not
Is helped by the regret
That those who know her, know her less
The nearer her they get.

St. Armand presents this poem as a prime example of Dickinson's expression of art as a haunted house. He explains that Dickinson "saw it as the artist's task to capture the 'likeness' or spirit or ghost that lurked within the Gothic castle of the landscape" and successfully convey this "effect" to readers (*Dickinson* 227). Lease similarly observes that through this "meditation on water" Dickinson dramatizes the "enormous difficulty of unraveling" the mysterious spirit or ghost to which St. Armand refers (115). Both St. Armand and Lease usefully position Dickinson within the context of spiritualist discourse, yet emphasize aspects other than the immediacy with which the poem speaks to readers about the universe they share with nature; St. Armand sees the poem as striving for a spe-

cific aesthetic effect, while Lease understands it as an aestheticized dramatic enactment.

A reading of the poem more directly responsive to the instability of nature
as expressed through the spiritualist references of the last two stanzas illuminates Dickinson's concern with the way nature informs utterance and contributes
to the incomplete embodiment that characterizes democratic personality. The
poem begins in the "other world" of nature—here signified by well water—and
metaphorically translates it into a commonplace jar, so that access to the mysterious abyss of nature acquires a domestic immediacy. The middle two stanzas
consider the way elements of nature—grass and sedge—manage to live in immediate proximity to such a mystery and not express the awe that so dominates
the speaker's experience. The poem then declares that the silence of grass and
sedge does not apply to the speaker because for her "nature is a stranger yet"; she
is both an extension of the natural world and an alienated observer of it. Those
who feel the power of nature's "haunted house" sense an awe-inspiring vastness
that makes talking about her a disturbingly reductive matter of simplifying "her
ghost."[31] The sense of awe that fills experience with as yet undisclosed spiritual
potential collides with the knowledge that comprehension will never encompass
this thrilling mystery: "those who know her, know her less / The nearer her they
get." The speaker therefore concludes by declaring the impossibility of succeeding in her objective of speaking about nature, thus setting in place the absent
presence vital to the spectral communication of the medium who simultaneously
affirms her inability to speak while speaking nonetheless.

Readers confronted with the paradox of speaking the unspeakable are invited
to decide for themselves where they stand in relation to nature. Will they sim-
plify nature and speak about her with ease or face her directly and accept the
incompleteness of utterance? The speaker in the poem models the latter choice
and in doing so asserts the incommensurability of nature and self that characterizes democratic responsiveness.[32] In Ruttenburg's terms, "the analytical and
conceptual difficulties of democratic personality must be seen as inhering not
in the intellectual substance of its utterances, which were often inarticulate if
radically persuasive, but in the individual act of utterance itself" (6). Such an
act retains a high degree of insubstantiality and hence disembodiment by incorporating within it an awareness of the unsimplified ghost that inhabits nature's
haunted house. Democratic personality, for Dickinson, required recognition of
the spectral incommensurability of all action as a precondition for resistance to
social convention and the continuous expression of an imperfectly contained,
antiestablishment voice.

The speaker of "Conscious am I in my Chamber –" (Fr 773B) delineates precisely this kind of incomplete embodiment through utterance that gives special

attention to the spirit's absent presence in democratic personality. The poem opens with the speaker's description of a "shapeless friend" who "doth not attest by Posture – / Nor confirm – by Word" and who is best known through "Hospitable intuition." Special emphasis is given to what the speaker cannot state for certain and how that lack of certainty is itself a component of encounters with the spirit world. Consequently, the speaker concludes that even though it is impossible to know if the spirit visitant appears to others ("visit Other") or even has any confirmable existence ("Do He dwell – or Nay"), what little is known is sufficient to affirm a spirit presence: "But Instinct esteem Him / Immortality."[33] The critical component of this relationship, though, is conveyed in the third stanza, where the question of presence is confronted directly:

> Presence – is His furthest license –
> Neither He to Me
> Nor Myself to Him – by Accent –
> Forfeit Probity –

The poem's attention to "Word" and "Accent" demonstrates that the spirit presence of the "shapeless friend" cannot be sustained by means of language; "Probity," or honest representation, may, however, be achieved when language points to but does not name that which cannot be embodied. Rather than foreclosing thought by definitively anchoring presence in the present moment, the speaker regenerates the meaning-bearing potential of language by affirming the open-ended, relentlessly responsive requirement of democratic thought that preserves the sovereignty of the individual by making individual choice an ongoing process.

One feature of spiritualist language that is of particular interest to scholars now investigating the democratic ramifications of spiritualism, and that may have also attracted Dickinson's attention, was the specific function of probity. Braude points to the "unaccountability of mediums" that resulted from their function as "merely passive vehicles" who could not be held responsible for the "content of their messages" (87). Spiritualists themselves held widely divergent views on such fundamental matters as the relation of God to nature (Carroll 87) and who were and who were not spiritualist practitioners. As R. Laurence Moore has observed, "It was not even entirely clear—even among its own partisans—as to who counted as a spiritualist" (41). An environment as thoroughly charged with instability as was the field denominated "spiritualism" would have been enormously attractive to a democratic writer who sought to promote the necessity of individual self-creation by affirming the incommensurate spectral nature of social identity. Allen Grossman's linkage of "'invisibility'" with what he de-

scribes as the "'*incommensurability* criterion'" lucidly accounts for the ghostly
presence of Dickinson's democratic utterance by explaining that there can be
"'no image of the incommensurable, as there is no actual social formation characterized by equality, and therefore there is no image of the person'" (qtd. in
Ruttenburg 387). Dickie similarly describes Dickinson's lyric expression of incommensurability as an "unaccountable surplus" that "cannot be made uniform,
narrated, and organized into a single individual" (19).

The awareness resulting from such expressions of incomplete embodiment
opens the self to multiple conflicting voices that challenge dominant discourse
in ways that become particularly pronounced in relation to questions of spiritual
identity. Thus Dickinson writes many view-from-the-grave and voice-from-the-
dead poems, like "Safe in their Alabaster Chambers –" (Fr 124F), "I felt a Funeral,
in my Brain" (Fr 340), "Because I could not stop for Death –" (Fr 479), and "I heard
a Fly buzz – when I died –" (Fr 591). As Lease has observed, one aim these poems
serve is that of introducing the possibility that the next life reflects an entirely
different sense of nature, one that is nothing anyone in this life expects (*Reading* 102–103). In Jane Eberwein's words, Dickinson's presentation of the afterlife
in "Safe in their Alabaster Chambers –" is designed to provoke readers by casting
the dead saints "as 'Safe' in imagery suggestive more of a bank deposit vault than
of anything holy" (132). In these and other descriptions of the afterlife, Dickinson presented readers with opportunities to regenerate language and thought by
imagining alternatives to orthodox accounts of death and the life of the spirit.

As this concern with mystery and incommensurability indicates, spiritualism figures in the writing of Emily Dickinson not only in her use of spiritualist language but perhaps more importantly when she explores the relationship
between utterance and embodiment in democratic identity. And the relationship to embodiment that Dickinson uses spiritualism to articulate may have
special meaning in the twenty-first century because we now debate more than
ever before the many challenges to institutional norms of embodiment that proliferate in Dickinson's literary corpus. R. W. Franklin's 1981 publication of *The
Manuscript Books of Emily Dickinson,* Marta Werner's 1995 publication of forty
late manuscripts in *Open Folios,* the formation of the Emily Dickinson Editorial Collective, the creation of the *Dickinson Electronic Archives,* the growing Internet availability of holograph manuscripts, the 1998 publication of Franklin's
new variorum, the 2003 publication of Eleanor Heginbotham's *Reading the Fascicles of Emily Dickinson,* the 2005 publication of Virginia Jackson's *Dickinson's
Misery: A Theory of Lyric Reading,* and the 2008 *Emily Dickinson's Correspondence: A Born-Digital Inquiry* all contribute to our sense that Dickinson left a
highly unstable body of work.[34] Unexpectedly, investigating Dickinson's uses of
spiritualism may illuminate the way her own aesthetic of incommensurability

complements emerging critical and editorial judgments that seek to honor the cultural currents of Dickinson's day while also identifying Dickinson's personal, political, and artistic aims. Manuscript resistance to print embodiment may be one facet of an aesthetic of incommensurability that informs many of the most enigmatic features of Dickinson's life.[35]

4

A Version of Fame

Dickinson's Correspondence and the Politics of Gift-Based Circulation

In this chapter I examine Dickinson's practice of circulating poems through her correspondence as an expression of personal sovereignty supported by nineteenth-century gift culture. I look at Dickinson's exchange of literary gifts as an alternative to print-based circulation that encouraged the formation of counter-publics through the collaborative affirmation of intransigent habits of thought. I focus on Dickinson's correspondence with Helen Hunt Jackson, Susan Gilbert Dickinson, and Thomas Wentworth Higginson because the letters and poems Dickinson exchanged with them pointedly address the issues of publication and Dickinson's relationship to a larger public. Dickinson's extensive epistolary relationships with Susan Dickinson and Higginson, especially, embrace many other subjects as well, but here I concentrate on those letters that best show how knowledge of gift culture further illuminates Dickinson's efforts to promote democratic personality. I approach Jackson as the correspondent who most vividly reveals Dickinson's dedication to gift-based circulation through her efforts to convince Dickinson to seek print publication and forego the intransigence that she perceives as an impediment to public acclaim. Susan, by contrast, is attuned to Dickinson's gift-based approach to circulation and shares her understanding of poetry's power to awaken the sovereign self, but balks in her efforts to circulate the full body of Dickinson's poems after Dickinson's death, at least in part because she anticipates a public backlash and in Dickinson's absence lacks the strength to go forward on her own. I give the most time to Dickinson's correspondence with Higginson because these letters and the relationship they limn demonstrate his responsiveness to the provocative power of Dickinson's literary gifts. More than any other, this correspondence makes clear the extent that Dickinson acted according to the logic of gift exchange, and that her doing so frequently jolted her recipient out of complacency through affirmations of shared values that resist containment in predictable patterns of thought and action.

   This chapter may be understood as providing historical reinforcement for Katha Pollitt's observation that Dickinson's writing is political because "every line [Dickinson] wrote is an attack on complacency and conformity of manners, mores, religion, language, gender, thought" (2). Examining Dickinson's letters as an extension of nineteenth-century gift culture significantly clarifies the extent that Dickinson's "attack on complacency" takes place within a broadly established system of gift exchange that potentially unites giver and receiver in a collaborative effort founded on each party's capacity for social resistance.[1] Read in this context, many of Dickinson's seemingly eccentric and inwardly directed observations acquire social and political content. As an example, her famous declaration to Higginson that publication is as "foreign" to her "as firmament to fin" and that if "fame" were hers she could not "escape it" (*L* 408) might now be read as an effort to provoke Higginson's reconsideration of what fame is and whether conventional publication is the best means to achieve it. By challenging basic assumptions governing Higginson's life as a writer and an editor, Dickinson's words have the potential to alter his social identity in ways that would significantly reshape his public conduct. Challenges similar to this one figure prominently in contemporaneous short stories by Constance Fenimore Woolson and Elizabeth Stoddard in which the failure of gift-based circulation reveals the receiver's inability to rise above the "complacency and conformity of manners" that Pollitt has identified as a hallmark of Dickinson's writing. A brief examination of these short stories sheds light on Dickinson's correspondence with Jackson, Susan, and Higginson, illuminating the extent to which Dickinson's participation in gift culture enabled her to launch the sort of attack on political, social, and religious conformity that critics such as Pollit have long found in Dickinson's poems.[2]

   Before going into those stories and their application to Dickinson's correspondence, though, I want to outline what the political implications of gift exchange may have been for nineteenth-century Americans. In *Sentimental Collaborations,* Mary Louise Kete makes the case that the circulation of literary gifts among isolated people in nineteenth-century America did indeed perform an important political function. Kete proposes that gift exchange translated "'the isolated, dysfunctional 'one' or 'I' into a 'we' able to act on and promote communal interests among the competing interests of other 'we's'" (54). These "'little societies'" collectively contributed to a larger "national and authoritative 'We,'" as in "We the people," through a process that invested private and predominantly middle-class Americans with the authority to shape civic culture.[3] Kete's linkage of correspondence to the language of founding documents is echoed by Elizabeth Hewitt, who demonstrates in *Correspondence and American Letters, 1770–1865* that the unifying force of the Declaration of Independence derives in part from its epistolary status and the capacity of letters to confer both independence and unity.

"Epistolary writing," Hewitt explains, "paradoxically emphasizes the individual sovereignty of the letter-writer, even as it harnesses the atomism or anarchy that might come from this model by ultimately connecting the individual to a matrix of other letter-writers" (12). Elizabeth Barnes makes a similar point about the Declaration of Independence, only she does so within the larger framework of sentimental culture: "What results is a surprising conflation of the personal and the political body—a vision of 'the people' as a single and independent entity, asserting its liberal privilege in a body at once collective and individual" (1).

Gift-based systems, like the one Dickinson participates in, influence public culture as special instances of both sentimental culture and epistolary politics, performing the additional role of reinforcing shared moral values precisely because gift exchange takes place apart from the practical demands of daily life. In anthropologist David Cheal's words, the gift economy is a *"system of redundant transactions within a moral economy, which makes possible the extended reproduction of social relations"* (19). These newly vitalized moral values then guide individual political acts, invigorating the civic self. Participants in gift circulation thus demonstrate their individuality through collaborative acts in which they disclose personal values that recipients affirm with acceptance and reciprocity. As Kete states, "The way to keep the self is to give it away" (53). Such a conflation of the personal and the political points to the way that even a private woman, like Dickinson, could have a hand in public politics through the declaration of shared values she achieved by the circulation of her literary gifts.

Dickinson would almost certainly have been attracted to the questioning of social conformity that was so central to participation in the "little societies" promoted within gift culture. Studies of gift exchange, including Kete's, acknowledge that gift donation proceeds by means of a distinct and often intransigent subjectivity that unites giver with receiver through mutual collaboration.[4] Cultural anthropologist Jacques T. Godbout helpfully describes this process as operating "according to rules that are not those of the public institution and differ from it essentially in not making a distinction between 'them' and 'us,' in not creating that radical split that always exists between . . . a producer and a consumer" (166). This merging of producer and consumer is one of the most important distinguishing features of a gift economy, a feature that Dickinson trades upon in her own efforts to engage correspondents as collaborators, as when she sends Higginson four poems in 1880 and urges him to "Reprove them as your own –" (*L* 681).[5] The specifically intransigent element in such collaborations is rooted in the participants' decision to resist institutionalized norms through their mutual affirmation of values perceived to be unique and unconventional. Geoffrey Sanborn describes just such an intransigent subjectivity in Dickinson's writing as her "emphasis on the subversiveness of intransitive existence" (1340). As I have indi-

cated in previous chapters, the activation of an intransigent subjectivity makes
political action possible but does not determine the nature of the action. In this
sense, intransigence might be thought of as "Revolution" in the latent or "Pod"
phase that becomes action "When the Winds of Will are stirred" (Fr 1044).

The Stoddard and Woolson short stories vividly represent the social and political pressures that must be resisted before attaining the intransigent subjectivity
essential to participation in gift circulation. Woolson's short story "Miss Grief"
describes a male author who receives an unsolicited manuscript from an unknown female writer and—as Higginson did with Dickinson—concludes that
the author desires print publication. The female writer, however, replies that his
opinion would be of little value "in a business way," though she would be grateful for a response that "might be—an assistance personally" (253).[6] The challenge
attached to the gift surfaces when the male writer recognizes both that the obscure woman's talent is superior to his own and that her originality will not yield
to conventional print standards: "her perversities," he concludes, "were as essential a part of her work as her inspirations" (265). Rather than questioning editorial orthodoxy and experimenting with modes of circulation more appropriate to
the unruly manuscript, he insists on making the work conform to public expectations. "'I like it,'" he claims, "'because my taste is peculiar. To me originality and
force are everything . . . but the world at large will not overlook as I do your absolutely barbarous shortcomings on account of them'" (259). Unable to imagine
literary success in accordance with the artistic taste he shares with the author he
calls "Miss Grief," he proves incapable of entering the gift economy. Frustrated
in his efforts to "alter and improve" the work "himself," he grudgingly admits, "I
could not succeed in completing anything that satisfied me, or that approached,
in truth, Miss Grief's own work just as it stood" (264). At last admitting that he
has "utterly failed," he abandons the effort and terminates circulation. This brief
cycle of earnest interest and failed effort effectively establishes the male author's
inability to perceive the nonconventional taste he shares with Miss Grief as the
basis for a viable alternative to conventional print norms, thereby demonstrating
that he lacks the intransigence essential to forming a "little society."

Stoddard's 1870 story, like Woolson's of 1880, also concentrates on the way superior literature is withheld from circulation when the recipients of the literary
gift prove incapable of thinking outside the norms of social convention. In "Collected by a Valetudinarian," two unassuming women, Eliza Sinclair and Helen
Hobson, contemplate the management of a literary estate that opens their eyes to
what Helen refers to as a "world of beauty and truth" (290). We learn that the deceased author of genius, Alicia Raymond, left in her estate an unpublished novel
in which she "dare[s] tell the truth about men and women" (298), a truth that
proves capable of reaching at least one audience member when Julia Beaufort,

fiancé to Alicia's brother, responds positively to a private reading: "'Oh, sister!' she cried, 'how dare you tell the truth about us women?'" (306). The dissemination of this daring truth about women, then, is what is at stake when Helen and Eliza contemplate the future dispensation of Alicia's literary gift.

Initially, they enthuse over the possibility of establishing Alicia's literary fame, comparing Alicia to Charlotte Brontë and imagining themselves as the chief exponents of her art. But the challenge they face is quickly expressed when Eliza asks, "'Dear Helen, how shall we idlers be taught this ideal happiness?'" (290). Helen's response illuminates the demand for an intransigent self that departs from the conventional values that have guided their lives up to this point: "'As soon as we can be made to believe that what is called material or positive happiness is no more truthful or exact than that named visionary or romantic happiness.'" This challenge to rethink the material terms of their lives proves too much for them. Eliza immediately acknowledges the futility of such an attempt by imagining how she and Helen would appear in the eyes of the male hotel manager, Mr. Binks, whose vision she associates with the culturally normative, "ordinary eye." Within the conventional social framework reinforced by the male gaze, Eliza sees no support for the artistic happiness she associates with Alicia's work: "We were a couple of faded, middle-aged women. . . . Why should such indulge in aspirations for happiness, or the expectation of doing any farther [*sic*] work in this gay world?"

Here, as in the Woolson story, circulation terminates when collaboration collides with social identity. Just as the male author of that story could not imagine his own participation in circulation that took place outside print norms, here Helen and Eliza are unable to imagine the intransigent subjectivity essential to their participation in the circulation of Alicia's literary estate. In the closing lines of "Collected," Eliza acknowledges, "if there were more minds among us" like Alicia's "we should have a better literature" (307). Yet when Helen quite logically asks if it "'is . . . not a pity she should be lost to the world?'" Eliza replies with the last words of the story, stating that the preservation of Alicia's memory by the two of them, plus Alicia's brother and wife, "'is enough.'"

The Correspondence with Helen Hunt Jackson

Read with the Stoddard and Woolson stories in mind, Dickinson's correspondence with Helen Hunt Jackson stands out as perhaps her most striking failure to win a collaborator.[7] The available letters clearly show that Jackson was impressed by the power of Dickinson's literary gift but failed to contribute in any significant way to the circulation of the poems because she was unable to accept gift exchange as a viable means to achieve literary fame. Despite her determination to win lasting recognition for Dickinson, she proved incapable of imagining the poems that first reached her as gifts in any terms but those codified within the economy of print publication. The correspondence falls roughly into three stages that effectively embody the cycle of initial enthusiasm and ultimate inaction that characterized gift reception in the Woolson and Stoddard stories. In the first stage, Jackson strives to educate Dickinson in the protocols of the printed page. Like the male author in "Miss Grief," she assumes Dickinson wants to appear in print and exhausts herself in the attempt to achieve that end. The second stage begins after Jackson acknowledges the failure of her efforts and Dickinson seizes the opportunity to draw Jackson into the role of collaborator essential to gift circulation. The third and final stage conveys an uneasy peace achieved once each woman has recognized and accepted the steadfast refusal of the other to adopt an alternative set of literary values.

Upon receiving her first literary gift from Dickinson in October 1875, on the occasion of her second marriage, Jackson immediately signifies her distance from the sensibility of gift culture by imposing the values of ownership and property that define print publication. Jackson does this by sending back Dickinson's letter, requesting clarification of the line "To Dooms of Balm –" that concludes the gift poem, and demanding that Dickinson view the letter as her (Jackson's) property and return it to her as the proper owner (L 544). On the blank last page of Dickinson's letter, Jackson writes, "This is *mine*, remember, You must give it back to me or else you will be a robber," leaving little doubt about her claim of ownership. This behavior plainly shows that rather than reciprocating in kind, as would be appropriate in gift exchange, Jackson requests that Dickinson redefine the gift as a conventional literary commodity. That Dickinson never did return the letter suggests her refusal of Jackson's terms. Perhaps because of Dickinson's refusal, Jackson begins her next letter by emphatically reiterating the conventional literary values she has imposed on the correspondence: "But you did not send it back, though you wrote that you would. / Was this an accident, or a late withdrawal of your consent? / Remember that it is mine – not yours – and be honest." Jackson's language here makes evident the conflicting values that will characterize the entire correspondence; she questions Dickinson's honesty, presumes the logic of consent hinged to ownership, and appears oblivious of alternative explanations. Within gift exchange, however, collaboration takes the place of ownership and honesty can become a factor of sincere response rather than action governed by consistency with prior statements. As Emerson has noted in "Gifts," "The gift, to be true, must be a flowing of the giver unto me, correspondent to my flowing unto him" (156–157). The "correspondence" part of gift-based epistolary correspondence is connected to resonance of character and the acceptance of departures from convention rather than adherence to widely held codes of conduct.

Writing specifically of gift exchange, Pierre Bourdieu gives particular attention to the way participants must avoid overt declarations of duty or the obligation to reciprocate: "To betray one's haste to be free of an obligation one has incurred, and thus to reveal too overtly one's desire to pay off services rendered or gifts received, so as to be quits, is to denounce the initial gift retrospectively as motivated by the intention of obliging one. It is all a question of style" (*Outline* 6). With gift-based correspondence, especially, expressions of gratitude and even the implicit or indirect acknowledgment of obligation must be carefully avoided or managed with stylistic flourish that makes the discourse of gratitude itself a gift. When perceived in this context, Jackson appears totally unaware that Dickinson could be seeking to establish an alternative basis for their communication, concentrating instead on her efforts to bring Dickinson into the fold of literary orthodoxy. She concludes this letter by affirming that Dickinson is a "great poet" while also accusing her of being "wrong to the day you live in" because she "will not sing aloud" (L 545).

The next letters in this first sequence show the two writers increasingly at cross-purposes: Jackson pushes more aggressively for the simplification and publication of poems while Dickinson seeks to change the subject. When Jackson next writes Dickinson in August, she opens her letter with the assurance that Dickinson has not offended her and asks that Dickinson submit poems to the upcoming Roberts Brothers "No Name" poetry volume. Whether or not Dickinson feared giving offense through her refusal to return the "Dooms of Balm" letter is not clear. Jackson appears to have concluded that Dickinson's hesitation has to do with fear of public exposure, not a reluctance to release poems that have failed to communicate. On the contrary, Jackson assures Dickinson of *"double"* anonymity (*L* 563) and ends the letter proper with the following two sentences: "Thank you for writing in such plain letters! Will you not send me some verses?" (*L* 564). These last lines give the impression that Jackson is attempting to mentor Dickinson,[8] an impression reinforced by her final letter of 1876 that contains her admission that upon rereading "the last verses" Dickinson sent her, "I find them more clear than I thought they were. Part of the dimness must have been in me" (*L* 565). Such qualified praise of poems that are "more clear" but not crystal clear, plus the acknowledgment of a partial "dimness" in her own reading may be designed to soften Dickinson up for the advice that follows. Jackson's declaration, "I like your simplest and [most direct] lines best," here functions as the verdict of the published poet who kindly guides the efforts of her fainthearted friend.

Despite Jackson's efforts to help, however, Dickinson felt her position had become impossible and requests Higginson's intervention in an October 1876 letter. Using language appropriate to the clash of gift and commercial economies,

Dickinson explains that during a face-to-face visit in Amherst Jackson "seemed not to believe" her statements that she "was unwilling" and "incapable" of writing for the "No Name" series (L 563). Asserting to Higginson that she "would regret to estrange her," Dickinson solicits his assistance as someone who speaks the language of the marketplace—like Jackson—and who will help her avoid the appearance of a snub: "if you would be willing to give me a note saying you disapproved it, and thought me unfit," Dickinson writes, "she would believe you."[9] Through this device, Dickinson strives to preserve her relationship with Jackson by having a mutually respected third party declare her "unfit," thereby elevating friendly regard for the other's strengths and weaknesses above the pursuit of an anonymous commercial audience.

The next three letters from Jackson demonstrate that far from being deterred in her efforts to see Dickinson in print, Jackson has probably already submitted "Success is counted sweetest" (Fr 112). In her October 25, 1878, letter,[10] Jackson takes a decidedly more aggressive tact, but one that at least takes into account Dickinson's demand that the poems be circulated as gifts rather than marketable commodities: "Now – will you send me the poem? No – will you let me send the 'Success' – which I know by heart – to Roberts Bros for the Masque of Poets? If you will, it will give me great pleasure. I ask it as a personal favor to myself – Can you refuse the only thing I perhaps shall ever ask at your hands?" (L 625). Tempting as it is to see Jackson's focused personal appeal as a recognition of Dickinson's insistence that the poems be treated as gifts, the possibility remains that Jackson is simply using all the tricks at her disposal to secure authorial approval. As Betsy Erkkila has noted, "The seeming desperation of Jackson's request is owing to the fact that in an act of rashness she had already submitted . . . 'Success' . . . and the poem was about to appear in print whether or not Dickinson gave her consent" (*Sisters* 91).[11] The final letter in this initial phase of the correspondence conveys Jackson's doubt that the end result was worth the effort she invested in having her friend published. After expressing her hope that Dickinson has "not regretted giving me that choice bit of verse," she admits that "on the whole, the volume is a disappointment to me" (L 626).

The first phase of the Jackson correspondence, then, set the terms of the two writers' debate over literary ownership and circulation. In the second phase, that of 1879, Dickinson sent Jackson a number of poems that clarify her own position on these issues, perhaps feeling that Jackson would be open to an alternative approach following her disappointment with A Masque of Poets. The poem "Before you thought of Spring" (Fr 1484C) can represent the general tenor of these poems and letters. In this work, Dickinson metaphorically equates the blue bird with the poet in an exploration of the relationship between poem, reader, and author that delineates a gift-based system of circulation:

Before you thought of Spring
Except as a Surmise
You see – God bless his suddenness –
A Fellow in the Skies
Of independent Hues
A little weather worn
Inspiriting habiliments
Of Indigo and Brown –
With Specimens of Song
As if for you to choose –
Discretion in the interval
With gay delays he goes
To some superior Tree
Without a single Leaf
And shouts for joy to Nobody
But his seraphic self –

Elizabeth Petrino effectively frames the poem's link to female poetic practice: "Given the common depiction of women's poetic voices as birdsong, this lyric may express Dickinson's attitude toward poetry and the marketplace: resisting the opinions of others and proclaiming its independence, the bird sets an example for his human counterparts" (183). The poet, like the gift, makes a sudden, unexpected appearance, and offers the reader choices—"Specimens of Song"— passing on to other locations after discrete but disinterested "gay delays," finally shouting for joy out of dedication to self-expression. Here the principles of gift circulation are clearly represented: the delight in both giving and receiving, the absence of reference to reciprocity, the freedom on the part of the recipient to collaboratively engage by selecting from among multiple "Specimens of Song." Perhaps it was Jackson's reading of the line, "As if for you to choose – ," that prompted her to choose a specific specimen in her May 1879 letter where she asked Dickinson to try her "hand on the oriole" (L 639).

With this gesture, Jackson goes further than at any other time in moving from an isolated "I" to a collaborative "we" and thereby accommodating Dickinson's gift-based system. Jackson's opening words in this same letter, "I know your 'Blue bird' by heart – and that is more than I do of any of my own verses" (L 639), implies a fusion of self and other consistent with sentimental gift collaboration. "We have blue birds here," Jackson writes in what is possibly the most unqualified of all her compliments to Dickinson, "I might have had the sense to write something about one myself, but I never did: and now I never can. For which I am inclined to envy, and perhaps hate you" (L 639). Such language points to the possibility that Jackson does indeed seek to collaborate with Dickinson through the promotion of poetry that she sees as representing a level of accomplishment that inspires her admiration but which she failed to realize on her own. Nevertheless, the emotional distancing of her language—even if it is jocular in tone—conveys the logic that motivates her two requests for permission to, in her words, "send [the poem] to Col. Higginson to read." These reiterated appeals for permission, accompanying such pronounced emotional declarations, may reflect Jackson's struggle to retain the tough-minded professional detachment so famously revealed in her 1870 letter to James T. Fields: "'I don't write for money, I write for love, . . . then after it is written, I *print* for money'" (Coultrap-McQuin 155).[12] The overall impression conveyed in this letter, then, is that while Jackson admits the appeal of gift collaboration, she simultaneously clings to the considerably cooler professionalism that she subscribed to in her own poetic practice.

The third and last letter in this second phase of the correspondence shows Dickinson responding with alacrity to Jackson's request, providing not only an oriole poem but an additional hummingbird poem as well. This response may demonstrate Dickinson's sense that Jackson's resistance is weakening, as well as her determination to offer Jackson choices among multiple poems, or specimens, as well as within poems themselves. The oriole poem, "One of the ones that Midas touched" (Fr 1488D), again describes the way poets and readers interact, this time giving special attention both to the multifarious guises assumed by the poet and the reader's role in selecting among them. Dickinson begins by drawing attention to the unreliability of the poet's self-representations through lines that describe the oriole/poet as "So drunk he disavows it," "A Pleader – a Dissembler – / An Epicure – a Thief –" and "He cheats as he enchants." At last, the poet leaves the recipient not with a resolved sense of identity but rather, in Dickinson's words, he departs "like a Pageant / Of Ballads and of Bards – ." The poem carries on for eight more lines in which Dickinson shifts to the subjunctive mood in postulating that the oriole is in fact the golden fleece sought by the Jason of Greek mythology, but the explicit association of bird and poet ends with the reference to "Ballads and . . . Bards."

The recipient, in the meantime, is repositioned from a collective "we," whose initial impression of the poet is "So dazzling we mistake him," to a singular "I" who enters into dialogue with the poem's "we" by selecting a personally appealing set of meanings from among those offered. In this case, the final eight lines suggest the rejoinder of a speaker who assumes the subjunctive mood in declaring that for her purposes the poet/bird performs as the mythic Jason's fleece: "if there were a Jason, / . . . / Behold his lost Aggrandizement / Opon the Apple Tree – ." In this way the poem models both the collective perception of the poem and the particular reader's response, demonstrating that all recipients make independent creative decisions that construct meaning for a collective "we" through a process of collaboration with the poet. A similar procedure is followed in the humming-bird poem (Fr 1489B) where the bird shifts from a "Route of Evanescence" to "A Resonance of Emerald" to "A Rush of Cochineal," leaving the speaker to venture a speculative interpretation of what is observed: "The Mail from Tunis, probably, / An easy Morning's Ride."[13]

Here it is worth mentioning that Dickinson engaged in gift-oriented selec-tions of her own, choosing to send the oriole poem to her Norcross cousins, as well as Jackson, and sending the hummingbird poem to five other correspon-dents, including Higginson (Johnson, *Poems* 1011–1012). It is in the letter to Hig-ginson that accompanied that poem and three others, that Dickinson requested he "Reprove them as your own –" (*L* 681), giving special emphasis to the recipi-ent's role as participant in a collaborative venture.

Following the above offering of poems that included Dickinson's famous hummingbird, the correspondence ceases from May 1879 to April 1883, at which time Dickinson clarifies for Jackson and Thomas Niles, the Roberts Brothers editor who oversaw the "No Name" series, her belief that poetic achievement was not dependent on widespread public recognition. In her 1883 letter-poem to Jackson, Dickinson speaks of memory and forgetting: "To be remembered what? Worthy to be forgot, is their renown –" (*L* 772). Her main message is simple: that she would like to hear from Jackson. But it is difficult and perhaps unreasonable not to approach this missive as a last comment on Dickinson's failure to initiate a more-enduring discussion of poems as gifts. After all, by this time each woman has failed to convince the other to adopt her method of circulating poems and must for this reason come to terms with the fact that each has rejected the other's preferred method of reaching readers and thus ensuring a place in communal memory. Read in this context, Dickinson's letter-poem may be interpreted as say-ing that some of the materials *currently* considered significant enough "to be re-membered" will in the fullness of time prove unworthy of recollection. When ap-plied to the correspondence that led to disappointing publication in *A Masque of Poets* and later to Dickinson's poems about the collaboration of poets and read-ers, these brief lines imply that officially acknowledged printed works may have a permanence that seems more enduring than gift-based manuscript poems, but that the time-bound nature of such materials can also contribute to their disap-pearance.

As if commenting on her detachment from the fashion of the moment, Dick-inson sent the poem "How happy is the little Stone" (Fr 1570E) to Niles in *"late April 1882"* (*L* 725) after having received a letter from him in which he joined Jackson in wishing that she "could be induced to publish a volume of poems" (*L* 726). Though the copy sent to Jackson is lost, the variorum editors Thomas H.

Johnson and Ralph W. Franklin agree that one was sent. In light of Niles's letter and her awareness of Niles through his involvement with the *A Masque of Poets* volume, Dickinson appears to be using the poem to inform both Niles and Jackson of her indifference to literary trends, thereby reducing Jackson's concerns about the quality of the volume and informing Niles that print publication was not essential to her poetic identity.[14] The opening three lines—"How happy is the little Stone / That rambles in the Road alone / And does'nt [*sic*] care about Careers"—introduce the independence of the undistinguished stone that later in the poem "Associates or glows alone" whether or not "A passing Universe put on" its "Coat of elemental Brown." Here Dickinson adopts the poetic equivalent of Benjamin Franklin's snuff-brown coat to emphasize the poet's willingness to accept a kind of intrinsic invisibility in the eyes of the world so long as doing so contributes to the larger poetic objective that the poem describes as "Fulfilling absolute Decree / In casual simplicity – ." With these lines, the poem tells Jackson and Niles that Dickinson is pursuing her poetic vocation unhindered by any present lack of public recognition.

In the exchange between Dickinson and Jackson that follows these 1882 and 1883 letters, Jackson moves back to her earlier, more-insistent commitment to commercial publication, while Dickinson continues, but more gently now, to promote the value of gift-based circulation. Perhaps because of Jackson's forced confrontation with her own mortality compelled by a serious leg fracture, when Jackson writes Dickinson in September 1884 she speaks about the management of Dickinson's literary estate. After imagining "[w]hat portfolios" Dickinson must by this time possess, she writes, "I wish you would make me your literary legatee & executor" (*L* 841). She also states that Dickinson perpetrates a "cruel wrong to your 'day & generation' that you will not give them light." Dickinson's September response to Jackson concludes with a prose sentence and the first three lines of a poem that together clarify the extent that her poetic vocation is an alternative to Jackson's: "Pursuing you in your transitions, / In other Motes – / Of other Myths / Your requisition be" (*L* 841; Fr 1664). Here the word "requisition"[15] performs a pivotal function in proclaiming that Jackson's efforts to enlist Dickinson's poems in her very different project have failed. Dickinson represents herself as dedicated to her friend's "transitions," but at the same time acknowledges that Jackson has engaged "other Myths." No doubt in part because of the clarity with which she declares her poetic independence from Jackson, Dickinson closes by signing herself "Loyally, / E. Dickinson."[16]

The final pair of letters reveal a Jackson who accepts Dickinson's wish for a friendship based on gifts and mutual support even though she remains interested in discovering the full corpus of Dickinson's work; Dickinson similarly appears dedicated to sustaining the friendship, but for her doing so involves openly conveying her poetic perceptions, trusting that the friendship can now accommodate the free expression of differences. Jackson's February 1885 letter begins by thanking Dickinson for a fan apparently sent as part of a lost letter, thus establishing the continued presence of gifts. All but the last line of the letter describes the slow mending of Jackson's broken leg and her physical surroundings. Her concluding clause, "I wish I knew what your portfolios, by this time, hold" (*L* 869), provides the only hint that she still regrets not having greater access to Dickinson's writing.

The two drafts of Dickinson's March 1885 final letter to Jackson include an extraordinary concluding comment on her preference for manuscript distribution over print publication. Read in the light of previous exchanges concerning publication, the most provocative portion of this letter is Dickinson's comment on having recently finished Jackson's novel *Ramona*. "Pity me," she writes, "I have finished Ramona," enigmatically adding, "Would that like Shakespeare, it were just published!" (*L* 867). Deliberately inverting historical fact by presenting Shakespeare as "just published" when in reality *Ramona* had just appeared may underscore Dickinson's belief that *Ramona* is already part of the past, whereas for her Shakespeare is eternally reborn in the eyes of readers.[17] More important, the lines may also be stating that it would have been better if *Ramona* had been published *like* or in a manner similar to Shakespeare. Given Dickinson's awareness of editorial disputes surrounding multiple scholarly editions of Shakespeare, she may well have considered his mode of publication a significant factor in securing public interest.[18] Charles Knight, editor of the Dickinson family edition of Shakespeare (Leyda 352), provided further precedent, if such were needed, when he described his own editorial position: "I have found it necessary," he writes in the "Advertisement" to volume eight, "to combat some opinions of former editors which are addressed to an age nearly without poetry" (B). Knight further explains the way editorial policy reflects transient reader taste: "These essays, therefore, are not to be received as the opinions of an individual, but as the embodiment of the genial spirit of the new school of Shakespearean criticism, as far as a humble disciple may interpret that spirit."

With this sort of editorial debate as background, the two meanings conveyed in Dickinson's comment on *Ramona* can be seen to work in tandem, collectively stating that an important source of Shakespeare's vitality comes from his having composed at a time when writers did not automatically seek print publication and thereby surrender authority to transient editorial norms. According to such logic, Shakespeare could in fact remain "just published" indefinitely, as publishers would never have access to a definitive, author-approved print text against which to measure the authority of their editions. In this sense, then, Shakespeare performs as a model for the sort of writing that Dickinson thinks most alive;

that is, writing that continuously acquires new life through the collaborative engagement of readers. The irony that has pervaded this correspondence and becomes most pronounced in this last letter is that Jackson discovered Dickinson's poems when Higginson showed her unedited manuscript poems he had received through his correspondence with Dickinson, thus validating the potential circulation available through a gift economy that Jackson never entered, despite Dickinson's efforts.

The Correspondence with Susan

The correspondent who provides the sharpest contrast with Jackson and whose intentions most consistently meet the challenge posed by a gift-based system of circulation is Dickinson's sister-in-law, Susan. The letters that passed between the two women over the course of nearly thirty-six years repeatedly affirm the shared values so central to the notion of a redundant morality and the corollary understatement of reciprocity that went along with the gift recipient's freedom to dispense, dispose, or distribute the gift without consulting the giver.[19] Not only is this Dickinson's most extensive correspondence, containing some 254 letters and letter-poems, it is also the correspondence that most clearly expresses the collaborative spirit that she fosters in her poetry.[20] These letters routinely communicate the shared understanding that the women were engaged in a joint enterprise that they viewed from the beginning as an effort to inject into American culture the habit of independent thought that they metaphorically associated with the liberating power of poetry, a power that they contrasted with the more pedestrian, rule-bound character of prose. Through the collaborative production of poetry within the context of gift culture, Susan received drafts of Dickinson poems as well as fair copies that she treated in various ways, sometimes commenting on them, sometimes reading them to friends, sometimes submitting them for publication, and at other times doing whatever came into her head. Dickinson never objected to any of these decisions, at least in part because the terms of gift exchange meant that the giver trusted the recipient to act in a manner consistent with the expansion of their little community of "we" that Kete has positioned at the heart of gift culture. Even though Dickinson did not herself seek print publication, she did not dispute Sue's freedom to do so as long as her motive reflected their shared sense of purpose. Unlike Jackson, who sought to convince Dickinson that she should accept her approach to circulation, Susan merely proceeded as she thought best and left Emily to continue with her preferred method of circulating poems through letters, a method that Sue also employed, only not so exclusively as Emily.

Even the earliest letters in this correspondence show that Susan and Emily were aware that their joint undertaking challenged prevailing cultural norms. In an 1851 letter to Susan, Dickinson imagines the two of them creating what she describes as "a little destiny to have for our own" (*OMC* 8)[21] and declares, "we are the only poets – and every one else is prose" (9).[22] Despite the apparent separation of self and other here designated by the metaphorical division of humanity into poetry and prose, Dickinson significantly stipulates that their overriding goal is that of drawing others into their destiny: "let us hope," she asserts, "they will yet be willing to share our humble world and feed upon such aliment as *we* consent to do!"[23] Ever aware of the challenge their invitation to collaboration poses for readers, Dickinson makes it clear that in their hands words can perform a kind of martial service, as if enlisted in a patriotic enterprise that must penetrate the defenses of conformity before collaboration can become a realistic possibility. In a letter-poem to Susan written in the "late 1850s" (79), she describes a "word / Which bears a sword" and "Can pierce an armed man" for which act the word will be remembered "On patriotic day." Susan extends this martial theme in March 1862 when she describes the publication of Dickinson's "Safe in their Alabaster Chambers –" (Fr124B) and possibly a poem of her own titled "The Shadow of Thy Wing" as a "Fleet" that she compares to General Burnside's "siege and capture of Roanoke Island in February 1862" (96, 97).[24] As early as February 1852, when Sue was teaching in Baltimore, Dickinson described her as "the precious patriot at war in other lands" (12), suggesting that they associated their artistic aims with both conflict and national interest from early in their correspondence.

One important example of the way Dickinson understood the project she undertook with Susan as provoking a potentially violent social transformation appears in the January 15, 1854, letter she writes to Susan just after returning home from Sunday morning services. Here she uses a favorite metaphor, the phoenix, as a figure for a dramatic sudden change that she connects with her own escape from the debilitating, objectifying force of religiously sanctioned social subordination. The letter begins, "I'm just from meeting, Susie, and as I sorely feared, my 'life' was made a 'victim' " (*OMC* 48). Quotation marks around "life" and "victim" point to Dickinson's refusal of what the church calls "life" and the demand that within the script founded on that life hers is the role of victim. Dickinson immediately reclaims her independent subjectivity: "I walked – I ran – I flew – I turned precarious corners – One moment I was not – then soared aloft like Phoenix, soon as the foe was by." Dickinson's careful placement of dashes serves to isolate the specific stages of her escape while also conveying her break with institutionally imposed identity in breathless, dramatic disjunctions. Much of the letter is filled with imagery of social and spiritual oppression that Dickinson similarly seeks to escape, provoking her wish that Sue or Vinnie would assume the righteous anger of "Goliah, or Samson – to pull the whole church down" (49). In what eventually emerges as a dizzying interweaving of varied cultural strands, Dickinson humorously illuminates what she sees as the pervasive cultural enforcement of patriarchal values by proclaiming that "the 'Secretary of War' will take charge of the Sabbath School," and that the viola that accompanies the church choir will become the Jill of the "Legend of 'Jack and Gill' [*sic*]" who tumbles after a reckless Jack. This rich bricolage of myth and legend is here presented as in league with patriarchal forces that seek to impose the drab prose of conformity, implying that Sue and Emily have their work cut out for them as they seek to expand their little society of poets.

At least as important as Susan's shared sense that the poetry of their particular little society could effect change in the larger world is the fact that Susan took significant steps to extend the circulation of Dickinson's poems. Martha Nell Smith observes that "Sue, as would Helen Hunt Jackson a couple of decades later, appears to have actively promoted Dickinson by seeking a wider audience for her poetry while the poet was still living" (*Rowing* 155). Most important, perhaps, was Susan's introduction of Dickinson's poems to Mabel Loomis Todd in 1882 (Leyda 361); yet there is compelling reason to believe Susan's efforts at circulation began much earlier. Thomas H. Johnson proposes that Susan was behind the 1866 publication of "A Narrow Fellow in the Grass" (Fr1096B; 713), and Smith has argued that Susan published both "Blazing in gold, and quenching in Purple" (Fr 321B) and "Success is counted sweetest" (Fr 112) in 1864 (*Rowing* 156), fourteen years before Jackson's publication of the latter poem.[25] Here it must be noted that seeking publication on her own initiative was not without risks for Susan. As Hart and Smith explain in *Open Me Carefully*, Susan's publication of "There came a Day – at Summer's full –" (Fr 325B) in the August 1890 issue of *Scribner's Monthly* did not sit well with Dickinson's sister, Lavinia. "After the publication," Hart and Smith point out, "Lavinia, who had a fascicle copy of the poem, objected to Susan's presumption. However, Susan maintained that she had the right to publish any poems that Emily had sent to her" (*OMC* 116). Such an assertion of rights is perfectly in keeping with the practice of gift circulation, if not the legal system, as through collaboration the poem becomes a joint production, not the exclusive property of a single author. Dickinson's astonishing 1864 letter stating of Susan, "When my Hands / are Cut, Her / fingers will be / found inside –" (131), figuratively affirms a shared authority consistent with gift collaboration while also hinting at joint authorship through the synecdoche linking both women to the same set of authorial "Hands."

The shared sensibility crucial to gift culture and pointedly captured in the graphic image of Sue's hands inside of Emily's is one of the most-pronounced features of this correspondence. In a letter written in February 1852, Dickinson observes to Sue, "How vain it seems to *write*, when one knows how to feel"

(*OMC* 12). Further on in the same letter Dickinson again communicates the redundancy of writing when one has certain knowledge of the other's interior
experience: "Never mind the letter Susie, I wont be angry with you if you dont
[*sic*] give me any at all. . . . Only *want* to write me . . . and that will do." The idea
conveyed here is that writing is important primarily as a gift that expresses depth
of feeling and reinforces shared values rather than as a means of communicating news. In a letter written *"about February 1852"* (18), Dickinson repeatedly affirms the redundancy of attempting to inform Sue about matters Sue already
knows. "Oh Susie," she writes, "I often think that I will try to tell you how very
dear you are . . . yet darling, you know it all – then why do I seek to tell you?" (15–
16). As if redundantly asserting her own redundancy, Dickinson cuts herself off
a few lines later, stating, "I shall not *tell* you, because you know!" (16). Through
language like this, Dickinson not only affirms her confidence in the community
of "we" that she and Sue inhabit, but she also reiterates the logic of nonrecipro-
cation that is a cornerstone of gift culture. As her own writing in these letters
makes clear, the giving and receiving of the gift are ends in themselves—to register an obligation to respond would be to admit that the circuit of the gift was
incomplete and that the gift had failed.[26]

In a series of letter-poems Dickinson sent Susan at a later stage of their correspondence, Dickinson presents what might almost be read as a catechism on
the logic of gift exchange. Writing to Sue in the *"mid-1860s"* (*OMC* 140), Dickinson spells out the circuit of exchange that begins and ends when the gift is both
given and received:

> Gratitude – is not
> the mention
> Of a Tenderness,
> But its' [*sic*] still
> appreciation
> Out of Plumb of
> Speech.

Dickinson's disavowal of speech—or in the case of letters, writing—is a textbook
instance of the completion achieved when giver and receiver merge. Dickinson
makes this point in an even more explicit manner in a *"late 1870s"* (222) letter-
poem:

> Susan –
>   The sweetest
> acts both exact

and defy, gratitude,
so silence is all
the honor there is –

Even into the 1880s, Dickinson reiterates the needlessness of saying thanks or acting in any way but content with the fullness of the moment. The following letter from the *"early 1880s"* (233) shows the way Dickinson delights in pointing out the redundancy of gratitude in a friendship that has repeatedly affirmed its enduring strength through gifts each has given to the other:

"Thank you"
ebbs – between us,
but the Basis
of thank you,
is sterling and
fond –

One of the most-interesting features of these particular letter-poems is the way they function simultaneously as the redundant thanks that Dickinson decries and as new gifts themselves that affirm the shared sensibility that is itself the reason thanks are not required. In this sense, letter-poems that celebrate the absence of thanks but give it anyway may be understood as a distinctive gift-culture trope that endlessly loops the affirmation and erasure of reciprocity thus compounding redundancy and magnifying the message that what is being given is free from obligation and thus an expression of unqualified affection.

The confidence, trust, and affection so vividly conveyed in these letter-poems about redundant reciprocity help establish and maintain the crucial foundation that enabled Emily and Susan to launch their fleet of poems as a collaborative venture. The best-known example of their working together on a poem appears in the correspondence that surrounds the March 1, 1862, publication of "Safe in their alabaster chambers" (Fr 124A) in the *Springfield Republican*. Ralph Franklin speculates that Susan gave a copy of the poem to Samuel Bowles, a close friend and publisher of the *Springfield Republican,* when he visited in June 1861. Hart and Smith agree but further speculate that Susan also gave Bowles a copy of her own poem, "The Shadow of Thy Wing," that appeared in the paper beneath Dickinson's poem. Hart and Smith base their judgment on the similarities that they see with other poems by Sue, though both poems were published anonymously in the *Republican* and no copy of "The Shadow of Thy Wing" appears in Susan's papers. Susan's letter to Emily, written after she had a chance to see both poems in the *Republican,* asks if Emily has *"read* [the] *Republican"* then delivers the line mentioned earlier about their mutual "Fleet": "It takes as long to start our Fleet as the Burnside" (*OMC* 96). Read in the context of gift culture, Sue's use of the pronoun "our" and the noun "Fleet" could easily mean either that a poem by each appeared in print, thus justifying the reference to a fleet, or that a single poem jointly produced is the first "ship" in a fleet of poems yet to be published. However, the fact that by this time two other Dickinson poems, "Nobody knows this little Rose –" (Fr 11) and "I taste a liquor never brewed –" (Fr 207) had already been printed in the *Republican,* and probably submitted by Sue (Franklin, *Poems* 67, 237), Hart and Smith are likely correct in assuming that Sue's "Fleet" reference points to the first occasion when poems by both women simultaneously appear in print. In any case, the difficulty demonstrated here of determining who possesses proprietary rights and when a poem might be referred to as "ours" is further complicated by the process of gift collaboration.

With "Safe in their Alabaster Chambers –" there is clear evidence that the poem was a collaboration, even though Dickinson remains the primary writer. As Martha Nell Smith has noted, "at least in the case of 'Safe in their Alabaster Chambers,'" Sue "critiqued the text while Dickinson was in the process of writing and in that way participated in the creation of the poem" (*Rowing* 182). Smith has in mind Sue's letter to Dickinson, written *"about 1861"* (*OMC* 99), in which Sue comments on a revision of the second stanza. Sue opens by stating, "I am not suited / dear Emily with the second / verse," then notes that "it does not go with the / ghostly shimmer of the first verse" and closes her critique by proposing that "the first verse / is complete in itself" and "needs / no other" (98–99). At this point in her letter, Sue expresses her admiration for the first stanza in words that Dickinson will very nearly replicate nine years later when describing the physical sensations she associates with poetry. Sue writes, "You never made a peer / for that verse, and I *guess* you[r] / kingdom does'nt [*sic*] hold one—I / always go to the fire and get warm / after thinking of it, but I never / *can* again" (99). Higginson reports that Dickinson's words to him during his August 1870 visit were, "'If I read a book [and] it makes my whole body so cold no fire ever can warm me I know *that* is poetry'" (*L* 473–474). Such striking similarity further magnifies the artistic interdependence that Emily expressed in her 1864 letter to Sue in which she wrote, "When my Hands / are Cut, [Sue's] / fingers will be / found inside –" (*OMC* 131). Dickinson's response to Sue's criticism is to send yet another stanza, further expressing her serious appreciation of Sue's aesthetic judgment. "Your praise is good," Dickinson writes, "because I *know* / it *knows*" (100).

To appreciate fully the representative nature of this particular correspondence, it must be seen in the context of a history of collaboration that runs through the letters that passed between Emily and Susan. As early as the late 1850s, Emily sent Sue a letter-poem containing a draft version of "Frequently the woods are pink –"

(*OMC* 78–79, Fr 24), a poem that she revised further and placed at the end of her first fascicle (Franklin, *Poems* 81–82). Hart and Smith identify the letter-poem as bearing an "'X' in Susan's handwriting on the verso" (281 n. 79). While there is no further record of Susan's response to this particular draft, we do get a vivid sense of one of the varied forms such a response might have taken in a *"mid-1860s"* letter-poem from Emily that contains verse responses in Susan's hand (*OMC* 152– 153). After reading Emily's letter-poem that describes cricket song and the coming of night ("The Crickets sang" [Fr 1104C]), Sue writes the following in pencil on the reverse of the sheet: "I was all ear / And took in strains that / might create a seal / Under the lids of death" (*OMC* 153). This, and another four-line response, also in pencil,[27] do not offer a critique of the sort provoked by "Safe in their Alabaster Chambers – ," but do suggest an ongoing conversation that could take many forms; in this case, a highly appreciative poetic rejoinder from Susan.

A *"late 1860s"* (167) letter-poem that Franklin has published as "The Face we choose to miss –" (Fr 1293) also contains a penciled note from Sue on the back, but this time she revises Dickinson's poem. Here is Emily's letter-poem:

> The Face we
> choose to miss –
> Be it but for
> a Day
> As absent as
> a Hundred
> Years,
> When it has rode
> away '   (*OMC* 167)

Susan's version of the poem makes it more conventional by eliminating unorthodox capitalization, indenting to show continued lines (or turnovers), moving the single dash to the end of the poem, and attaching Emily's name.

> The face we
>   choose to miss
> Be it but for
>   a day
> As absent as
> A hundred years
> When it has
> rode away –
>   Emily

Susan's modification of the poem may indicate that she was considering sending it out for publication, in which case the inclusion of Emily's name could have
served as a reminder that the poem originated with Emily, even though Susan
has copied it in her own hand.

These and many additional examples of collaboration can be found in *Open
Me Carefully*, where Hart and Smith usefully describe the usually penciled comments Susan makes. One of the most intriguing of these is a letter-poem from
"*1870 or later*" (176) that contains a draft version of "Who were 'the Father and
the Son'" (Fr 1280). Hart and Smith note that the "ink draft has many penciled changes and is further evidence of Emily and Susan working over poems"
(176). What these many examples of collaboration finally show is that Susan and
Emily's community of "we" formed a collective identity that depended on the
individual contributions of each even as it eclipsed individuality through shared
dedication to the patriotic transformation of their world from prose to poetry.
In Kete's terminology, each gained her self by giving it away.

By far the biggest challenge Susan faced as a collaborator came after Dickinson's death, when Lavinia requested that she edit a volume of Emily's poems for
publication. Quite unlike the selective placement of isolated poems that she had
pursued on a small scale in the past, Susan now faced the prospect of launching
an extensive collection that would conceivably advance the patriotic project she
shared with Dickinson by unveiling before the public an unconventional poetic
body, much of which may have been new to her.[28] Key considerations would certainly have included both the creation of an appropriate print format and managing the potential social fallout she imagined in 1891 when she described herself as
"'dreading publicity for us all'" (qtd. in Smith, *Rowing* 213). Her circumstance in
this sense mirrored the tribulations not only of the male writer in "Miss Grief"
who confronted manuscript resistance to print demands but also that of the two
women in "Collected by a Valetudinarian" who faced the hardship of imagining the new social role they would have to create for themselves. Understandably,
Susan hesitated.

The little we now know of her efforts to meet this challenge is conveyed in an
1890 letter to Higginson explaining that she envisioned a book of Dickinson's
writing "'rather more full, and varied'" (qtd. in Bingham 86) than the one he had
undertaken with Mabel Loomis Todd. In their analysis of Susan's efforts, Hart
and Smith conclude that "Susan wanted to showcase the entire range of Emily's
writings: letters, humorous writings, illustrations—in short, everything left out
of the Loomis Todd and Higginson collections" (xvi). This would have been a
daunting undertaking indeed, one almost certainly guaranteed to bring Susan
into the public spotlight and associate her not only with Dickinson's own innovations but, if her book appeared after the Higginson and Todd volumes, would

also identify her as an editor willing to exceed the limits of taste adhered to by Higginson, a nationally known writer and political activist.[29]

Sue's inability to realize the ambitious project she envisioned for Dickinson's poems may be best explained by Dickinson's absence. What the preceding overview of the Susan and Emily correspondence shows is that they gathered strength through mutual devotion to a shared undertaking. Their little community of "we" was in this sense stronger than either woman could be when acting independently. While it is impossible to know for certain why Sue did not progress further with her "'more full, and varied'" book of Emily's writings, gift culture does provide a logical explanation (qtd. in Bingham 86). The primary assumption behind the concept of a redundant morality is that it expresses a communal value system that acquires its unique power precisely because it is communal. The reception of the gift in this sense affirms values the giver expresses in the face of doubt and uncertainty. With Emily's passing, Susan possessed rich memories, certainly, plus a fabulous body of literary work, but she had lost forever the one person who could grant her the communal strength to confront the world. Martha Nell Smith speculates that Susan's "reading through the manuscripts" while suffering grief at the loss of her dear friend "may well have been emotionally trying and inhibiting for her," perhaps leading to feelings of anger: "it is highly likely, then, that Susan was angry at Emily's death, and editing the latter's poems would only exacerbate frustrations and feelings of abandonment" (*Rowing* 213). However we account for Susan's inaction, what is clear is that when the "we" of Susan and Emily became the "I" of Susan, their jointly imagined poetic fleet lost its way.

The Higginson Correspondence

Though Higginson ultimately did more than any other correspondent to promote the circulation of Dickinson's literary gifts, his means of doing so was decidedly less ambitious than the multigenre project Sue may have had in mind; yet he also balked at the prospect of publicly aligning himself with poetry that he viewed as highly unruly and politically charged. As Dickinson's 1862 "I have no Tribunal" letter surely indicates (*L* 409), he knew from the beginning that Dickinson exercised a sovereignty antagonistic to conventional editorial expectations. In that letter her words, "you suggest that I delay 'to publish,'" reflect his reluctance to see her enter print (*L* 408). That reluctance is reiterated almost thirty years later in the opening sentence of his preface to the 1890 first edition: "The verses," he writes, "belong emphatically to what Emerson long since called 'the Poetry of the Portfolio'—something produced absolutely without the thought of publication" and, notably, without "whatever advantage lies in the discipline of public criticism and the enforced conformity to accepted ways" (Higginson, "Preface" 13). Higginson's reference to Emerson here, as many scholars have observed, places Dickinson's poetry in a distinct democratic tradition by drawing on Emerson's identification of portfolio poems with what he termed a democratic "revolution" that gave "importance to the portfolio over the book" ("New Poetry" 220).[30] Higginson recalls his reluctance to seek print publication in his essay on Dickinson that appeared in the October 1891 issue of *Atlantic Monthly*, where he writes that her poems "were launched quietly and without any expectation of a wide audience" ("Emily Dickinson" 543). Clearly, to be associated with a literary revolution gave him pause, just as the male writer in "Miss Grief" paused when confronted with a parallel prospect. That Higginson was willing to proceed where that writer was not may be the primary indication that Dickinson succeeded over time in winning some degree of unconscious collaboration through her gift of 103 poems (Franklin 1552). After all, we do know that he never received any compensation for his labors (Horan 89).

Perhaps the most remarkable aspect of the Higginson correspondence is the evidence that he did in fact act in accordance with the dictates of a gift economy, even though there is no indication that he knew he was doing so. His 1891 *Atlantic Monthly* account of the correspondence supports this notion in several instances, most strikingly through the distribution of individual authority evident in Dickinson's persistent reference to herself as "Scholar" and, in Higginson's words, "assuming on my part a preceptorship which it is almost needless to say did not exist" ("Emily Dickinson" 554). What is interesting here is the unstated agreement to maintain a hierarchical vocabulary of "scholar" and "preceptor" while in fact introducing a set of contrary private meanings. This mutual creation of a private linguistic code is fully consistent with Higginson's restructuring of the terms of their relationship, so that a shared sensibility consistent with a distinct community of "we" replaces the initial hierarchical imbalance. "I soon abandoned all attempt to guide in the slightest degree this extraordinary nature," he writes, "and simply accepted her confidences, giving as much as I could of what might interest her in return." Surely his efforts to confer items that would be of interest to Dickinson constitutes that most essential of all gifts: the mutual affirmation of equality possible when customary cultural barriers are first resisted and then transgressed by shared assertions of individual authority.[31] How could this experience not have had some influence on Higginson's decision to exercise his own sovereignty by doing what neither the male writer in "Miss Grief" nor the two women in "Collected by a Valetudinarian" could: risk censure by expanding the circuit of literary distribution.

In keeping with the inverted linguistic code that configured Dickinson as "scholar" and Higginson as "preceptor," when in fact authority was far more balanced than such terms would suggest, is the manner in which Dickinson consistently used Higginson to avoid publication. Difficult as it may be to discern Dickinson's original intent in writing him after reading his 1862 essay "A Letter to a Young Contributor," it is hard not to imagine her as being interested in at least discussing the question of publication. Higginson's essay specifically addresses the "many of those who read the 'Atlantic Monthly' [and] have at times the impulse to write for it also" with the explicit aim of offering practical advice about publication ("Letter" 528). Such a statement understandably predisposed Higginson to assume, at least for a time, that Dickinson wanted his advice about publication, thus his early and consistent advice that she not attempt to do so. Curiously, in Dickinson's famous third letter to Higginson, her "smile" at his suggestion that she "delay 'to publish'" and her dismissal of his early charges that her verse is "'spasmodic'" and "'uncontrolled'" do not lead to a schism in their relationship (*L* 408–409), though Higginson may have wondered at times what exactly the ground rules were that governed the conduct of his new correspondent. While Dickinson aggressively dismisses Higginson's critical advice in her June 7, 1862, letter, she also pleads with him to give her more instruction: "But, will you be my Preceptor, Mr Higginson?" (*L* 409). That her wish to correspond with him is not connected to print publication becomes stunningly clear in Dickinson's *"early 1866"* letter where she informs Higginson that her poem "A narrow Fellow in the Grass" (Fr 1096B) appeared in the February 17 issue of the *Springfield Weekly Republican* purely because "it was robbed of me" (*L* 450). Dickinson is emphatic here about removing any false impression that she set out to "deceive" him after having previously announced her refusal to print: "I had told you I did not print" (*L* 450).[32] In light of this adamant stand and her determination to appear consistent in her opposition to print publication, it is not surprising that she accepts Higginson's opposition to print publication without treating it as a blow to their burgeoning friendship. Neither is it a surprise that Dickinson appeals to Higginson in 1876 to "give me a note saying you disapproved" of Helen Hunt Jackson's efforts to print Dickinson's poems (*L* 563).[33] What Dickinson's responses show is that her interest in sustaining a correspondence with Higginson did not grow out of a wish for his assistance in getting her poems into print. Her decision to open a correspondence with Higginson when she did, but not for the purpose of achieving print publication, is but the first of many instances of Dickinson's inviting Higginson to search beyond normative expectations in the process of understanding their relationship.

What Dickinson did want from Higginson was for him to save her life. Twice Dickinson writes to Higginson that he has indeed saved her life though he may not have known that he had done so. In a letter written in *"June 1869,"* she observes, "You were not aware that you saved my Life" (*L* 460). A decade or so later, *"about 1879,"* she repeats this observation while asking why she has not received any recent letters: "Must I lose the Friend that saved my Life, without inquiring why?" (*L* 649). Precisely what Dickinson had in mind when she writes about having her life saved is no doubt beyond recovery, but the logic of gift culture does provide a possible, if only partial, explanation. In the same letter in which she first declares that Higginson saved her life, Dickinson's opening paragraphs express the concern with redundant morality and grappling with expressions of gratitude that so characterize her letters to Susan:

> A letter always feels to me like immortality because it is the mind alone without corporeal friend. Indebted in our talk to attitude and accent, there seems a spectral power in thought that walks alone – I would like to thank you for your great kindness but never try to lift the words which I cannot hold.
>
> Should you come to Amherst, I might then succeed, though Gratitude is the timid wealth of those who have nothing. I am sure that you speak the truth, because the noble do, but your letters always surprise me. My life has been too simple and stern to embarrass any.   (*L* 460)

Dickinson's initial description of "immortality ... without corporeal friend" celebrates the achievement of a shared sensibility not encumbered by gender codes grounded in cultural constructions of their male and female bodies. Her succeeding reference to "spectral power" reiterates this appreciation for a relationship not bounded by bodies while addressing the imaginative independence such boundlessness makes possible as "thought that walks alone."[34] Dickinson's use of the term "spectral" also evokes her understanding of language as disembodied expressions of meaning incommensurate with the self that I explored in the previous chapter as crucial to her incorporation of spiritualist terminology. When she then goes on to tell Higginson "your letters always surprise me," she affirms her reception of the gift that is his uniquely independent thought. Her surprise here is crucial, as it confirms her communion with another outside the boundaries of predictable intellectual or imaginative processes. The language of gratitude and indebtedness that accompanies these expressions of delight is entirely appropriate to gift exchange because it sets in motion the redundant cycle of giving the gift of thanks it claims it is incapable of giving, thereby provoking a vision of expanded future gratitude while simultaneously offering an understated version of thanks in the present.

Where with Susan the redundancy of gratitude was achieved by repeatedly asserting that no gratitude was necessary, here the redundancy is achieved when Dickinson declares her incapacity to give it. That Dickinson should assume this approach is perfectly consistent with the coded language of inverted authority that runs through her correspondence with Higginson. According to this code, she in actuality expresses the same attitude toward gratitude with him that she does with Sue, only in his case she proclaims an inability belied by her introduction of the subject of gratitude. In one sense, then, Higginson saves her life by forming a friendship that enables her to invert the customary language of female subordination so that even her own diminished expressions of her life acquire a grandeur by implying what they appear to deny. The closing line of her second paragraph that protests, "My life has been too simple and stern to embarrass any" (*L* 460), may for this reason be read as an expression of complexity and personal power that could indeed embarrass were it widely acknowledged.[35] Such an enigmatic declaration may indeed have provided Higginson the jolt of surprise and delight that Dickinson so valued in his writing to her.

Higginson's gift of friendship might have been especially welcomed by Dickinson in 1862 due to her own reevaluation of the domestic publication she had been engaged with since at least 1858 (Franklin, *Poems* 20). According Ralph W. Franklin, Dickinson's approach to fascicle construction went through a period of "disorder that came into her workshop from late 1860 until early 1862" (22). Following the particularly stressful months of "early 1862," when "the fascicle idea had itself come apart," and after Dickinson had probably composed in the neighborhood of 300 poems and eleven fascicles, she writes Higginson for the first time. After opening this correspondence with Higginson, Dickinson enters what Franklin estimates to be her most productive years, completing 227 poems in 1862 and 295 in 1863 (1533). This upsurge in the creation of manuscript poems suggests that an additional explanation for the "life" Higginson saved is that through his open expression of both interest and awe he helped restore her confidence in herself as a writer and gave her the courage to move forward with the daring experiments she was contemplating in her manuscript books. Franklin draws a clear picture of Higginson's probable influence: "In the summer of 1862, perhaps under the innocent influence of Higginson, whom she later called her 'safest' friend, one who had 'saved' her life, a new sense of order took hold in Dickinson's workshop, lasting until 1864" (24).[36] What Dickinson sought from Higginson, then, was indeed assistance with publication, but not the print publication he had in mind; her aim instead was the development of a friendship that would motivate her to eclipse even further the limits of conventional poetic form in the pages of her manuscript books.[37] Higginson provided Dickinson precisely the impetus she needed through his repeated expressions of surprise and delight at his reception of her literary gifts.

There can be little doubt that Higginson was indeed frequently jolted over the course of his long correspondence with Dickinson. In the May 11, 1869, letter he sent to Dickinson that provoked her to compose the above paragraphs and state for the first time that he had saved her life, Higginson details the powerful effect her language has had on him. His letter begins this way: "Sometimes I take out your letters & verses, dear friend, and when I feel their strange power, it is not strange that I find it hard to write & that long months pass" (*L* 461). To receive such an uninhibited admission of her ability to overwhelm an established public figure and widely published male writer must have been deeply gratifying for Dickinson. As Higginson's letter progresses, his language ever more clearly conveys the reversal of conventional male and female roles that may have been one of the primary sources of pleasurable surprise for Dickinson. "I should like to hear from you very often," he writes, "but feel always timid lest what I *write* should be badly aimed & miss that fine edge of thought which you bear. It would be so easy, I fear, to miss you."[38] With these words, Higginson presents himself as the dumbstruck reader of the other's words who admits to timidity in the face of her accomplishment.

Higginson's assumption of a passive and self-effacing posture in response to Dickinson's linguistic potency unmistakably casts him in the role of feminine recipient. However, he rapidly moves to balance the perhaps discomforting fluidity of their relationship, reclaiming the male subject position in the opening of his final paragraph. There he invites her to visit him in Boston, pointedly declaring, "All ladies do" (*L* 462). Higginson devotes the rest of the paragraph to the many events in Boston that she might find enticing. A particularly intriguing passage conveys Higginson's hesitation as he first invites Dickinson to come when he is scheduled to give a paper "on the [Gre]ek goddesses" at the "Woman's [Cl]ub" and then seemingly retracts his invitation: "I should still rather have you come on some [da]y when I shall not be so much taken up – for my object is to see you, more than to entertain you." Higginson's apparent concern with making Dickinson the object of his gaze rather than allowing himself to be the object of hers suggests his awareness of the gender ambiguities in their relationship, as well as his determination to balance the distribution of authority.

When Higginson visits Dickinson for the first time in August 1870, he is jolted many times as Dickinson repeatedly anticipates and undermines his assumptions about their proper roles, surprising him again and again with a deft juggling of authority that requires much from him as he struggles to maintain his equilibrium. The note Higginson writes to his wife reflecting on the visit contains the following understandable admission: "I never was with any one who drained my nerve power so much" (*L* 476). Rather than reading this statement as an expression of relief founded on repugnance or a desire to escape Dickinson's presence, it should be read instead as the confession of exhaustion associated with extended exposure to a remarkably intense personality who made extraordinary demands on him. The extensive list of startling interactions that precedes this statement suggests more than anything else that Higginson's visit was characterized by the powerful physical sensations that both Dickinson and Sue understood as defining qualities of poetry. In words that echo and expand upon Sue's earlier observation about the power of the first stanza of "Safe in their Alabaster Chambers –" (Fr 124F), Dickinson delivers one of her most-famous definitions of poetry. These words registered with such force that Higginson repeats them *verbatim:* "'If I read a book [and] it makes my whole body so cold no fire ever can warm me I know *that* is poetry. If I feel physically as if the top of my head were taken off, I know *that* is poetry. These are the only way I know it. Is there any other way'" (*L* 473–474). Considering Higginson's remarks in the context of this definition points to the likelihood that his physical distress registers his reception of Dickinson's gift of sumptuous destitution, the poetry she previously gave him in her written words alone and has now provided in her person. One of the reasons Dickinson may have so valued Higginson's friendship is his willing admission of her power to unsettle the predictable pattern of his life. By doing so, he became one of her most important collaborators.

Higginson's account of Dickinson's conduct in their first meeting lends credence to the view that Dickinson sought to merge herself with her poetry and by doing so make Higginson's visit the physical enactment of gift exchange that up to this time had been achieved exclusively through the written word. Dickinson's initial gesture of appearing with "two day lilies" that she hands to Higginson stating, "'These are my introduction'" immediately collapses the separation of poetry and person by openly employing actual blossoms, one of her own favorite figures for poetry, as representative of who she is (*L* 473). When Dickinson then asks Higginson to forgive her breathless conduct, stating, "I never see strangers & hardly know what I say," the stage is set for multiple unanticipated disclosures. As if it weren't awkward enough to be referred to as a stranger after having corresponded for eight years and collectively planned the visit now unfolding, Higginson is further confounded when Dickinson talks "continuously – & deferentially – sometimes stopping to ask me to talk instead of her – but readily recommencing." This deferential silencing of the other is shortly followed by her response to Higginson's asking her if "she never felt a want of employment, never going off the place & never seeing any visitor" (*L* 474). "'I never thought,'" she replies, "'of conceiving that I could ever have the slightest approach to such a want in all future time' (& added) 'I feel that I have not expressed myself strongly enough.'" Had Higginson known the full extent of Dickinson's domestic publication and the scope of her correspondence, he may not have been as surprised as he apparently was to learn that a virtual recluse could find her time so fully employed.

Other passages recorded by Higginson that seem designed to urge thought beyond familiar channels include Dickinson's asking him, "'Could you tell me what home is,'" even though they are standing in her home; and her startling revelation that "'I've never had a mother,'" despite the fact that at the time of Higginson's visit in 1870 both parents were alive and her mother quite possibly present in some other region of the house (L 475). These and the other statements like them characterize Higginson's visit, casting the whole of this initial encounter with Dickinson as a series of largely unanticipated observations delivered by Dickinson for the purpose of distilling "amazing sense / From Ordinary Meanings –" (Fr 446). By giving herself to Higginson as a poem, Dickinson effectively invests what he might well have anticipated as a social encounter that would place their relationship on a more ordinary footing with the properties of gift exchange that evolve by a process of surprising revelations, each repeatedly affirming the power of poetry to shed new light on the familiar world.

Of the many examples of gift exchange that surface in the letters between Dickinson and Higginson, none are more revealing than those surrounding their epistolary discussion of Higginson's poem "Decoration." From the beginning of their correspondence, Dickinson sent Higginson poems along with letters and letter-poems, while she made note of and commented on published works of his that she discovered in the world of print she so avidly explored.[39] She eventually became so adept at identifying his style that she could even spot his anonymous publications.[40] The ensuing joint discussion of the other's writing became itself a form of gift exchange as the aim was not analysis or critique but rather the expression of personal appreciation. In this way each affirmed the values they saw conveyed through the writing of the other, often delighting in the surprising turns each discovered. Nowhere is this more apparent than in Dickinson's poetic response to Higginson's poem and his approval of that response. After having first encountered "Decoration" around Memorial Day 1874 in *Scribner's Monthly* (L 525), Dickinson provides Higginson with a single quatrain distillation of his poem in June 1877. Higginson in turn copies Dickinson's revision of his poem and sends it to Mabel Loomis Todd in May 1891 with the following declaration of his admiration: "She wrote it after re-reading my 'Decoration.' It is the condensed essence of that & so far finer" (Bingham 130). With this gesture, Higginson extends the circulation of Dickinson's gift to him, effectively acting on his prerogative as the recipient. This inclusion of Todd and eventually the public who would read the second volume of Dickinson's poems that he and Todd were then collaboratively editing, exemplifies the way that gift exchange can transgress the boundaries of what Mary Loeffelholz has described as the often restrictive unilateral relationship scholars too often treat as the determining structure of familiar correspondence ("'Decoration'" 664). As Loeffelholz has noted in her careful analysis of Dickinson's 1877 letter that contains her revision of Higginson's poem, "Dickinson's letter . . . everywhere foregrounds the scene of writing and of writing's circulation" (680).

Viewing all four of the Dickinson-Higginson letters that deal with "Decoration" as expressions of gift culture lends further strength to Loeffelholz's conclusion while also illuminating the pugilistic stance Dickinson often struck in her efforts to jolt Higginson's perceptions. This is made especially clear when Dickinson conflates herself with the biblical Jacob at the close of the last of these four letters by describing the Old Testament Jacob as "Pugilist and Poet" and then declaring that "Jacob was correct" in blessing the angel with whom he wrestled (L 903).[41] With these words, Dickinson notably revises the famous passage from Genesis to tell Higginson that her unanticipated moves and abrupt surprises constitute a form of linguistic wrestling predicated on the power of each to bless the other.

This wrestling metaphor that concludes the exchange surrounding "Decoration" has a long foreground in the letters discussing Higginson's poem. This can be seen in Dickinson's opening remarks on the poem where she builds on the fluidity of gender roles previously established with Higginson while also acknowledging the reception of redundant values so central to gift exchange. Her initial line, "I thought that being a Poem one's self precluded the writing Poems, but perceive the Mistake" (L 525), represents Higginson as both assuming and defying the traditional female role as passive object, thereby attributing to him the power she herself exhibited during his 1870 visit. Loeffelholz identifies the gender play in this opening sentence, concluding that with these words Dickinson "defensively imagines Higginson himself in the generically feminine condition of being a poem but not writing poems, the condition of mute lyric womanhood" (" 'Decoration' " 675). The very next sentence of the letter, however, militates against such an assertion of defensiveness on Dickinson's part: "It seemed like going Home, to see your beautiful thought once more, now so long forbade it – Is it Intellect that the Patriot means when he speaks of his 'Native Land'?" (L 525). Acknowledging the gift function in these lines, Loeffelholz argues that through them Dickinson accepts " 'Decoration' as a gift on something like its own terms: as offering her, through Higginson's mediating 'Intellect,' a sense of patriotic location in her 'Native Land.' "[42]

An alternative, though in many ways complimentary reading, is urged when the letter is framed by the history of gift exchange as traced through Dickinson's correspondence with Higginson. In that context, being referred to as a poem can imply a defiance of culturally imposed silence, as clearly reflected by Higginson's response to Dickinson's poetry and physical presence. For Dickinson to assert that Higginson is a poem might just as easily be her way of applauding his poetic resistance to culturally imposed gender expectations, a resistance that might apply equally to her.

The part of Higginson's poem that most captured Dickinson's interest is the concluding stanza, where the speaker breaks with the established Decoration Day (now Memorial Day) practice of commemorating dead soldiers, and instead places lilies on the grave of a woman. After having surveyed the graves of fallen soldiers, the speaker, "bearing lilies in my hand" (Franklin, *Poems* 1248), chooses not to honor the grave of a departed comrade, expressing his departure from expectation in the following final quatrain:

> Turning from my comrades' eyes,
> Kneeling where a woman lies,
> I strew lilies on the grave
> Of the bravest of the brave.   (1249)

Loeffelholz astutely discerns that the *mise-en-scène* constituted by the speaker's placement of the lilies on a woman's grave poses unavoidable parallels with Dickinson's conduct on the occasion of Higginson's first visit: "Although this significance could not have been available to Higginson's audience . . . in the 1874 *Scribner's*, many aspects of Higginson's poem entitle us to wonder whether Dickinson's private writing or her private being . . . had not already inscribed itself inside Higginson's other motives for 'Decoration'" ("'Decoration'" 670).[43] With this association firmly in mind, Loeffelholz interprets Dickinson's reference to "Patriot" and "'Native land'" as an ironic acknowledgment of "the obscurity to which Higginson was content to assign her in his unsought role as her literary mentor" (676).

An additional interpretive wrinkle appears, however, when Dickinson's response is analyzed in terms of gift logic. Accordingly, Higginson's linguistic reenactment of Dickinson's conflation of self, poetry, and lilies stands out as a mutual defiance of gender containment expressive of a shared sensibility. Dickinson's reference to intellect as "'Native Land'" therefore redundantly reiterates her reference to "going Home," further establishing her reception of Higginson's gift. When Dickinson next states, "I should have feared to 'quote' to you what you 'most valued'" (*L* 525), her words convey her appreciation for Higginson's daring incorporation of what *she* most values through his public departure from a culturally normative mourning practice. Where Loeffelholz presents Dickinson as defensive about Higginson's metonymic association of her with the silence of the grave, my alternative reading presents Dickinson as confirming Higginson's public declaration of the patriotic cause they both further through resistance to social codes. Unlike Loeffelholz's reading that interprets Higginson's final stanza as a patronizing commentary on Dickinson's brave but terminally private poetic effort, this reading understands his poetic gesture as a future-directed collaboration that publicly expands the category of acceptable patriotic action to embrace the dauntless efforts of women like Dickinson whose participation in gift-based systems of exchange can ultimately influence public conduct.

The third of the four Dickinson letters that touch on "Decoration" includes Dickinson's own four-line poetic response to Higginson's printed poem, in this way providing evidence that she was interested in extending the gift exchange that now includes his contribution to their joint collaboration. Bearing in mind that Higginson's poem is itself a linguistic response to Dickinson's physical enactment of poetry that took place during his first visit, Dickinson's short quatrain can be understood as the third phase in an ongoing exchange that demonstrates the power of language to incorporate and thus perpetuate the memories of others. In this June 1877 letter, Dickinson leads up to her mention of Higginson's poem by posing questions about immortality. She introduces this topic by recalling a funeral she attended when a child where "the Clergyman asked 'Is the Arm of the Lord shortened that it cannot save?'" (*L* 583). Sensing uncertainty in the preacher's use of the word "cannot," Dickinson appeals to Higginson for an explanation of the uncertainty that troubles her own belief in immortality. "I was told you were once a Clergyman," she writes, then states her conviction that he will provide comfort by redundantly affirming that he has also known such uncertainty: "It comforts an instinct if another have felt it too." Only now, after having established immortality as her subject, does she tell Higginson "I was rereading your 'Decoration.'" Placing the poem in the context of this discussion magnifies the poem's central concern with immortality, particularly in connection with the ritual act of memorializing the dead on Memorial Day. In this way, Dickinson frames her response to Higginson's poem in the context of a discussion that associates immortality with memory, thereby suggesting that uncertainty about immortality in the afterlife is enforced by the awareness that memory in present life is fleeting. Absence from memory is equated with departure from mortal life, and both are viewed as impenetrable mysteries. Within this associative web, Dickinson's observation that she was "rereading" Higginson's poem can be interpreted as her way of telling him that he is not forgotten and hence retains the potential for immortality. Her very next line, "You may have forgotten it," now magnifies the gift of her recollection by implying that poets can forget their own creations even when their poetry is about memory and immortality.

When Dickinson then presents Higginson with her response to his poem, her doing so points to the way memory can be perpetuated in the words of another, implying that the impression one makes on the memories of others can achieve immortality through language that persists even after all distinct memories of the creator have faded. This is in fact the core message of her poem to Higginson:

Lay this Laurel on the One
Too intrinsic for Renown –
Laurel – vail your deathless Tree –
Him you chasten, that is He! (Fr 1428C)

Enduring memory, and hence immortality, comes to those whose impression on the language of their culture is so pervasive that it becomes intrinsic; that is, their impact is so far reaching that it registers in the foundations of language and is no longer associated with a distinct individual. The laurel that symbolizes renown, or the cultural perpetuation of a distinct person's achievement, provides only the illusion of achievement. The "Him" that the laurel chastens by withholding tribute is actually the "He" most truly honored by becoming an intrinsic and thus immortal part of his culture's primary memory—its language.

As she did in her assertion that a poet can be a poem and still create poems, Dickinson here proposes the possibility of defying objectification. Loeffelholz describes Dickinson's stanza as holding "out the hope that 'He/Him' can be both reader and writer, both the reader and what is read" ("'Decoration'" 677). In terms of the gift exchange carried out between Higginson and Dickinson, one might say that the collaborative process requires that the reader/receiver of the gift also be a writer/giver of gifts. In this instance, Dickinson gives Higginson a poem in which her writing is the celebration of his creativity, thus preserving his subjectivity while making him the object of her own linguistic creation. Dickinson's poetic encapsulation of Higginson's poem in this sense offers him the gift of immortality by presenting him as intrinsic to her poem.

The last of Dickinson's letters to Higginson that include mention of "Decoration" is also very much concerned with the question of immortality, this time through association with the recent death of Helen Hunt Jackson. Writing Higginson in "spring 1886" (L 903), Dickinson begins her letter with a misquotation from "Decoration" as part of an initial, effusively elegiac paragraph. Dickinson alters Higginson's line, "Mocks the sacred loneliness" (Franklin, Poems 1249), so that it reads "Mars the sacred Loneliness," drawing attention to the way Higginson's poem casts doubt on the sincerity of some mourning rites. Higginson's preceding line, "And no stone, with feign'd distress," declares the insincerity of empty ritual, implying that the truly grieved or most deeply missed are, at least in some instances, those whose remains lack the conventional vestments of sorrow.[44] By underscoring these particular lines in Higginson's poem, Dickinson in effect asks him to recollect the part of his poem that most clearly makes the point she emphasized in her own rewriting of it: that memory is better served by acts too intrinsic for renown. Beginning her own letter with these particular lines makes clear her sensitivity to the hollowness of ritual overstatement that she herself mocks by a series of emphatic ejaculations heralding "Decoration" as an elegy for Jackson and juxtaposing it with language from the elegy President Humphrey delivered on the occasion of Jackson's father's death twelve years previously. After presenting her version of Higginson's line from "Decoration," she appears to applaud him with the words, "What an Elegy!" that are followed by language from President Humphrey's earlier elegy: " 'From Mount Zion below to Mount Zion above'!" (*L* 903). Dickinson then ends the paragraph with the words, "Gabriel's Oration would adorn his Child," as if to hail Higginson as Gabriel and say that "Decoration" and the sonnet he sent Dickinson in which he paid tribute to Jackson are her ultimate adornments.

Interpreted as a gift, this opening paragraph performs in two ways: first it contributes to the accumulation of elegiac tributes to Jackson and therefore collaborates with Higginson; secondly, it overplays the elegiac mode in a manner designed to remind Higginson of his own observation that excessive protestations of mourning may in fact signal a hollow sentiment and speed the departed person's passage from memory. This second function of the paragraph is also a collaboration, of course, but one meant to inform Higginson that their joint participation in the spectacle of mourning runs the risk of delighting in its own display rather than sincerely feeling the loss of a loved one. The writing of the letter close to Decoration Day incorporates the memory of Dickinson's own father's death—that she previously associated with "Decoration" (*L* 528)—while intensifying awareness of another father's passing through reference to Jackson's father's funeral, indicating that Dickinson is thinking about multiple deaths and the way mourning rites in general relate to memory and immortality.

Dickinson follows this opening with a recollection of her last encounter with Jackson, then thanks Higginson for sending her a copy of his sonnet "To the Memory of H.H." to which she responds with verse of her own that in many ways challenges Higginson's more conventional poem by presenting Jackson as an intrinsic part of Dickinson's present. Higginson's poem imagines Jackson's soul passing through a "disembodied world" where she consorts with "ethereal women (born of air / and poets' dreams)" such as "Cleopatra," "Shelley's Helen," and "Rossetti's Rose Mary" ("Memory" 47). In sharp contrast to Higginson's ethereal imaginings founded on notions of remote worlds and poetic visions of female perfection, Dickinson imagines a spirit presence capable of assuming many forms in the here and now:

Not knowing when Herself may come
I open every Door,
Or has she Feathers, like a Bird,
Or Billows, like a Shore – (*L* 903)

Dickinson's powerful language of anticipation, especially her opening of "every Door," reads almost as a rebuke, as if she were chiding Higginson for forgetting his own assertions about rituals of memory that are really acts of closure.[45] The sentence that immediately follows her quatrain appears to contrast her respect for what she views as Jackson's wishes with the conventional alternative she associates with Higginson's poem: "I think she would rather have stayed with us, but perhaps she will learn the Customs of Heaven, as the Prisoner of Chillon of Captivity." Equating heaven with prison and enforced conformity to customs could be Dickinson's way of telling Higginson that he has indeed slammed the door on their mutual friend.

Such rough treatment further demonstrates the absurdity of the "Preceptor" and "Scholar" pretense that both maintain through the length of their extensive correspondence. It may also explain why Dickinson concludes this letter with reference to Jacob and the angel. "Audacity of Bliss, said Jacob to the Angel," she begins, as if in admission of her own too transparent audacity in trusting to Higginson's angelic nature (*L* 903). When she then states, "'I will not let thee go except I bless thee,'" she seems to be saying that the wrestling she has imposed on him is an expression of love and respect she associates with the divine. Her final words, "Pugilist and Poet, Jacob was correct," confirm her assumption of the Jacob role and leave Higginson with the message that she was right in compelling him to confront the accuracy of his own insight into mourning that he expressed in "Decoration." The letter ends, then, with an assertion of redundant values, achieved by Dickinson's returning to Higginson the gift he gave her in his poem.

Dickinson's final letter to Higginson, written within a month or two of her letter about Jackson's death and scant days before her own, provides an extraordinary symmetry to their twenty-four-year relationship by reinforcing the reversal of the roles each originally assumed in their first letters and once again broaching the subject of immortality. Dickinson's two-line letter-poem reads as both an appeal for a response from Higginson and a metaphoric extension of the previously established trope that people can be poems: "Deity – does He live now? / My friend – does he breathe?" (*L* 905). These lines so closely resemble Dickinson's first words to Higginson in her April 15, 1862, letter that it is difficult not to think that she had that first letter in mind. She opened that letter by asking Hig-

ginson if he is "too deeply occupied to say if my Verse is alive?" and further stating, "Should you think it breathed – and had you the leisure to tell me, I should
feel quick gratitude –" (*L* 403). By shifting her questions about living and breath-
ing from her own poems to the mortal man, Dickinson in effect asks Higginson
to verify *his* life, inverting her original request that Higginson verify *her* life.

That she was associating poetry with mortal life at this early stage of their relationship is established through her two letters to Higginson affirming that by
taking her writing seriously he had saved her life. The repeated fusions of self and
poetry that emerged in her correspondence with Higginson build on Dickinson's
early linkage of poetry with life so that her question in this last letter is not limited to the health of the mortal man but extends also to his stature as immortal
poetry. Dickinson's initial address to "Deity" identifies her concern with immortality, while her reference to her "Friend" completes the union of mortal with immortal that has been the poetic gift at the core of their friendship.

Higginson's final response to Dickinson, his last and most enduring gift, was
to overcome his own trepidation and use his literary authority to advance her
immortality. He did this by acting as the authorizing agent whose literary stature
and experience guided Mabel Loomis Todd's final selection and editing of Dickinson's poems and secured a publisher for the 1890 first edition. In her account of
Lavinia's early efforts to draw Higginson into the project, Millicent Todd Bingham describes Higginson's initial resistance to print publication: "He wrote that
he was extremely busy, and that the confused manuscripts presented nearly in-
superable obstacles to reading and judging such quantities of poems. Though
he admired the singular talent of Emily Dickinson, he hardly thought enough
could be found to make an even semi-conventional volume" (18). Concern with
the unorthodox nature of Dickinson's poems and his fear that they might not
be made sufficiently palatable for the reading public inform Higginson's 1890
preface where he writes, "Such verse must inevitably forfeit whatever advantage
lies in the discipline of public criticism and the enforced conformity to accepted
ways" ("Preface" 13). Fortunately, the public reception of Dickinson's work exceeded all expectation, and Higginson's joy as well as relief registers forcefully in
his December 15, 1890, letter to Todd. "Pardon me if I bore you," he writes, "but
I often wish for your sympathy, because you are the only person who can feel as
I do about this extraordinary thing we have done in revealing this rare genius. I
feel as if we had climbed to a cloud, pulled it away, and revealed a new star behind it" (Bingham 81). Higginson's obvious delight, together with his rhetoric of
cosmic revelation, mark this as the final and greatest surprise that comes to him
as Dickinson's last gift.[46]

The opening paragraph of his 1891 *Atlantic* essay shows that by this date Higginson had begun to understand that he has participated in a major literary event

of historic proportions. He begins by acknowledging the unanticipated nature of her success: "Few events in American literary history have been more curious than the sudden rise of Emily Dickinson . . . into a posthumous fame" ("Emily Dickinson" 543). Then he confirms the extent to which the magnitude of her success overwhelmed all expectations, including his own: "But for her only sister, it is very doubtful if her poems would ever have been published at all; and when published, they were launched quietly and without expectation of a large audience. Yet the outcome of it is that six editions of the volume have been sold within six months, a suddenness of success almost without a parallel in American literature." Perhaps Higginson appreciated the irony that Dickinson should at last achieve the fame she claimed she could not escape if it were hers and that he should be the dumbfounded collaborator who reluctantly changed the landscape of American poetry.

No matter how misguided we now judge Higginson's editorial efforts, what we know of his correspondence with Dickinson and his decision to coedit the first edition tells us that he went forward with a pronounced sense of dread and lent his name to a publication he fully expected to create an altogether different sensation. Even though the form Dickinson's texts take today differs rather markedly from the versions Higginson and Todd produced in 1890 and 1891, the presence of a sovereign self has remained consistent. When Katha Pollitt states that Dickinson is more political than Walt Whitman and Langston Hughes, her words reflect the history of Dickinson's initial gift-based method of circulation, according to which she intransigently resisted the tribunal of print, insisting instead on the power to unite distinct sovereign selves. Higginson's willingness to risk censure through his role in bringing Dickinson to the larger public reflects the responsiveness to Dickinson's insistent defiance of cultural codes that typifies his long relationship with her. That our memory of Higginson's distinct contributions to her published presence should fade with the emergence of new editorial practices may mark his final transition from "Preceptor" to the "He" she described as "Too intrinsic for Renown" in her verse response to "Decoration."

5
Copyright, Circulation, and the Body

In this chapter I explore Dickinson's aesthetic of intrinsic renown and consider how her decision not to seek print publication is yet another reflection of her democratic sensibility. As I demonstrated in the preceding chapter, the phrase "Too intrinsic for Renown" played an important role in Dickinson's correspondence with Thomas Wentworth Higginson as part of their ongoing conversation about publication (*L* 583). My aim there was to show that Dickinson behaved in a manner consistent both with the dictates of gift culture and her own conviction that the literature most worthy of admiration is that which is readily absorbed by the writer's culture. Intrinsic fame, she believed, would come to those whose thought entered the fabric of American culture, not as a result of efforts to market their work and limit public access. The point I have been making throughout this book is that Dickinson actively sought the collaboration of readers in the creation of reading experiences that enact democratic assertions of sovereignty through independent choice. Now I want to look at Dickinson's preference for intrinsic rather than extrinsic renown as consistent with the stance toward publication that she developed during a historical period when Americans were very much concerned with the question of copyright and the ownership of literary property.

Fame, as constituted by authorial ownership, set authors apart from the promiscuous circulation of thought in the public domain and for this reason promoted an understanding of authorship very different from that advocated by Dickinson. The public debates that surrounded copyright legislation during Dickinson's lifetime revolved around the issue of literary circulation and the extent that the interests of democratic culture were best served by the limitations imposed on literary reproduction when authorial property rights were established through copyright. Using the language of twentieth- and twenty-first-century scholarship, I describe the way Dickinson treated the written text as a porous container that metaphorically represents the author's body as informed by the currents of culture and not as an isolated entity capable of originating new ideas in the manner required by copyright. My aim is to show how Dickinson promoted an awareness of the public and democratic origins of knowledge that was very much at odds with the monopolizing impulses that motivated copyright advocates.

One of the most intriguing features of Dickinson's writing that emerges when it is viewed through the lens of copyright debate is her recognition that the female writer in nineteenth-century America was simultaneously present and not present as a public figure.[1] Key poems dealing with questions of ownership and publication reflect Dickinson's concern that a broadly held public understanding of female experience performed as a precedent for the literary representation of women's lives that severely limited what counted as genuinely female. As a consequence, it was all too often the case that American women writers retroactively affirmed only those experiences that comported with public expectation. This is essentially the point Stacey Margolis makes in *The Public Life of Privacy in Nineteenth-Century American Literature* when she argues that in novels of the period public assumptions about the private self, or "publicness," acted "as a condition of intelligibility" (14). Rather than viewing the public "as a space of exposure, surveillance, or discipline," Margolis urges us to consider this space "as a condition of intelligibility for individual action." The consequence is of course the denial of subjective experience that cannot be verified retroactively by reference to public norms. Dickinson's poem "To my quick ear the Leaves – conferred –" (Fr 912), in which the speaker complains that she "could . . . find a Privacy" nowhere, registers this sense of having been formed in the likeness of the public image. Conversely, Dickinson's poem "Ended, ere it begun –" (Fr 1048) illuminates authorial awareness of a "story" that "perished from Consciousness." The "story" referred to here is not so much a story of the private female, though it could be that, as it is the story of female experience that falls outside the public parameters of acceptable female conduct, thus drawing attention to the isolated female whose presence is not an acknowledged feature of public life.

Developments within the nineteenth-century debate over copyright inform what might be thought of as a literary narrowing of female experience that takes place as copyright advocates advanced ever-more expansive claims about the fundamentally private nature of the creative process itself. My point here is that as the emphasis on originality essential to the establishment of literary property became more pronounced, the more closely print expressions of female experience became equated with the interior lives of women. This development is central to the general argument Grantland S. Rice makes in *The Transformation of Authorship in America* where he describes changes in the cultural understanding of authorship as constituting "the legal transformation of a public and political activity into one that was private and productive" (7). Throughout the nineteenth century, Americans observed the efforts of authors to extend proprietary rights over literary productions by grounding their arguments in natural rights as established in Lockean notions of property. One of the most active proponents of authorial copyright was Noah Webster, who, as an Amherst resident of considerable fame, author of the dictionary owned by Dickinson's family, and grandfather of Dickinson's friend Emily Fowler, would have brought this debate close to home. Siva Vaidhyanathan makes the case in *Copyrights and Copywrongs* that Webster was instrumental in establishing the Copyright Law of 1831 that extended copyright protection from fourteen "to twenty-eight years (renewable for fourteen more)" and that he was a tireless advocate for "perpetual copyright protection" (45).

Driving efforts like Webster's was the conviction that authors ought to enjoy the same natural rights to property ownership that the legal system associated with the ownership of landed estates or other forms of material property. Copyright advocates perceived authors as intellectual laborers whose exertions transformed the world of ideas by making a part of that world an extension of their intellectual bodies. In Rice's analysis, this understanding of authorship required the cultural promotion of "unique, elite, and therefore antidemocratic personalities who were outside the pressing concerns of society" (78). According to this view, the nineteenth century was characterized by movement away from a utilitarian approach to authorship that gave preference to the reading public who benefited from the democratic circulation of ideas expressed by authors. As a consequence, the author-centered view that authors owned their literary productions and had the right to control public access became more and more dominant through the course of the century.

What most interests me in this shift from public circulation to private ownership is the way public debate defined the creation of original ideas and the role of the author's body in the process of original creation. Virtually all scholarly accounts of the nineteenth-century copyright debate acknowledge that the core question centered on how to balance public access to knowledge with the need to provide authorial incentives. Much of the nineteenth century was absorbed in very public debates surrounding revisions of the copyright law that sought a legal distinction separating a collective intellectual commons from the particular expressions of ideas achieved by individual authors.[2] Legal scholars Monroe E. Price and Malla Pollack describe "the complexity of copyright in a free society" as posing a particularly vexing legal challenge: "how does one calibrate a legal structure so as to provide adequate incentives for creativity without, at the same time, discouraging the inventive scholarship that comes from the exploitation of existing ideas?" (452). Through a series of copyright acts that began with the 1790 Copyright Act and—as far as Dickinson is concerned—ended with the 1870 Copyright Act, the American judicial system increasingly sided with authors, extending protection for literary property based on the Lockean understanding of natural law, according to which ownership is founded on the principle that individuals own their bodies and can acquire additional property by investing the labor of their bodies in the natural world.[3] Melissa J. Homestead succinctly describes the legal status of authorship based on Locke:

> Thus, according to Locke, man acquired property rights by mixing his labor with common materials, and civil government had a fundamental duty to protect those property rights acquired through labor. Advocates of copyright transformed Locke's laboring body and hands into the author's laboring mind. Similarly, they transformed Locke's material objects removed from the state of nature and made a man's own through physical labor (such as trees transformed into lumber to build a house) into words and ideas from the common store transformed by the author's intellectual labors of invention, arrangement, and selection into works of literature. (26)

Within this framework, the writer's mind derives its power to acquire property from the precedent provided by the labor of an isolated and thereby original body. What is more, the focus on originality made possible through isolated acts implies that authority for the ownership of literary property depends on the privacy of individuals whose labor generates products that bear the imprint of a unique, natural, and unmediated self. As a consequence of this logic, the productions of authors were viewed as the unencumbered expressions of the private self.[4]

The resulting tendency to perceive women's writing as the natural expression of a private self might well have been particularly appalling to Dickinson, not only because she viewed writing as a collaborative undertaking but because she understood nature to function as a tool in the cultural perpetuation of social and political power. This is a point I made in chapter 3 where I examined Dickinson's uses of spiritualism and that I approach in this chapter as Dickinson's recognition of the essential circularity that guides the cultural construction of female authorship when only those expressions of female experience that conform to a previously codified set of cultural expectations are seen as "natural." In her discussion of the Copyright Act of 1909, Homestead hints at such a restriction of authorial expression when she describes the expansion of copyright protection as arising from the mistaken authorial expectation that legal protection would lead to "increased freedom and power for authors," when in fact "publishers instead increasingly 'managed' authorial production" (259). Based on their assessments of market demand, "publishers increasingly intervened in the artistic process" so that what seemed at first an "expansion of author's rights was thus ultimately a triumph of corporate interests." I believe that Dickinson observed a similar process in her day and sought to combat the exclusion of unconventional expressions of female experience from print culture through her democratic circulation of literature achieved through a collaborative process that did not limit creation to an isolated authorial body.

Public Privacy and the Unpublishable Female Story

One of Dickinson's chief aims was to clarify the extent that the public perception of the female body was itself a cultural creation and that women readers had to begin questioning broadly held cultural assumptions about female nature if they were to begin imagining forms of female experience not dictated by cultural precedent. As Domhnall Mitchell has argued in his perceptive analysis of Dickinson's participation in the culture of nineteenth-century Amherst, "The poem therefore serves as a complex interface between an urgent and personal formulation of what are essentially social allegiances and priorities (the desire for distinction, permanence, privacy), and other views that were still in the process of defining themselves at that time (the ideas of equality and democracy, mobility, public opportunity and achievement)" (*Monarch* 13). In "To my quick ear the Leaves – conferred –" (Fr 912), Dickinson pursues this aim by presenting the natural world as an antagonist who robs her speaker of her private experience.[5] In doing so, Dickinson again asserts the ambivalent attitude toward nature earlier affirmed by the speaker of "This is my letter to the World" (Fr 519) who states that nature's "Message is committed / To Hands I cannot see – ." In this poem, though, the speaker is unable to distance herself so easily from nature's message, claiming instead that "I could not find a Privacy / From Nature's sentinels – ."

> To my quick ear the Leaves – conferred –
> The Bushes – they were Bells –
> I could not find a Privacy
> From Nature's sentinels –
>
> In Cave if I presumed to hide
> The Walls – begun to tell –
> Creation seemed a mighty Crack –
> To make me visible –

The idea that nature requires sentinels reinforces the notion that nature is limited and that its domain must be protected, yet even in the womb-like seclusion of a cave, certainly among the most feminine and private of all landscape features, the speaker feels exposed. Significantly, it is "Creation" that exposes her, as it is the biblical story of creation that provides the primary cultural foundation for the public view of woman as divinely ordained to be man's helpmeet. Indeed, the poem might be read as a contemporary reenactment of the biblical expulsion from the garden where the "Leaves" of line one are both part of the natural world the speaker inhabits and the pages of the Bible and literary works that determine how she interprets her circumstance.

Within such a reading, the speaker, as Eve whose "*quick* ear" underscores her newly acquired life, seeks the solitude of a cave to escape the scrutiny of the Creator but in so doing discovers to her dismay that she has entered more fully that which she seeks to escape. Indeed, if the "Bushes" of line two are "Bells" the speaker associates with public experience—as with bells that signal the passage of collective time or summon worshipers to church—then the "Walls" of the cave that begin "to tell" in line six signify that she has actually entered the bell that symbolically structures public experience. With the implacability of nightmare, the poem states that for women even the most-private recesses of the female body have been appropriated as expressions of public experience. Woman, the poem tells us, is inseparable from nature, and public understanding of the female self as founded on the story of nature's creation is inescapable. This devastating discovery reveals that independent thought in the free space of the woman's interior self is an illusion; the interior self is no longer separable from its public representation. Yet, as the poem indicates by means of the speaker's dismay, a sense of privacy persists, undermining the delineation of a strict binary whereby privacy is absolutely displaced. Creation is a "mighty Crack," not full disclosure, certainly, but suggestive of an inability to affirm the reaches of self that exceed public intelligibility.

The set of circumstances detailed in "To my quick ear" provide a rough outline of the cultural forces at bear on the conduct of nineteenth-century women writers that I want to look at as even further constrained by the increasing focus on the writer's body promoted by copyright advocates. Nancy Cott's analysis of the ministerial incorporation of Eve's experience in the Garden of Eden as the basis for a religiously informed view of the "natural" woman in nineteenth-century New England provides one important strand in the logic linking Eve to nature that Dickinson magnifies in her poem. "Writers later in the eighteenth century dropped the references to Mother Eve," Cott notes, "and focused instead on the religious inclination 'naturally' present in female temperament" (128). This

model of naturally occurring religious inclinations that defines women as subject to male authority and as passive recipients of spiritual power coincides with
Joanne Dobson's argument that female writers formed part of a "community
of expression" within which a posture of female reticence dictated female literary self-expression. "I propose that the writing of nineteenth-century American women at mid-century, particularly in the manifestly 'literary' genres of
poetry and fiction, shows characteristics of just such an expressive community—
constituting a discourse distinctively and discernibly patterned by cultural assumptions regarding the nature of womanhood and her 'divine reticence'" (Dobson 9). In making her argument, Dobson draws on Nina Baym's conclusion that
nineteenth-century literary reviewers judged as most accomplished those literary characterizations of female experience that "approximate[d] the woman to
a type" (*Novels* 98). To be more precise, "The 'best' women characters are not individuals, are not mixed, and certainly have no secrets to be laid bare." In other
words, the world of print culture encouraged the authorial presentation of female characters whose conduct denied the existence of a private self capable of
departing from public norms.

At the same time that public perceptions of nature and religion were being
combined to produce uniform and predictable expressions of female character
in the work of women writers, trends in medical science were further defining
the female body in ways that corresponded directly with Dickinson's suggestion
that even the womb had been appropriated as a public site for the determination
of female conduct. This is a point that Carole Smith-Rosenberg famously made
in *Disorderly Conduct* when she stated, "as the nineteenth-century progressed,
male physicians pictured women as fragile creatures, dominated by their repro-
ductive processes. From puberty to menopause, these processes established the
reason and the rhythm of women's lives" (23). Popular medical handbooks like
Edward H. Dixon's *Woman and Her Diseases, from the Cradle to the Grave* made
explicit the extent that the uterus dictates female experience. In one of the best-
known passages from this text, he presents woman as largely at the mercy of her
uterus:

> It was said by the ancient physicians, that "the uterus was an animal
> within an animal," so well were they convinced of its surprising power over
> the affections and the sentiments. Nor does it seem at all inconsistent with
> the perfect harmony of nature's laws that it should be so. When we reflect
> on the inconceivable wonders of its functions—that within its cavity na-
> ture, with her plastic hand, gives the first evidence of her power to attach
> an immortal spirit to those very elements of which the meanest insect,
> or even a blade of grass, is also formed—we may with great propriety de-

mand, why the whole organism should not respond to its slightest affection. (195–96)

In her discussion of Dixon's medical handbook, Diane Price Herndl acknowledges the extent that the complexities surrounding the medical diagnosis and treatment of uterine fluctuations increasingly defined women as incapable of interpreting their own bodies. "The rhetorical impact of Dixon's book," she argues, "which continually lists symptoms that only the physician will be able to interpret accurately, is to convince his reader that she is in constant peril of mortal disease and must consult her physician over every bodily vicissitude" (38). The question that this version of nineteenth-century medical science poses for the middle-class woman writer contemplating her position within the debate over copyright centers precisely on whether or not she possesses the capacity to produce original work if the metaphorical foundation for literary originality is the isolated labor of the physical body. For if women writers had to rely on the expertise of male physicians in order to interpret their own bodies, and if that expertise is the product of medical science, to what extent can such a body meet the standard of privacy that is the prerequisite for original creation?

Dickinson approaches this question by urging readers to imagine the female body as a contested space not determined by the totalizing image of the culturally condoned "natural" woman promoted by religion, medical science, and literary convention. She achieved this indirectly in "To my quick ear" through reference to "Nature's sentinels" at the end of the first stanza. The presence of guards presupposes a realm of experience beyond the boundaries of nature that the speaker acknowledges in her language but may or may not be capable of entering. All we know is that her choice to seek privacy in a "Cave" proved unproductive. As readers, we wonder what lies on the other side of the sentinels' field of vision and what might have been the case if the speaker had chosen to go there. Dickinson more directly addresses the possibility of experience embodied outside the reach of nature in "Ended, ere it begun –" where the speaker witnesses the retroactive erasure of a story situated outside the protocols of print culture.[6] Read in the context of copyright debates that increasingly emphasized the isolated authorial body at the same time that biological and religious definitions of the female body increasingly reduced the potential for private and original thought, the poem presents the productions of the nonconformist female writer as literally unreadable.

Ended, ere it begun –
The Title was scarcely told

When the Preface perished from Consciousness
The story, unrevealed –

Had it been mine, to print!
Had it been your's [*sic*], to read!
That it was not our privilege
The interdict of God –

The poem's focus on "The story" as a possession establishes the three figures most prominent in nineteenth-century disputes over literary ownership: author, publisher, and reader. The speaker's knowledge that a story exists, even though it was ultimately "unrevealed," points to the possibility that the speaker is actually the writer, as no one else would be in a better position to determine that there was a story that somehow never materialized. If the speaker is the writer, then the poem tells us that her aim is that of making the story available to the reader—which could include the general public—through an act of publication performed for the public good: the speaker seeks to promote "our privilege," not her personal property rights.

By structuring the first three lines of the second stanza so that they progressively advance from "mine" to "your's" to "our," Dickinson presents the untold story not as the writer's exclusive property but rather as a creation that is realized through acts of reading that define the published work as the product of multiple bodies, as an expression of incompletely isolated and democratic personalities who see themselves reflected in collective experience. As such, the published work would not be understood as a product commensurate with a singular, isolated, and static body but rather as the fluid expression of a dynamic process incommensurate with any particular material expression. What the poem tells us, though, is that this kind of reading is not possible; instead, the poem describes a desired form of democratic reading that the speaker somewhat grudgingly admits to be impossible within the terms of print culture.

Read as a poem that emphasizes reading rather than authorial rights, the poem may be seen as advocating a utilitarian approach to copyright that privileges reader experience over that of authors and that sees publication as tracing the passage of a democratic personality rather than bearing the imprint of a discretely embodied elite self. The metrical composition of the poem lends force to this approach by situating the greatest metrical irregularity in the first three lines of the first stanza where the story that can't be told is wrestled into submission and either erased from consciousness or withheld from public scrutiny. The most interesting line from a metrical point of view is the third in the Franklin edition, where the line extends to ten syllables and utilizes metrical feet not terribly common in Dickinson's poems. As I read it, the line begins with a pyrrhic foot, moves to a trochaic foot, and concludes with two dactylic feet. In Dickinson's fascicle manuscript, the concluding dactyls appear on a line of their own, perhaps in this way drawing additional attention to the heaviness of the only three-syllable feet in the poem and thereby magnifying their role in squashing the story that can't be revealed. From this point on, the lines in print versions of the poem all conform to iambic trimeter or tetrameter, reinforcing the sense that the metrical unruliness of the first three lines of the poem have now been brought under control, along with the content they attempted to communicate.[7]

With this metrical reinforcement in mind, we can see more clearly that the first three lines represent a struggle during which the speaker is stripped of the story and forced to conform to a more regular pattern, as if to say that the unrevealed story was somehow less regular, less predictable. We don't know anything else about the lost story except that its loss illuminates the pathos of the female author, magnifying the mangling of her subjectivity, or what Virginia Jackson refers to as the separation of "a life" from "its 'proper' representation" (223). As Jackson understands it, these sorts of divisions of the self are "perhaps the signature characteristic of the subjectivity Dickinson bequeaths to literary history." What is most interesting about Jackson's analysis for my purposes is her recommendation that we view "the riddle of subjective experience" posed by divided subjectivity as a challenge Dickinson "most often portrayed as a problem for lyric *reading.*" I agree that lyric reading is exactly what takes over in "Ended, ere it begun – ," and that this reading has everything to do with the female body. Jackson states her position in language that applies directly to the argument I am also making, only I make it in terms of copyright and authorial originality: "We might go so far as to say that the anticipation of that reading is exactly what fractures the subject: she experiences at the level of her person the fate of her representation, and it is a fate consistently figured as a crisis of or for bodily identity." What I am suggesting is that authorial ownership requires the same sort of body presupposed by lyric reading and that Dickinson responds to both by repeatedly urging readers to concentrate on what is not contained in the poem, to direct their energies instead to experiences that register in their own bodies but that are not as visible as they should be in the published works of women writers.

But the poem also expresses the challenge faced by female authors who may wish to present unorthodox dimensions of female experience that are stricken from the print record by an "interdict of God." In this instance, the power of the divine is associated with strict adherence to social codes that determine the acceptable range of female experience through appeal to a divinely ordered natural

5. "Ended, ere it begun –" (J 1088/Fr 1048) *MBED* 1257. By permission of the Houghton Library, Harvard University. *MS AM 1118.3 (192c)* © The President and Fellows of Harvard College.

world. God, then, directs what goes into print through the agency of the publisher whose job it is to see that published works reach the broadest possible market by meeting public demand. What the poem asks of us, though, is that we see this "interdict of God" as at odds with the best interest of the woman writer who wishes to alter marketplace values by presenting alternative versions of female experience. As in "To my quick ear," our reading experience is directed to that which lies beyond the speaker's power to represent on the printed page: awareness of life beyond nature's sentinels or what might be thought of as the subject of a story that actually exists but cannot be rendered in print. In order to imagine what does not appear in the poem, readers have to turn to their own experience and read the pages of their own bodies, thus collapsing author and reader roles. As readers authorize unprintable aspects of their own experience through the process of reading the published poem, their reading embraces personal experiences not accommodated by public codes governing the private experience of "real" women.

Sensitivity to acts of erasure of the sort witnessed by Dickinson's speaker would have been particularly acute among women authors who regularly confronted restrictive editorial demands that routinely narrowed the acceptable range of female experience. When writing of the motivation behind the political ambitions of nineteenth-century American women poets, Paula Bernat Bennett identifies this very sense of being excluded from official print culture as a primary impetus. Bennett argues that the socially engaged writers she examines in *Poets in the Public Sphere* questioned "whether the refining and redemptive qualities literary sentimentality and domestic ideology ascribed to women were in fact qualities that defined—or should define—women. . . . To what extent, if at all, women should identify with these qualities was, perhaps, for the poets I discuss, the single most important question driving them to write" (*Poets* 23). Though Bennett might well resist including Dickinson among the writers she discusses because of Dickinson's emphasis on the epistemological dimension of democratic personality, I would argue that the difference is more apparent than real.

Women writers who resisted confinement within the terms of femininity enforced by print culture had to be capable of thinking outside those terms and working around the efforts of publishers. This is precisely what the speaker of "Ended, ere it begun –" seems incapable of doing. A reading of the poem that concentrates on the institutional power that overwhelms at least some nonconventional women writers might interpret the speaker as a female author who witnessed the rejection of her story by an editor who refused to read beyond the title and the beginning of the preface. This would account for the exclamation points following the lines "Had it been mine, to print!" and "Had it been your's [*sic*], to read!" This would also underscore the fact that even if female writers produced stories that they knew others would want to read, they still had to negotiate a male-dominated publishing world within which males understood the proper labor of their own male bodies to include the profitable management of works produced by female bodies. Through what amounts to a critique of the woman writer's vulnerability within America's gender-based economic hierarchy, Dickinson's poem can be seen as exposing paternalistic class interests imbedded within the legal concept of exclusive ownership.[8] In this, her interrogation of Locke's philosophical position proceeds along lines that anticipate the legal historian Alan Hyde, who points out that "For Locke the property-as-autonomy-and-freedom claim is a claim to dominate others. Any system of property is necessarily a map of the domination of some who lack by others who have" (56).[9] Given the importance of the body-as-property metaphor to copyright law, Dickinson's concern with this metaphor can be understood as central to a poetics that seeks to redress the antidemocratic and legal muting of the female literary voice.[10]

According to a reading of "Ended, ere it begun –" that views the speaker as a female writer who has her story taken from her, the poem's critique of the principle of copyright focuses on the unintelligibility of the female American author. As I have been arguing, one of the central problems a market-driven textual economy posed for the woman writer was the Lockean legal requirement that the textual body be identifiable as the stable product of individual labor. In *Emily Dickinson and Her Contemporaries* Elizabeth Petrino demonstrates that for nineteenth-century women writers the textual body was expected to conform to the widespread cultural belief that biology suited women for emotional expression but limited their intellectual potential. "In claiming that women poets expressed their emotions naturally and spontaneously," Petrino writes, "critics considered their best poems to be those in which the meter is correct and which appear to issue without forethought; conversely, they disparaged metrical innovations in women's verse, claiming that they gave the impression of laborious labor" (28). Women writers who sought the economic and cultural benefits of publication were pressured to accommodate editorial norms designed to erase all destabilizing textual features.

Petrino clarifies the bind in which women writers found themselves as they attempted to produce texts acceptable to the public but also expressive of selves not predicated on social convention. Citing the words of an anonymous critic writing for *The Nation*, Petrino explains the paternalistic impulses that drive his assessment. This critic begins by objecting that Helen Hunt Jackson's 1870 collection of poems, *Verses*, made her " '[seem] more intellectual' than she is" and then proceeds to make the stunningly dismissive observation that " 'the feeling is clothed in a somewhat enigmatic form, and one finds it almost laborious to unclothe it and discover it.'" Petrino asserts that the attitude expressed here is characteristic of that held by many critics and editors: "in fact," she observes, "so often were women's lives and books compared that their poems came to be referred to as 'embodiments,' 'waifs,' and 'children,' which needed to be 'fathered' under the auspices of a male ... before appearing in public" (21). What this choice of terminology suggests is that the female body, as represented by the product of its labor (writing), was critiqued by male critics and appropriated by male editors through gestures constructed as acts of kindness but that in reality subsumed the female body within the male.

In this context, Dickinson's reference to a "story" that is known by at least some women but incapable of being published for public consumption, may be understood as pointing to other stories that are likewise unpublishable because they reflect unruliness in the manner of telling as well as in content. By positing a story perceived but not possessed, seen but not read, known and yet unintelligible, the poem points to the way systems of publication and distribution can fail both the author whose story never reaches the public and the public that senses the presence of stories that they never see in print. It also suggests that the story not revealed by publishers is a story the publishing establishment may well be incapable of reading.[11] Both the "enigmatic" elements objected to in Jackson's poems, and the "'spasmodic,'" "'uncontrolled,'" and disorderly features Dickinson refused to eliminate despite Higginson's recommendations that she do so,[12] were seen as unruly gestures because they represented a body that undermined its own integrity, that asserted a perpetual refusal to consolidate its parts in a manner consistent with public assumptions about the female body and the legal demand for originality. Because women writers who retained such anomalous elements in their works were subject to severe forms of editorial intrusion, their published texts functioned as culturally palatable accounts of female experience that affirmed the public expectation of innate female privacy even though they may have contained hints of public experience that eluded the editor's eye.[13] For this reason, even women who enjoyed the monetary benefits of publishing risked sacrificing their *literal* bodies in the process of producing an acceptable *literary* body.

One of the most troubling implications of "Ended, ere it begun –" is that for Dickinson and many other American women writers the much-vaunted freedom of the press so close to the heart of democracy had become an ideological instrument that all too often exercised its power by foreclosing, rather than expanding, the range of voices admitted into print.[14] According to the terms set forth in Dickinson's poem, the emergence of female literary voices during the first half of the nineteenth century may be less significant than we would like to think, if indeed publication was governed by public expectations that constrained the sort of female self granted an official voice. As Lora Romero succinctly observed, "even if (as it indeed appears) the best-selling novels of the period written by women outsold the best-sellers written by men, the book-selling industry was almost entirely in the hands of men, a fact that greatly complicates the issue of who 'controlled' the literary marketplace" (13). By drawing attention to the economic and legal exclusion of voices that readers would like to see on the printed page, Dickinson illuminates the real political implications following from a highly artificial and institutionally informed distinction between the published version of womanhood and the public's actual experience of women, a distinction itself dependent on a specific interpretation of the Lockean body-as-property metaphor.[15]

The Epistemology of Female Authorship

In her efforts to extricate the woman writer from public constructions of the female body and the limited narratives supported by those constructions, Dickinson reveals her sympathy for the utilitarian side of the copyright wars that raged around her. Looking closely at the principles that guided utilitarian thought casts important light on Dickinson's understanding of the authorial body that logically follows from Locke's presentation of humanity as property of the divine creator and therefore vehicles for the expression of divine thought, not original sources. At the heart of the utilitarian position was the view that authorship was an activity understood as "communicative and participatory" (Rice 92), drawing on the circulation of ideas already present in the public domain and not susceptible to exclusive ownership. Thomas Jefferson presented a classic utilitarian summary of authorship in an 1813 letter to Isaac MacPherson: " 'If nature has made any one thing less susceptible than all others of exclusive property, it is the action of the thinking power called an idea, which an individual may exclusively possess as long as he keeps it to himself; but the moment it is divulged, it forces itself into the possession of everyone, and the receiver cannot dispose himself of it' " (qtd. in Vaidhyanathan 23).

In opposition to this view, copyright advocates magnified the material dimension of authorship, giving particular weight to the literary product of the writer's labor. This understanding of authorship urged greater appreciation for authorial originality and encouraged the view that authorial production was the result of intellectual labor that could be equated to that of an autonomous body. Melissa Homestead cites the 1830 House of Representatives report promoting copyright legislation as plainly stating the material argument made by those who would extend the terms of copyright protection: "'Though the nature of literary property is peculiar, it is not the less real and valuable.... [T]he literary man ... writes and labors assiduously as does the mechanic or husbandman. The scholar who se-cludes himself, and wastes his life, and often his property, to enlighten the world, has the best right to the profits of those labors: the planter, the mechanic, and the professional man, cannot prefer a better title to what is admitted to be his own'" (qtd. in Homestead 86). As the preceding discussion of "Ended, ere it begun –" makes clear, an important reason for Dickinson's opposition to copyright and the view that literature be understood as the property of a distinct individual was her recognition that such a view sought to confine the isolated authorial body within social conventions that limited the body's freedom of expression. More than that, even, Dickinson appreciated the extent that equating the individual mind with a fabricated, socially acceptable body severely compromised the indi-vidual's capacity to exercise intellectual sovereignty.

To understand Dickinson's position in relation to the mind of the author, it is helpful to look directly at the language used to establish the body-as-property metaphor in the second of Locke's *Two Treatises of Government:* "Though the earth, and all inferior creatures be common to all men, yet every man has a prop-erty in this own person. This nobody has any right to but himself. The labour of his body, and the work of his hands, we may say, are properly his. Whatsoever then he removes out of the state that nature hath provided, and left it in, he hath mixed his labour with, and joined to it something that is his own, and thereby makes it his property" (128). Copyright advocates seized on this language as pro-viding a foundation for claims that authors could treat intellectual creations as property over which they held monopolistic power. As Hyde has pointed out, however, democratic as this association of body and property may seem, there is in fact "nothing inevitable about Locke's association of the owned, body as prop-erty, with any claim of autonomy and freedom in the self that owns that body" (55–56). This is very nearly the conclusion that Dickinson urges in "Ended, ere it begun – ," when she presents the speaker as being denied the power to tell her story by an "interdict of God." If the authorial self is subject to cultural assump-tions that determine what is intelligible, that very self may declare her own prop-erty unintelligible if it does not conform to those assumptions. This is at least one way of accounting for the absence of the story that remains unrevealed in Dickinson's poem. Locke's words give persons rights over the products of their labor, but do not stipulate that the persons who possess bodies also possess the intellectual freedom to make responsible choices about the uses and outcomes of their labor.

Once questions of epistemology surface as crucial to the mind's ability to accurately perceive the world, the focus of "Ended, ere it begun –" can be seen to shift from a primary concern with publication, *per se,* to an analysis of the political and ideological assumptions that sanction particular representations of women's lives. As a consequence, questions about what exactly the "it" in "Ended, ere it begun –" represents become increasingly vexed. "It" at first appears to be a book, a lost story, the elements of that story, or possibly the bodies of people who have met untimely deaths, but the rest of the poem deconstructs any simple identification of "it" with book, body, or story. Instead, the poem asks readers to admit that conventional notions of books and bodies rest on a dubious separation of self from other. That is, if the "story" is in fact concealed and not "ended," which is to say rejected but not destroyed, then its absence is the result of a blindness built into the protocols of print publication and literary propriety. By drawing attention to the artificiality of published representations of female experience, the poem implies that there are additional stories of female "others" also capable of having ended ere they begun.

At the same time, though, that the poem illuminates the relativity of all stories by questioning naïve trust in the possibility of original thought, it also affirms the authority of readers to evaluate stories for what they are: transient accounts of human experience that serve temporary and imperfect political purposes. It delivers this affirmative message by placing the reader in the position of weighing alternatives through a process that achieves the democratic aim of maximizing rather than diminishing reader participation in the determination of meaning. This is most clearly seen through the poem's articulation of both the Lockean formulation that, in Rice's words, "rendered authorship the private activity of unique, elite, and therefore antidemocratic personalities who were outside the pressing concerns of society," and the utilitarian position that "reduced writing to 'inventions' assembled from the public realm of ideas by commonplace literary 'producers'" (78). When the speaker identifies the discrepancy between the stories female authors would like to publish and accounts of female experience that enter print, she positions herself in the utilitarian camp; her concern is with printing and reading, acts that give a text value through its participation in the public domain. At the same time, though, she acknowledges the power of the Lockean position through her inability to imagine an alternative. Readers who witness the speaker's self-silencing recognize that what prevents her story from achieving public circulation is the rigid conception of female experience that the publishing world insists upon as critical to the successful marketing of female writers.

This logic once again illustrates the poem's interest in shifting the focus of publication away from author-based considerations grounded in the body-as-property metaphor to the utilitarian demand that literature be understood as the fluid expression of a dynamic body politic. For this to happen, literature itself must be viewed as the incomplete expression of a personality that defies containment within the singular body presupposed by the body-as-property metaphor. Dickinson contributes to this desire for a more utilitarian understanding of literary origins through her practice of writing poems that draw reader attention to experiences that do not appear on the page. Doing so encourages readers to imagine for themselves what those experiences might be, thereby breaking down the separation of author and reader, private and public, by asking that readers draw from their own bodily experience in collaboration with authors. Such an understanding would view individual published works as the product of multiple bodies that collectively shape authorial perception, ultimately yielding a vision of print culture as the dialogic presentation of equally authoritative voices that vie for reader consent.[16]

By increasing reader awareness of muted voices like that of the unintelligible woman writer and thereby signaling a departure from institutionally determined public codes of privacy, Dickinson's poem points out the ontological impossibility of achieving isolated and hence original privacy. All voices admit of intelligibility by virtue of their relationship to others. Although the speaker confidently asserts the transferability of literary property, this belief is belied by the "interdict of God" that prevents that transfer and stymies public circulation of the story. Crucially, the term "interdict" has ancient associations with the law, particularly ecclesiastical law that as far back as the thirteenth century used the term to designate an "authoritative sentence debarring a particular place or person . . . from ecclesiastical functions and privileges" (*OED*). Thus Dickinson's choice of terms suggests that the speaker's wish for publication represents a violation of religious law. Nonetheless, the fact that it apparently requires an act of God to repress the unruly female story reveals a weakness in the orthodox notion of authorial privacy. In this instance, divine authority is similar to nature's sentinels who patrol the boundaries of orthodox thought, simultaneously imposing order and exposing the precariousness of that order. Dickinson's inclusion of God as a participant in this matrix of textual exchange is for these reasons especially ironic, as it suggests that in order to perceive even their own bodies as exclusive property, individuals must paradoxically believe that all bodies are simultaneously the "property" of a divine creator.[17] Were this not the case, God's interdict would have no authority.

The precedent for this claim can be seen in another statement that appears in the second of Locke's *Two Treatises of Government,* where humanity is described as "the workmanship of one omnipotent, and infinitely wise Maker" and there-

fore "his property, whose workmanship they are, made to last during his, not one
another's pleasure" (117). Here Locke's language pointedly establishes humanity
as an extension of God and subject to divine will. This means that if we treat
Dickinson's poem as the representation of an author/speaker in conflict with the
body-as-property metaphor that provides the foundation for authorial originality
and ownership, we have to conclude that the speaker is mistaken in thinking that
her exclusion from print culture is due to an act of God. In drawing this conclusion, the speaker wrongly attributes authority to the human body and the creative power of the human intellect presumed within the body-as-property metaphor and silences herself because her story does not conform to an institutional
definition of the female body that she incorrectly associates with the will of
God. Through this speaker's thought, Dickinson identifies a fundamental epistemological inconsistency within the emerging understanding of authorship that
grants the authorial body a legal standing by displacing divine authority with a
culturally constructed view of the female body. The final challenge, then, that
Dickinson issues in this poem is that readers cease to think of authorial rights
as grounded in the body-as-property metaphor and instead perceive this crucial
metaphor as an ideological tool that thwarts the proper aims of art in a democratic culture. Readers are encouraged to recognize that authors, printers, and
readers who persist in claiming that literature is capable of becoming anyone's
exclusive property do so in the absence of divine support, despite claims to the
contrary.[18] But more important, the poem correlates the ontological with the
aesthetic by provoking reader desire for a story not admitted to the public realm
on the basis of artistic and professional norms. Powerful as the legal and philosophical arguments in support of copyright are, Dickinson's poem ultimately
presents reader desire for a fuller and more democratic proliferation of cultural
stories as the preeminent consideration appropriate for a democratic citizenry.[19]

Selling the Royal Air

How then is a utilitarian author to proceed in a culture that extends copyright
protection to authors through a distortion of philosophical and religious precedent? I believe that this question, or one similar to it, was very much on Dickinson's mind when she wrote "Publication - is the Auction / Of the Mind of
Man -" (Fr 788) in around 1863. More than any other poem in the Dickinson corpus, "Publication - is the Auction" provides insight into the mind of the woman
writer who imagines how best to elude entrapment in the authorial body demanded by copyright. Produced in fair copy form during the difficult middle
years of the Civil War, the poem's concern with ownership and the body may also
be understood as Dickinson's effort to think through the implications of prop-

erty rights in general and the extent that ownership and slavery are intertwined. In this poem, what begins as a dismissive rejection of the commercial motive for publication quickly becomes a much more thoughtful assessment of democratic poetics, the literary marketplace, and the limits of authorial property rights:

Publication – is the Auction
Of the Mind of Man –
Poverty – be justifying
For so foul a thing

Possibly – but We – would rather
From Our Garret go
White – unto the White Creator –
Than invest – Our Snow –

Thought belong to Him who gave it –
Then – to Him Who bear
It's Corporeal illustration – sell
The Royal Air –

In the Parcel – Be the Merchant
Of the Heavenly Grace –
But reduce no Human Spirit
To Disgrace of Price –

The analysis of publication conducted through this poem may be understood as passing through three phases, each of which constitutes a specific option within the authorial contemplation of literary ownership. Taken together, these contemplative postures, or voices, focus the poem's discussion of publication on the issue of originality, or what Mark Rose describes as the "doctrine of originality" that arose "as a central value in cultural production . . . in precisely the same period as the notion of the author's property right" (6). Rose's observation that "the representation of the author as a creator who is entitled to profit from his intellectual labor came into being through a blending of literary and legal discourses" affirms the primary role attributed to privacy as a necessary adjunct to original creation. It is in response to this assertion of privacy that Dickinson speaks most powerfully in this poem.[20]

All three of the perspectives sketched in the poem treat as a given the role that economics plays in imagining approaches to publication, but each position offers a radically different understanding of the author's relationship to that re-

ality. The opening stanza presents a speaker who appears to disdain the economics of publication while paradoxically retaining confidence in the larger system
of exchange: the problem is one of taste that carries with it implications of class
and gender. A genteel woman would never permit her private writing to enter the
marketplace, but perhaps the demands of poverty would justify such degrada-
tion. In this case, the speaker grants that donning the commercial female body
may be justified for those whose need is great, but that the process of accepting
the public determination of that body is a form of commodification and hence
slavery that the speaker will not accept for herself. In a curious inversion of the
"author-slave analogy" that Homestead associates with the arguments in favor of
copyright (9, 49–51), Dickinson presents copyright as enabling authors to profit
by their labor, but in doing so entering economic slavery by assuming a commercialized female body. Here it is important to note that the speaker is capable
of imagining herself taking on the female body as a public commodity; if she
could not imagine herself on the auction block, she would not find the transaction so offensive.[21] Beginning the poem in this way may obliquely signal Dickinson's own contemplation of commercial publication during the early years of fascicle composition, an option that she distances herself from through the speaker
of this poem.

The voice that opens the second stanza is more contemplative; the speaker appears to weigh her initial judgment then reject it as unsuited to her particular
preferences. She chooses not to be enslaved within the body of the conventional
female author, but signals her refusal by an act of denial that reifies the economic and legal system that negatively defines her. The language of the stanza
holds open the possibility that the speaker is rethinking her position even as she
declares it. When she uses the plural pronouns "We" and "Our," she conflates
the royal "we" with the idea that she is acting for others. Unlike the speaker of
"Ended, ere it begun – ," this speaker anticipates her fate at the hands of publishers and openly admits her distaste for such an outcome. She understands all
too clearly that to "invest – Our Snow" would be to "invest" in both the monetary sense and in terms of dress—it would require tainting the pure snow of the
publicly unintelligible female story by assuming the guise of conventional female authorship. The problem is that her refusal to risk publication is presented
as perpetuating the protocols of property and ownership through inaction and
a snooty superiority; consequently, she remains secluded within property she
perceives as safe ("Our Garret") and takes into that retreat property that she believes she can protect in the interest of herself and others ("Our Snow"). At this
point in the poem, the repetition of the word "White" in line seven significantly
magnifies the racial implications of such a choice, suggesting that the speaker

subscribes to a racist ideology that understands creation as supporting the race-based privilege of whites. Such a position is ultimately unacceptable not only because it fails to make the actual experiences of women publicly intelligible but because it also reveals the speaker's complicity in the cultural definition of nonwhites as "Other." This the speaker cannot do because she is altogether too aware that her interest in publication is motivated by a desire to escape the category of "Other" imposed on women writers who stand outside the protocols of print culture. The logic of the first two stanzas demonstrates that the speaker's inaction perpetuates the auction of the female writer by placing unintelligible women in the same category of "Other" that denies the humanity of nonwhites. Karen Sanchez-Eppler makes this point in a different but related context when she writes that Dickinson "does not project her fears onto the bodies of some poor 'Other,' safely cordoned off by class or race. Rather, she recognizes this dangerous body as her own" (130).

The third and fourth stanzas introduce yet another voice that builds on the first two by continuing in the idiom of capitalist discourse but with the added twist of suggesting that items of greatest value can never be the property of distinct individuals. Instead, the body is presented as the vehicle for "Thought"—a commodity that receives value prior to embodiment through the agency of "Him who gave it"—that originates in an invisible source that exceeds the apprehension of "Him Who bear[s] / It's Corporeal illustration." Read in the context of copyright debate, this source of thought acts as a divinely inspired intellectual commons out of which the "Royal Air" emerges as the utilitarian circulation of "Heavenly Grace." The body is not the creator of literary property after all; instead, the body is the vehicle for already created "Thought" and therefore incapable of becoming the locus for private and hence original creation.[22] The legal construction of the human subject whose labor translates the body into property and then establishes ownership in the world by means of that body's labor is here represented as without foundation. This speaker offers what amounts to a renunciation of authorship as defined by the legal system.

The injunction delivered in the final seven lines instructs authors in the honest and democratic fulfillment of their duties. They are to "sell / The Royal Air –"; that is, the contents of the "Parcel" and not the parcel. This is a direct reversal of the basis for copyright that presents authors as justified in marketing the particular expression they give to ideas extracted from the intellectual commons. Such a finely drawn distinction between the corporeal poem and the message conveyed through linguistic embodiment insists that the article of value is not human creation but "Heavenly Grace"; not the body but that which is never more than partially embodied or always emerging out of invisibility. The clear implication is that to market the body is to "reduce . . . Human Spirit / To Disgrace of Price – ," to engage in a form of misrepresentation that erases knowledge of the true source of value.[23] The confusion that adheres in elevating the body of the poem above its message and then reifying the body *as* message is precisely the confusion that prevents the "story" of "Ended, ere it begun –" from ever being told. The marketplace demand that value be placed in the textual body affirms a form of ownership that confuses the true origin of thought with the human artifice that served as its momentary habitation. To market the artifice, the poem tells us, is to presume the power to make static the circulation of thought that is the primary utilitarian aim of publication in a democratic culture.[24] Moreover, to market the poem by legally defining its value in terms of property is to prevent a democratic proliferation of voices by subsuming the public and suprapersonal within the private individual.

As I indicated above in my reference to Rose and the concept of "author as creator," the larger cultural significance of Dickinson's opposition to the idea of authorial property lies in her rejection of the relatively new principle of literary originality. In her study of the legal foundations of copyright legislation in England and America, Martha Woodmansee explains the newness of this concept: "the notion that the writer is a special participant in the production process—the only one worthy of attention—is of recent provenience. It is a by-product of the Romantic notion that significant writers break altogether with tradition to create something new, unique—in a word, 'original'" (16). Citing William Wordsworth's 1815 argument in *Essay, Supplement to the Preface,* that "'Genius is the introduction of a new element into the intellectual universe,'" Woodmansee concludes that "our [present] laws of intellectual property are rooted in a century-long debate which culminated in pronouncements like Wordsworth's" that have led us to the legal belief that writing "*ought* to be solitary, or individual" (27). Dickinson's refusal to accept this proposition can be interpreted as both a democratic leveling of all participants in the circulation of literary works and an effort to avoid bondage within the female textual body demanded by commercial publication.

Dickinson most clearly achieves this last objective by proposing that publication can cease to be the auction "Of the Mind of Man" when and if readers stop confusing the textual body with the meaning of the poem. This is most clearly seen by unraveling the two apparently contradictory declarations that frame the poem: "Publication – is the Auction / Of the Mind of Man –" that begins the poem and "sell / The Royal Air // In the Parcel – Be the Merchant / Of the Heavenly Grace – / But reduce no Human Spirit / To Disgrace of Price –" that ends the poem. The final declaration, which is perhaps better understood as twin imperatives, stresses the necessity of not confusing literary value with the work of the author because doing so threatens to enslave the human spirit by reducing it to a price.

The question, then, is how might the goal of marketing the "Royal Air" be achieved? Dickinson provides no direct answer to this question, though an answer of sorts is available when the final lines are read in the context of copyright debate and the commodification of the female authorial body. Accordingly, Dickinson's point would be that publication fails to perform its proper duty precisely because the "Corporeal illustration" that is also referred to as "the Parcel" is what is in fact being sold in place of the "Royal Air." This confusion takes place because copyright replaces the actual body of the writer with an intellectually acceptable model that satisfies the legal demand for originality. For the female writer, this means that the body required for intelligibility within print culture is not an actual woman's body at all, but rather a patriarchally inspired simulacrum with which published representations must exhibit retroactive compliance. The way to escape entrapment within the "Mind of Man" is by making the textual body more representative of the actual body; that is, more clearly the product of competing cultural tensions and social currents that impact each actual woman's body differently. By this means, publication ceases to be the retroactive confirmation of female sameness achieved by approximating conformity with a prefabricated female body and instead becomes the unfolding story of the particular reader's body that she discovers through collaboration with the writer. The "Royal Air" thus becomes the intellectual commons that expands as the female reading public imagines stories of female experience that have not yet been told and that require the real bodies of others before their meaning can be known. When the female writer's textual body becomes the transient vehicle for the communication of ideas that are then absorbed and given new meaning in the lives of readers, the author's fame indeed becomes too intrinsic for renown.

The Body of the Text

The record of Dickinson's relationship to print publication demonstrates that she did not see commercial publication as a means to achieve the intrinsic renown that she desired. Her distribution of poems through her correspondence shows that she did, however, seek to circulate her work and—as I demonstrated in the previous chapter—that questions surrounding poetry and publication were subjects she frequently addressed. I now want to examine Dickinson's changing approach to manuscript production that is itself an adaptation of textual practices promoted through popular culture. A brief overview of the most obvious features of Dickinson's manuscript record shows that she was interested in the textual body from the beginning and sought various means to make the body of the text more clearly a part of the world inhabited by readers rather than the extension of an isolated authorial body capable of originality and ownership. I will conclude with a close reading of "That sacred Closet when you sweep –" (Fr 1385) that interprets it as a poem about the female body and the kinds of choices women must begin addressing in order to think independently about their own bodies and escape entrapment in the domesticated female body promoted by polite society and codified within print culture.

When considered in terms of their overall development, and viewed with an eye toward broad changes suggestive of a general trajectory, Dickinson's experiments with manuscript design suggest a tendency to loosen the connective tissue of the textual body as a way of making that body more responsive to the interventions of readers. Dickinson sought in this way to enable the reader's body to mingle with the author's and thereby generate the poem through a dialogic interplay of reader and author. In doing so, she builds on what Jed Deppman has described as "Dickinson's profoundly conversational, other-dependent conception of poetry" within which particular poems "collaborate or compete with real or implied readers" (*Trying to Think* 28). As Dickinson's manuscript experiments advanced, she increasingly departed from a vision of the poetic body as separable from the surrounding world, promoting instead an increasingly fluid and utilitarian concept of the poem as perpetually in circulation, as continually being absorbed by readers and through them disseminated throughout the body politic. In a manner very nearly sacramental in character, Dickinson sought to reduce the imprint of her body on the material poem and achieve intrinsic renown by maximizing the circulation of her thought in the lives of others. That Dickinson's textual body has excited reader fascination from the moment her work became public testifies both to the elusiveness of that body and Dickinson's failure to escape appropriation within the body-as-property metaphor so much at the heart of copyright legislation.

In what has emerged as a general consensus among scholars and critics, Dickinson's manuscript practice may be understood as falling into four discernible stages, each of which marks a step away from the ideal of a fully stabilized poetic body. Franklin's introduction to the 1998 variorum edition of Dickinson's poems provides the most authoritative outline of these stages. Briefly stated, the manuscript record suggests that fascicle composition between 1858 and 1860 is dedicated to the creation of fascicle books composed of sheets of folded paper (bifolia) that Dickinson stacked one on top of the other and stab bound. These poems are the outcome of multiple drafts that Dickinson meticulously destroyed and appear in fair copy on fascicle pages free from the variants that will surface

later (Franklin, *Poems* 20–21). During this stage, Dickinson most closely approxi-
mated the coherent textual body desired by print culture, even though she already
included unruly features such as her dashes and her capitalization that significantly unsettled that body, making it unsuitable for commercial publication.

The second stage begins in "early 1861," at a time when, in Franklin's words,
"the goal was no longer finished poems" (22). While in this stage, Dickinson
opens her correspondence with Higginson and continues to produce fascicle poems after having stalled for a time. In the previous chapter, I argued that Higginson's responsiveness to her writing helped her emerge from this temporary
paralysis and led her to claim on two separate occasions that he had saved her
life. During this stage of manuscript creation, Dickinson begins including variants as part of her fair copy poems, thereby introducing what may have been her
most-daring departure from the concept of the poem as an internally coherent
poetic body. Marta Werner has identified this period as beginning "[a]round
1860" when "the first variant word lists appear along the fringes of Dickinson's
poems like an alien voicing, disturbing set borders and summoning into her work
'the spell of difference'" (3). Later changes in manuscript organization would be
even more radical, but this first step away from coherent embodiment may have
been the most traumatic. It should be noted that even though the inclusion of
variants defines this new stage, Dickinson did not include variants in all of her
poems; the point is that at this stage the inclusion of variants first became an
option that she continued to implement as she saw fit for the rest of her writing
life. This stage continues somewhat erratically until 1866, the year Franklin refers to as marking "the effective end of fascicle making" (26).

The third stage commences in 1870 when Dickinson resumed the composition of fascicle sheets with variants but ceased binding them (26). This stage extends for five years, to 1875, after which time she ceases to write on the special
paper designated for fascicle poems and instead composes on a variety of miscellaneous writing surfaces. Writing of this period, Werner observes of the manuscripts that "the end of linearity is signaled not in their apparent disorder but,
rather, in their apprehension of multiple contingent orders. No longer marking
a place in a book, the loose leaves of stationery and scraps of paper are risked to
still wilder forms of circulation" (3). Franklin notes that in this final phase Dickinson ceased the process of producing and destroying multiple early drafts, "and
near the end grew indifferent to making even second copies" (27). This abandonment of revision through multiple drafts could signal that in her last decade
Dickinson chose to limit even further the mediating influence of the authorial
hand and mind.

As this brief overview shows, Dickinson progressively departed from a book-
dominated concept of poetry composition beginning as early as 1861, when she

6. "Exultation is the going" (J 76/Fr 143B), "I never hear the word 'Escape'" (J 77/Fr144B), "These are the days when Birds come back –" (J130/Fr122C) *MBED* 100–101. These poems show the clean manuscript page that characterizes the first stage of Dickinson's manuscript production (1858–1860). By permission of the Houghton Library, Harvard University. *MS AM 1118.3 (10d–e, 11a)* © The President and Fellows of Harvard College.

These are the days when Birds come back.
A very few. A Bird or two.
To take a backward look.

These are the days when Skies resume
The old. old sophistries of June.
A blue and gold mistake.

Oh fraud that cannot cheat the Bee.
Almost thy plausibility
Induces my belief.

Till ranks of seeds their witness bear.
And softly thro' the altered air
Hurries a timid leaf.

Oh sacrament of summer days,
Oh Last Communion in the Haze.
Permit a child to join.

7. The last two stanzas of "One need not be a Chamber – to be Haunted –" (J 670/ Fr 407) and "Like Some Old fashioned Miracle –" (J 302/Fr 408A) *MBED* 448–449. These poems show the presence of variants that begin to appear in the second stage of Dickinson's manuscript production (1861–1866). By permission of the Houghton Library, Harvard University. *MS AM 1118.3 (65a, 65b)* © The President and Fellows of Harvard College.

o X 3

Like some Old fashioned
Miracle -
When Summertime is done -
Seems Summer's Recollection
And the Affairs of June -

As + infinite tradition - as
Cinderella's Bays -
Or Little John - of Lincoln -
Green -
Or Blue Beard's Galleries

Her Bees - have an illusive Hum -
Her Blossoms - like a Dream
Elate us - till an almost woe -
So plausible - they seem -
    + Memories   + Review -
Her Memory - like Strains - Enchant -
the Orchestra + is + a Dumb -
the Violin - in Baize - replaced -
And Ear, and Heaven - numb -

+ Exquisite + Bagatelles !

8. "That sacred Closet when you sweep –" (J 1273/Fr 1385) *MBED* 1376. This poem is from the third stage of manuscript production when Dickinson continued to use fascicle paper but ceased to bind the pages (1870–1875). A 94-1/2, Amherst College Archives and Special Collections.

began regularly including variants. Her manuscript record may for this reason represent a deliberate movement away from the clean page of the bound book to an increasingly unruly text that finally refuses containment within either her own version of a traditional binding or the specialized writing surfaces of the conventional book. In Werner's words, Dickinson's manuscripts trace "the trajectory of her desire to inscribe herself outside all institutional accounts of order" (4). This distancing of text from fixed systems of order reaches final form in the sorts of responses to miscellaneous nonliterary texts described by Melanie Hubbard in "Dickinson's Advertising Flyers: Theorizing Materiality and the Work of Reading." In that essay, Hubbard identifies a democratic collaboration of reader and author that emerges in response to the "demand that the reader enter into the creative process in order to get the poem," a procedure that "forces into bloom a certain kind of reading responsive to accident and choice" (32). This last textual gesture, one that comes in the final years of her life, makes even clearer Dickinson's determination to elude containment within the body-as-property metaphor upon which the concept of exclusive ownership depended.

In his essay meditating on the twenty-four-year correspondence he maintained with Dickinson that appeared in the October 1891 issue of the *Atlantic Monthly*, Higginson provides a rather striking sense of the central role played by embodiment in the language both of them used to discuss the unruly features of her writing. Near the beginning of that essay, he writes that in response to her first letter he "ventured on some criticism which she afterwards called 'surgery,' and on some questions, part of which she evaded . . . with a naïve skill such as the most experienced and worldly coquette might envy" ("Emily Dickinson" 545). Higginson's evident surprise at Dickinson's behavior is in large part due to his assumption that Dickinson's April 15, 1862, first letter to him was a request for editorial advice triggered by "A Letter to a Young Contributor," his essay giving advice to aspiring writers that was published in the April issue of the *Atlantic Monthly*. As a consequence, Higginson behaved as a responsible editor in recommending how she might prepare the sort of textual body best suited for commercial publication. Higginson's words seize on Dickinson's sensitivity to criticism that she expressed in language linking the textual body to the physical body in a manner consistent with her awareness that editorial demands reflected an artificial and distorted view of the female body, as if Dickinson were saying to Higginson that female conformity to editorial expectations can produce serious and even painful repercussions in the writer's body. We also see that Dickinson practices an evasion designed to prevent direct confrontation, thus enabling the correspondence to continue. That Higginson interprets her actions as resembling the conduct of a worldly coquette gives additional emphasis to the importance of Dickinson's body and expresses his early inclination to define her according to a suspect female type broadly depicted in popular literature.

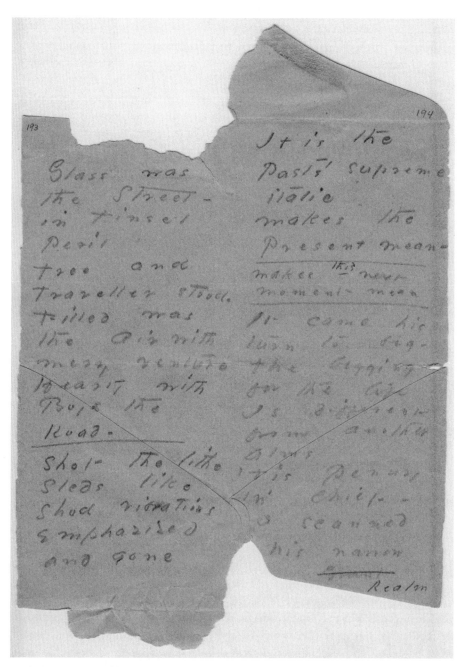

9. "Glass was the Street – in Tinsel Peril" (J 1498/Fr 1518). This is the recto and verso of the manuscript that shows the miscellaneous surfaces Dickinson wrote on in the fourth stage of her manuscript production (1875–1886). A 193 and A 194, Amherst College Archives and Special Collections.

Western Union Telegraph Co.

WILLIAM ORTON, Pres't.

Jennie Dickenson

Bears Judge found

No. _____   *I gave him leave*

Charges. *paid*   *to live .*

lost gratitude

though,   revive the snake

Smuggled   ~~thought~~ see ~~~my~~~~ ~~blood~~

my - his   o ~~twenty~~

Reprieve   ~~0~~ ~~love~~

os ~~Death~~

try if

him leave

I gave

Higginson's initial assumption that he is dealing with a female who can be identified according to familiar literary types quickly fades as he is repeatedly baffled by Dickinson's unpredictability. Reflecting on his changing view of Dickinson, Higginson remarks that after having received a fourth letter from her he continued to offer advice despite the fact that he had already begun to delight in her unorthodox style and that he had come to interpret the anomalous features of her textual body as an indication of her spiritual status: "It would seem that at first I tried a little—a very little—to lead her in the direction of rules and traditions; but I fear it was only perfunctory, and that she interested me more in her—so to speak—unregenerate condition" ("Emily Dickinson" 551). Higginson's admission that he is interested in the "unregenerate condition" of a woman he has previously described as a coquette points to a surprisingly sexual and even illicit undercurrent in this emerging relationship. That he is attracted to a woman he describes in such terms points to Higginson's willingness to accept behavior that deviates from cultural norms that as an editor it is his business to enforce on the printed page. In this particular relationship, Higginson well knew that the text was designed to stand for the body. Dickinson had made this clear to him in her July 1862 letter when she refused his request for a picture. Higginson quotes her as asking, "'Could you believe me without?'" and then providing a verbal description of herself that she hopes will serve in the place of a picture, asking, "'Would this do just as well?'" (549).

Further evidence that Dickinson seeks to fuse the textual body with her own actual body as part of a collaborative circulation of mutually generated thought can be seen in Higginson's previously cited reflections on the first full year of their correspondence: "Always glad to hear her 'recite,' as she called it, I soon abandoned all attempt to guide in the slightest degree this extraordinary nature, and simply accepted her confidences, giving as much as I could of what might interest her in return" (554). Again we see Dickinson's insistence on the physical dimension of written poetry through her use of the word "recite" that calls to mind the spoken rather than the written delivery of verse. And we see that Higginson now expresses a determination to win her approval; instead of concentrating on what interests *him* about her, he now desires to appear interesting in *her* eyes. Higginson's efforts to participate in a reciprocal exchange means that he is taking her interest into account as he shapes his textual response, allowing his textual body to be informed by hers, so that each contributes to the expansion of a collective intellectual commons. Perhaps this is what both Susan and Emily had in mind when they referred to poetry as having the capacity to chill the body (*L* 380, 473–474), and what led Dickinson to elaborate further by stating, "If I feel physically as if the top of my head were taken off, I know *that* is poetry" (*L* 747).

These few brief excerpts from Higginson's *Atlantic* essay provide important information about the sort of collaboration Dickinson sought to establish with readers that Higginson reinforces with language that shows how Dickinson preserved the independent sovereignty of each. One of the first and most important discoveries Higginson made is that Dickinson did not view her departures from conventional norms as accidents, or as errors in need of correction. When recalling his reading of "Your Riches – taught me – Poverty" (Fr 418C), a poem that Dickinson sent him with her second letter, Higginson comments on Dickinson's deliberate departure from poetic norms: "Here was already manifest that defiance of form, never through carelessness, and never precisely from whim, which so marked her" ("Emily Dickinson" 547). Equally significant is the way Dickinson appears undeterred by his criticism at the same time that she makes no apparent effort to change the way he views her writing. Higginson writes that she "recognizes the endeavor" but evades his critical efforts "with her usual naïve adroitness" (551). Some of the letters included in Higginson's essay do show that Dickinson is not afraid to state opinions about writing that differ rather markedly from his, but she is at all times more interested in responding to his words and clarifying her position than she is in discrediting his opinions. She appears more dedicated to providing an alternative view of poetic value that he can consider alongside his own and do with as he chooses. This mutual respect is an essential feature of gift exchange that I examined in the previous chapter as part of Dickinson's correspondence with Higginson that receives reinforcement in this essay. His responses to Dickinson provide evidence of her ability to promote the independent sovereignty of others while at the same time steadfastly expressing her own views as part of an ongoing conversation.

Higginson's words also reflect Dickinson's willingness to allow others to enter her texts and reshape them according to their own aesthetic tastes. We do not have a clear record showing that Dickinson adopted Higginson's recommendations, but that absence is balanced by the even more telling fact that she continued to send Higginson poems with full knowledge that he would dissect them and recommend revisions—at least in the early phase of their correspondence. And we know from history that even after he stopped making suggestions for revision, he remained devoted to the textual norms he would impose on her literary corpus after she was dead. From the vantage point of today, we find it easy to condemn Higginson as insufficiently sensitive to the textual body Dickinson left to future readers, yet Higginson's anxiety about being associated with what he viewed as unruly poems indicates that he was willing to take risks in order to honor the textual body of his friend. The uneasiness Higginson expresses in his introductory comments to the first edition of her poems, qualifying Dickinson's writing by describing it as removed from criticism and best understood as part of the portfolio tradition, implies that he had departed to some extent from normative and comfortable editorial conduct. This tells us that in presenting Dickinson to the public Higginson may have sought a middle ground between Dickinson's more radical textual innovations and his own understanding of what readers would find palatable.

In the end, Higginson was surprised by the eagerness with which the public embraced Dickinson's poems, perhaps revealing his blindness to the reading public's willingness to accept deviations from the conventional textual body. Such insensitivity may have come in part from his failure to appreciate the extent that the reading public was prepared to welcome poetry that incorporated the far more flexible approach to textual embodiment practiced in the portfolio tradition and other approaches to the collection and arrangement of written work that proliferated in literate middle-class culture. Even though he usefully associated Dickinson's writing with the portfolio, Higginson appears not to have fully grasped the many ways such a tradition linked Dickinson to popular textual practices that violated the terms of literary ownership so closely associated with copyright.

Dickinson was certainly not alone in her desire to contest the legal determination of exclusive literary rights and to promote alternative models of democratic writing and reading. Her circulation of texts to people like Higginson, Susan, Elizabeth Holland, and Helen Hunt Jackson betrays an attitude toward ownership that links her work to other developments within nineteenth-century women's culture that challenged the legal concept of authorial ownership. As recent research into women's clubs by Anne Ruggles Gere, Annette Baxter, Karen J. Blair, and Theodora Penny Martin has shown, middle-class American women of all stripes treated literacy as part of a broad political effort to bring women's lives into the public arena.[25] Gere's careful analysis of the last three decades of the nineteenth century specifies that by 1906 between 25,000 and 50,000 women's clubs regularly violated the boundaries of authorial property in a manner that closely replicated what individual women were doing through portfolio collections and scrapbooks in the privacy of their homes ("Common Properties" 385–386). In Gere's words, "The reading aloud of woman's clubs offered resistance" (390) to both "the book dominated view of discourse" and "the boundaries between texts [through] acts of appropriation, imitation, and general playfulness" (392). That these behaviors were meant to situate textual production within a communal and public rather than an individual and private context is made particularly clear through the practice of circulating unsigned and thus non-attributed texts. "In producing and circulating texts without the mark of ownership," Gere writes, "clubwomen signaled their preference for an ideology of communal ownership of texts" (Gere, *Practices* 107).

Dickinson's withholding of titles and signatures from her fascicle gatherings may form part of a parallel strategy to avoid claims of ownership. Even the storage of poem manuscripts in the trunk of Margaret Maher, her Irish house servant, suggests a willingness to place personal property within the private space of another as a gesture clearly antithetical to the aims of exclusivity.[26] The 1884 letter from Helen Hunt Jackson that refers to Dickinson's "portfolios of verses" (*L* 841) may similarly reveal a willingness to share poetry, this time of one or more portfolios or fascicles. The sharing of poems also comes up in accounts provided by Louise and Frances Norcross, where Dickinson is described as composing and reading poems aloud at the Homestead.[27] As has been seen, the free and unencumbered circulation of poems that Higginson refers to in his 1891 *Atlantic Monthly* essay demonstrates strong parallels with the activities regularly practiced in women's clubs. Moreover, the discussions of literary works conducted by Dickinson through her correspondence with Susan and others, especially the playful appropriations of textual materials gathered from well-known published authors, indicate that she shared the utilitarian view of textual property that Gere describes.[28]

As implied above, these utilitarian reading and writing practices can further be linked to popular culture through the method of composition Higginson identifies in the preface to the 1890 first edition where he describes Dickinson's poems as participating within the genre Emerson called "'Poetry of the Portfolio'" ("Preface" 13). Barton Levi St. Armand may have been the first scholar to appreciate the implications of Higginson's observation by linking it to Emerson's analysis of the portfolio as a "largely female art form" (*Culture* 5) intimately connected "to the rise of democracy" precisely because the works promoted by such an art do not convey the sealed off and polished structure associated with "mid-Victorian formalism" (4). This lack of finish that makes for open-ended and unstable texts may be thought of as a literary option particularly appealing to women writers who sought to promote utilitarian fluidity by inviting reader intervention in their enigmatic textual bodies. In other words, the portfolio performs both as the unique textual body of a specific author and as a model for reading that invites public intervention in that body. Dickinson might well have drawn on the portfolio genre with the expectation that doing so would stimulate just the kind of reader intervention common in nineteenth-century women's clubs.[29]

In addition to the portfolio tradition and forms of textual circulation practiced in women's clubs, Dickinson would certainly have been familiar with the widely accepted appropriation and transformation of texts encouraged by the keeping of commonplace books, autograph albums, and scrapbooks. This is a point Alexandra Socarides makes in "Rethinking the Fascicles: Dickinson's Writing, Copying, and Binding Practices" where she argues not only that "Dickinson was surrounded by women" who maintained commonplace books and autograph albums, but that "her own methods and decisions must have been at least partially informed by them" (76). What interests me most about Socarides's presentation are her descriptions of the ways American women collected and arranged writing produced by others in a manner reflecting both their own sensibility and their acknowledgment that individual identity is a collective creation. In commonplace books, "contents were most often taken from diverse sources and copied by the owner's hand" (71); autograph albums "were always blank books into which the compiler, as well as friends and family, copied prose, poetry, and drawings" (72); scrapbooks included elements of both previous forms of collection: "the scrapbook maker often varied her process, sometimes copying, but more often clipping and pasting" (76). All three of these methods are fragmentary in nature, frequently including within the compilation process written and printed matter distantly removed from the printed text of the legally established author and not treated as if governed by copyright law. In *The Scrapbook in American Life*, Susan Tucker, Katherine Ott, and Patricia P. Buckler make the important observation that "'no scrapbook can present meaning without the collaboration of a reader, yet no reader (aside from the scrapbook maker) can know enough to interpret it authentically and definitively'" (qtd. in Socarides 77). This is to say that these methods of textual collection exist so that the organizer or compiler can collaborate with readers through a limited process of circulation in the course of which the meaning intended by the owner is immediately transformed by readers. Such a process of circulation is possible because participants understood texts not as timeless works of art that forever bear the imprint of a distinct authorial body but rather as expressions of ideas already in circulation that acquire additional significance through engagement with the many particulars of the world experienced by the reader.

Socarides's analysis builds on the work of other scholars who have also been intrigued by the potential influence these popular traditions of assemblage and circulation may have had on reader engagement with Dickinson's writing. St. Armand was the first to connect Dickinson's manuscript compositions with the scrapbook tradition when he identified Dickinson's practice of attaching clippings to her manuscript poems and letters in *Emily Dickinson and Her Culture* (26). He even conjectured that Dickinson kept a scrapbook that has "long since disappeared." In the absence of this work, St. Armand recommends looking to the scrapbook of one of Dickinson's closest friends, Mary Warner.[30] Doing so, he asserts, will open our eyes to "the ephemerality of our own tastes, the elitism of our own judgments, the failings of our own popular prejudices" (31). Martha Nell Smith has also done important early work with scrapbook features of Dickinson's manuscripts, noting in *Rowing in Eden* that Dickinson "did not regard works as untouchably sacred" and "sometimes went so far as to cut up others' works to take an illustration or group of words to append to her own" (52). The result, Smith argues, has profound implications for how we understand Dickinson's texts: "Imagining readers who interact with works to produce texts, . . . does not put anxiety over or battles for meaning center stage, but spotlights the meaning producing processes of give and take between author and text, text and reader, reader and author, inevitable in reading." This give and take acquires a distinctly physical dimension when texts are understood as part of an ongoing circulation of ideas dependent on readers who actively inflect meaning according to their own bodily experience.

Viewing Dickinson's textual fluidity as an invitation to reader intervention consistent with writing and reading practices established within nineteenth-century women's culture can be extraordinarily helpful in explaining the physical alterations that have come to define the historical development of Dickinson's manuscript compositions. With the understanding that Dickinson's approach to manuscript composition was moving away from the model of the book toward increasingly direct forms of engagement with readers that ultimately situate poems on found scraps and documents designed for other purposes, we can read "The sacred Closet when you sweep –" as a poem that exposes the perils of aspiring to a publicly prescribed form of privacy while also inviting the reader's physical intervention in the text. Probably composed around 1875, during the third stage of manuscript production, it provides a marvelous illustration of the way Dickinson used material features to illuminate the arbitrary character of corporeal textual boundaries and the reading expectations fostered by them (see figure 8).

That sacred Closet when you sweep –
Entitled "Memory" –
Select a reverential Broom –
And do it silently –

'Twill be a Labor of surprise –
Besides Identity
Of other Interlocutors
A probability –

August the Dust of that Domain –
Unchallenged – let it lie –
You cannot supersede itself,
But it can silence you.

By directing attention to "other Interlocutors" within the memory of the woman who is on the verge of sweeping her "sacred Closet," the poem alerts us to the presence of muted voices that were more prominent within a preexisting self out of which the present self seeks to extract a less-cluttered and unruly identity. In this regard, the speaker serves as a complement to the speaker of "Ended, ere it begun –" who witnessed the silencing of voices that accompanied publication. In this poem, though, the speaker owns up to the process of becoming owned by the public version of female experience that determines what is intelligible and worth preserving. The poem also reiterates the presence of unrevealed stories that are somehow familiar but silenced by the domestic self.

One objective of the poem, then, is to challenge the positive cultural valuation of female privacy by revealing that culturally condoned privacy is in reality a public act; that in truth women's "privacy" performs an essential public and political function by removing half the human population from direct competition within the male-dominated marketplace. Stacey Margolis's observation about the highly valued but ultimately destructive force of privacy in nineteenth-century sentimental culture applies directly to the aims of this and the other Dickinson poems that I have been examining in this chapter: "This 'sacred discourse' which sanctifies privacy and intimacy, serves ultimately to disguise or make more palatable the power that is always at work in these supposedly 'protected' places" (13). Read in the light of these remarks, "That sacred Closet" illuminates the surrender of female sovereignty perpetuated through the pursuit of culturally prescribed domestic privacy. Just as the speaker in "To my quick ear the Leaves – conferred –" found herself exposed when seeking refuge in a cave, the sweeping woman in this poem will discover that even the isolated space of her mental closet requires conformity to public norms.

The choice Dickinson presents her readers in "That sacred Closet" is to accept or reject the advice offered by the speaker who advocates that the "August" dust of memory be preserved. In terms of the extended metaphor that figures the mind as a house within which dust collects in a particular closet, the speaker can be understood as saying that the mind is best served by what amounts to bad housekeeping. Such unorthodox advice challenges readers to consider the possibility that domestic habits as primary, practical, and seemingly self-evident as the removal of dust may in fact be harmful to the intellectual development of the sweeper. The speaker's awareness that this advice is likely to be met with resistance is reflected in her sequence of aggressive and insistent commands. Opening with a reference to "you," in the clause "when you sweep" that appears in the first line, and closing with a second and last reference to "you" in the last line ("it can silence you"), the poem reads as a series of directives. The reader is instructed to "Select," "do it silently," and "let it lie." Despite the somewhat rebellious objective of letting the dust "lie," a degree of submission to proper domestic hygiene is presented as inevitable. The first observation—that the reader will indeed sweep—indicates that the impulse to sweep is inescapable; from this point to the end of the poem, the speaker is concerned with the nature of the sweeping, not whether it will take place. This is important because it defines the reader as a domestic American female habituated to housekeeping and does not assail that attribute of female identity. Instead, the speaker draws attention to other voices that might also shape that identity: "Besides Identity / Of other Interlocutors / a probability – ." Crucially, the question of other interlocutors, other voices, remains open; these are what the reader must provide. It is at this stage of the poem that the reader must decide if her memory houses the "other Interlocutors" that the speaker sees as probably but not certainly present. If the reader concludes in the affirmative, she is then in the position of accepting or rejecting the speaker's advice.

Dickinson's final stanza then makes the point that if such "Interlocutors" exist, they should be left alone. Her speaker's point is that the dust that threatens the cleanliness of the house is equated with the unruliness of the self that stands in tension with the mental conduct of a proper housekeeper. The final two lines, "You cannot supercede itself, / But it can silence you," require that the reader agree with the speaker that the complete self, or the true "you," is composed of these other voices that exceed containment within the tidy confines of domestic identity. If the speaker proves convincing, and the reader chooses to preserve the dust of memory, she does so by evaluating something that is not contained in the poem: the aspects of her own self that correspond to the speaker's "other Interlocutors" but that register in her own mind and body, not that of the speaker. As a device constructed with the aim of opening the reader's eyes to her own experience so that she will resist erasure of that experience, the poem becomes effectively absorbed by the reader, forming an intrinsic component of the self the reader affirms through an assertion of sovereignty predicated on that self.

The dimension of the poem manuscript that most materially opposes submission to cultural codes of privacy is its presentation of script that climbs up the right-hand margin and runs upside down across the top of the page (see figure 8). The following observation by Hubbard applies to this aspect of the poem: whenever "the reader must literally turn the page—must switch from reading down the vertical axis to reading along the horizontal axis" the reading experience becomes part of "Dickinson's commentary on the material conditions of signification" (35). The consequence is that in this particular poem the reader's experience of reading enacts the challenge the speaker poses for the sweeper. Just as the speaker wishes the sweeper to depart from conventional domestic practice by listening to the marginalized "Interlocutors" of her memory and not sweeping, so also the poem asks that readers suspend judgment of its departure from conventional scriptural practice and instead listen not only for their own marginalized voices, but for those cultural voices that have been silenced through a codification of publishing practices that have overly determined reading behavior by making it subservient to books, the printed page, and the isolated textual body.

By taking seriously Mitchell's observation that "the visual characteristics of Dickinson's handwriting are not determinate" (*Monarch* 227), we can more fully appreciate the role we as readers play in the creation of poetic meaning.[31] The inevitable result of such an undertaking is a much less encumbered reading experience, one founded on respect for the unique qualities of the textual body as a stimulus to voicing possibilities that are at once more individualized and more public. By "public" I mean that poems seek to represent more accurately the experiences of actual readers through the publication and circulation of stories incommensurate with conventional literary types. One of the messages delivered by "That sacred Closet" is that as readers and authors collaborate through less determined, unorthodox reading experiences reading itself becomes a dialogic "Labor of surprise" out of which reader and author create new expressions of shared and hence public forms of literary meaning. In this way the *vox populi* is enriched by an elevation of individual voices that defies the undemocratic notion that authors can be the sole owners of literary property.

Reading Emily Dickinson as a poet who seeks to liberate the many cultural voices silenced by the body-as-property metaphor that served the legal aims of possessive individualism can have significant implications for the way she is understood in relationship to her moment in history. Initially, it means that we can begin to conceptualize her withdrawal from the public eye as a measure she was willing to take not only because it suited her emotional disposition, but because doing so allowed her more deliberately to address aesthetic concerns central to the perpetuation of democratic society. More important, her presentation of the logical inconsistencies within legal definitions of private and public experience that serve to exclude voices from print publication suggests that for her literary labor within the home could be conceived of as even more public than print publication.

But the feature of her writing that surfaces with greatest force when viewed as part of an effort to make writing more democratic, is the way that her manuscript compositions so clearly defy containment within the legal category of private property. Her dedication to unsettling the textual body, and by that means breaking down boundaries between self and other, makes her poetry a kind of self-destructing artifact that continually takes new form as it is consumed by her readers. That her efforts to promote a more utilitarian circulation of textual property position her in the company of other Americans who similarly sought to achieve a greater circulation of ideas is also important, as it allows for a greater appreciation of her status as a writer whose philosophical approach to copyright shows that she engaged in a major nineteenth-century debate within which such well-known figures as Thomas Jefferson and Noah Webster took opposing sides. At the same time, the most-enduring benefit of reading Dickinson as a democratic writer may be that doing so allows us to see her textual innovations as the deliberate incorporation of literary practices already established within a vital female literary culture that regularly violated the sanctity of the published textual body by dismantling, redistributing, and incorporating it in works of their own creation. If through her work we are better able to appreciate the democratic voices of her literate sisters, then she will have served to make the presence of female resistance to socially expedient forms of female silence even more central to our understanding of nineteenth-century culture. In this way, then, Dickinson will have helped to reveal the stories of female readers and writers that may have been titled and even prefaced but that all too often "Ended, ere [they] begun – ."

Appendix

A Preliminary List of Poems with Spiritualist Implications

Fr 124, "Safe in their Alabaster Chambers –"
Fr 132, "Just lost, when I was saved!"
Fr 212, "A transport one cannot contain"
Fr 229, "Musicians wrestle everywhere –"
Fr 274, "Again – his voice is at the door –"
Fr 285, "The Love a Life can show Below"
Fr 292, "I got so I could take his name –"
Fr 293, "A single Screw of Flesh"
Fr 306, "A Shady friend – for Torrid days –"
Fr 307, "A solemn thing – it was – I said –"
Fr 313, "You see I cannot see – your lifetime –"
Fr 331, "The only Ghost I ever saw"
Fr 337, "Of nearness to her sundered Things"
Fr 340, "I felt a Funeral, in my Brain,"
Fr 341, " 'Tis so appalling – it exhilirates –"
Fr 342, "How noteless Men, and Pleiads, stand,"
Fr 407, "One need not be a Chamber – to be Haunted –"
Fr 428, "We grow accustomed to the Dark –"
Fr 430, "A Charm invests a face"
Fr 479, "Because I could not stop for Death –"
Fr 498, "I lived on Dread –"
Fr 515, "There is a pain – so utter –"
Fr 518, "When I was small, a Woman died –"
Fr 584, "We dream – it is good we are dreaming –"
Fr 591, "I heard a Fly buzz – when I died –"

Fr 630, "The Soul's Superior instants"
Fr 739, "Joy to have merited the Pain –"
Fr 767, "One Blessing had I than the rest"
Fr 773, "Conscious am I in my Chamber –"
Fr 868, "Fairer through Fading – as the Day"
Fr 902, "Too little way the House must lie"
Fr 964, "Like Men and Women Shadows walk"
Fr 976, "Besides this May"
Fr 1004, "There is no Silence in the Earth – so silent"
Fr 1052, "It was not Saint – it was too large –"
Fr 1074, "What did They do since I saw Them?"
Fr 1129, "I fit for them – I seek the Dark"
Fr 1176, "Nature affects to be sedate"
Fr 1218, "The Bone that has no Marrow,"
Fr 1342, "No man saw awe, nor to his house"
Fr 1380, "The last of Summer is Delight –"
Fr 1391, "I sued the News – yet feared – the News"
Fr 1400, "The worthlessness of Earthly things"
Fr 1433, "What mystery pervades a well!"
Fr 1437, "Shame is the shawl of Pink"
Fr 1455, "Perhaps they do not go so far"
Fr 1513, "'Tis whiter than an Indian Pipe –"
Fr 1524, "Could that sweet Darkness where they dwell"
Fr 1530, "Facts by our side are never sudden"
Fr 1537, "'And with what Body do the come'?"
Fr 1555, "The Life that tied too tight escapes"
Fr 1586, "Image of Light, Adieu –"
Fr 1592, "Cosmopolites without a plea"
Fr 1612, "Witchcraft was hung, in History,"
Fr 1627, "The Spirit lasts – but in what mode –"

Notes

Introduction

1. Jack Capps's study of Dickinson's reading supports the idea that her knowledge of periodical literature enabled her to remain conversant with social and political events: "Even though books were the principal means by which Emily Dickinson extended her horizons, most of her knowledge of the detail and action in a world thus discovered came through her habitual reading of periodicals" (128). Capps states that the Dickinson family subscribed to and read the following six publications: the *Springfield Republican,* the *Hampshire and Franklin Express,* the *Amherst Record, Harper's New Monthly Magazine, Scribner's Monthly,* and the *Atlantic Monthly.*

2. R. McKinley Ormsby provides an interesting contrast to Edward Dickinson in his 1860 *History of the Whig Party.* In that work, Ormsby, unlike Edward Dickinson, openly expresses profoundly racist views (359) that contribute to what can only be described as a hatred for abolitionists. What he shares with Dickinson is his fear of sectional factions and a desire to preserve the union (358). Comparing Ormsby with Dickinson is helpful in establishing the range of political perspectives accommodated within the Whig party.

3. For good summaries of the political and civic lives of the Dickinson men, see Betsy Erkkila ("Class" 1–2), Cynthia C. Wolff (545–546n45), and Domhnall Mitchell (*Monarch* 62–63).

4. The symbol, "Fr," refers to the 1998 edition of Dickinson's poems, *The Poems of Emily Dickinson: Variorum Edition,* edited by R. W. Franklin. The numbers following "Fr" indicate the number Franklin assigned the poems. In all references to poems, I will also include the entire first line or key words from that line so that the reader can locate the poem in alternative editions.

5. See also the contrary perspectives evident in later poems such as "My country need not change her gown" (Fr 1540C) and "My Wars are laid away in Books –" (Fr 1579).

6. Unless otherwise indicated, all references to Dickinson's letters refer to the Thomas H. Johnson and Theodora Ward edition, *The Letters of Emily Dickinson.* Ci-

tations for this edition appear with a capital *"L"* followed by the Johnson and Ward page number, as in (*L* 687).

7. Marietta Messmer provides an insightful discussion of Dickinson's refusal to accept female reform efforts as part of a "more and more explicit resistance to the roles prescribed by the discourses of domesticity and orthodox Congregationalism" (74).

8. See also the contradictory positions Dickinson assumes in relation to that most iconic of American political figures, George Washington (*L* 319 and *L* 849), and her shifting and at times apparently unconscionable attitudes toward Irish immigrants (*L* 113 and *L* 827).

9. Like Messmer, Erkkila acknowledges Dickinson's rejection of "the middle-class notion of woman's writing as an extension of woman's domestic work" ("Emily Dickinson and Class" 19–20), but concludes that in doing so Dickinson adheres to "an essentially aristocratic and Carlylean notion of literature as the production of mind and genius for eternity" (20). Paula Bernat Bennett steadfastly privileges the conservative dimension of Dickinson's response to female reform: "for all its seeming libratory character, this double-sided poetics left traditional gender roles intact and Dickinson batting irresolutely between them" ("American women poet peers" 218). Mitchell also affirms that "Dickinson's writing can be seen as a site of political resistance and reaction," while concluding, "it is difficult to accept the image of Dickinson as a champion of *women's* rights because there is so little direct evidence that she had any sympathy whatsoever for the plight of other women" ("Emily Dickinson and Class" 195). Even though I agree that there is a pronounced conservative strain in Dickinson's writing, I also insist that the liberal strain is equally present. The position Mitchell articulates at the end of *Emily Dickinson: Monarch of Perception* is in line with the view I advocate (though it does differ from the position he asserts in the above passage): "No matter how much Dickinson sought to claim a patent on her language, she inevitably includes an alternative network of interpretive possibilities. The result is a diversity of voices, which includes preferences different from, and even opposite to, her monarch of perception" (257).

10. In *Inflections of the Pen,* I argue that Dickinson "provides conflicting perspectives that the reader is then obliged to resolve, if indeed resolution is desired" (52).

11. In *Inflections of the Pen,* I also draw attention to capitalization, line breaks, and other features of the text, as they appear in both print and manuscript formats. Here, I concentrate on the dashes alone, not because I think they operate in isolation from other significant features, but because I want to be as efficient as possible in making a focused point about multiple voices.

12. I provide an explanation of Dickinson's dialogic poetry in relation to Bakhtinian theory in *Inflection of the Pen,* 175n6. Mitchell also argues in support of Dickinson's dialogic poetry in *Emily Dickinson: Monarch of Perception,* when he acknowledges her departure from the monologic propensity Bakhtin links to lyric poetry in "Discourse and the Novel": "In my view," Mitchell writes, "Dickinson's work is pervaded with other voices and vocabularies, which suggest that it comes closer to

Bakhtin's definition of the dialogic imagination as this is manifested in *prose* discourse" (229). Messmer makes the case that Dickinson's correspondence also displays dialogic features (141–143).

13. I should mention here that this particular prose fragment has attracted much scholarly interest. Erika Scheurer may be the first to connect the passage to Bakhtinian dialogics, when she quotes it in the opening of her 1995 essay, " 'Near, but remote': Emily Dickinson's Epistolary Voice." Scheurer goes on to describe "Dickinson's literary project" as a "project that is realized in her quintessentially dialogic voice" (87). I refer to the passage in *Inflections of the Pen* in relation to both prose and poetry. Most recently, Messmer alludes to this prose fragment in her 2001 book, *A Vice for Voices: Reading Emily Dickinson's Correspondences,* in which she states her aim of throwing "into relief the complexity of [Dickinson's] epistolary art, including dialogic polyvocality as well as the high degree of performativity within her texts" (18).

14. W. C. Harris writes that "the slogan *e pluribus unum* was finally adopted as a national motto in 1872" (202). In *E Pluribus Unum: Nineteenth-Century American Literature and the Constitutional Paradox,* Harris examines the way American writers like Poe, Whitman, and Melville actively addressed the constitutional problem of uniting the one and the many. Harris makes an argument similar to mine when he states, "Constructing the relation of the many to the one, whether in terms of the relation between the states and the Union or between the individual citizen and something like a ruling principle of citizenship, is a preoccupation of the American text" (6–7). For Dickinson, choice plays a crucial role within the citizen's democratic duty to assert the sovereign self and therefore sustain a tension between the one and the many that ensures the one will make a distinct contribution to the many. As I explain in chapters 4 and 5, the distinct contribution of the individual may be absorbed by the many, making fame "Too intrinsic for Renown."

15. In *Class Structure in the Social Consciousness,* S. Ossowski cites the classic example of "classless but non-egalitarian society" as "the community of Athenian citizens . . . portrayed in Pericles' speech of 431 B.C." (99). Ossowski explains the form such "non-egalitarian classlessness" took in America: "Civic equality, which is a tenet of the American Creed, is supposed to be based on such classlessness, and not on a leveling-out of social status or income. Each citizen has equal rights and in a certain sense equal opportunities to aspire to lower or higher positions. It is assumed that inequalities of economic or social status are determined not by class affiliation but by personal qualifications, but nobody denies the existence of these inequalities" (107). As I make clear in chapter 1, like many Americans in the nineteenth century Dickinson may or may not have consciously registered all the class differences that appear rather striking to modern readers, even while she demonstrated a dedication to democratic values.

16. Kerber clearly states that the practice of locating female politics in the domestic sphere that was so central to Republican Motherhood was not restricted to the late eighteenth or early nineteenth centuries: "From the time of the Revolution until our own day, the language of Republican Motherhood remains the most readily

accepted—though certainly not the most radical—justification for women's political behavior" (12).

17. John Stuart Mill also emphasizes the importance of choice in *On Liberty:* "The human faculties of perception, judgment, discriminative feeling, mental activity, and even moral preference, are exercised only in making a choice. He who does anything because it is the custom, makes no choice. He gains no practice either in discerning or in desiring what is best" (105). Mill's words help establish the fact that a concern with choice was very much in the air at the time Dickinson was writing.

18. Definitions of democracy are useful in clarifying a generally accepted understanding of the term, but do not convey the broad range of public opinion that surrounded the slow and often contentious implementation of democratic principles that characterized the early years of the Republic and the nineteenth century. In *Sentimental Democracy,* Andrew Burstein provides a wonderfully helpful overview of the hopes and fears attached to the idea of democracy during this period (143–153). Writing specifically of the phrase "We the people," he explains one source of broad agreement that united the framers of the Constitution: "Democracy was meant to indicate a constitutional delegation of power that technically belonged to the people—the meaning of the term 'popular sovereignty'" (145). At the same time, the prospect of handing power over to the people sparked such fears of anarchy or *"mobocracy"* (248) that widespread acceptance of the framer's intentions would be a long time coming. "It would be some time yet," Burstein affirms, "before *democracy* ceased to arouse fears of 'democratic' tyranny" (147). Tocqueville's account of the spread of democracy in America reveals a similar discrepancy between the assertion and the realization of democratic ideals. Having declared that the "social state of the Americans is eminently democratic" (50), and that the Americans are "more nearly equally powerful, than any other country of the world" (56), he immediately qualifies these remarks by describing the grudging acceptance of democracy by the upper classes following the Revolution: "It was not even permissible to struggle against it any longer. So the upper classes submitted without complaint or resistance to an evil which had by then become inevitable" (59). Tocqueville tellingly follows this acknowledgment of persistent class difference with the prediction that changes in voting laws already undertaken have opened the door to a future expansion of suffrage: "Once a people begins to interfere with the voting qualification, one can be sure that sooner or later it will abolish it altogether." These comments tell us that for Tocqueville full introduction of popular sovereignty was fraught with uncertainty and achieved by degree in the face of public resistance.

19. Scholars regularly argue that the introduction of popular sovereignty is a logical impossibility. Edmund Morgan acknowledges the logical difficulties of achieving popular sovereignty, but argues that it performs as a useful fiction: "the sovereignty of the people, like the divine right of kings, and like representation itself, is a fiction that cannot survive too close an examination" (256). F. R. Ankersmit expands on the role of imagination as integral to the aesthetics of government: "To put it metaphorically, when a population unfolds itself into a group of people that is represented and

another group of people representing the former one, legitimate political power wells up, so to speak, in the hollow between the two groups. Hence, the origin of all legitimate political power must be situated in the aesthetic gap between voter and representative (state). This would justify, to begin with, the probably amazing and certainly unorthodox conclusion that *in a representative democracy all legitimate political power is essentially aesthetic*" (118).

Commenting specifically on the problem of sovereignty in America, Harold Laski bluntly declares that sovereignty has no role at all: "A peculiar historical experience has . . . devised the means of building a State from which the conception of sovereignty is absent" (49).

20. The *OED* defines "consent" as, "The action of granting; the thing granted." This focus on the act of "granting" draws attention to the deliberate and conscious element of consent that implies choice on the part of the individual granter.

21. Hooker's distinction between positive and implicit consent, or what has been described here as immediate or ongoing consent, is effectively captured in John Locke's discussion of consent in his influential "Second Treatise of Government": "For when any number of men have, by the consent of every individual, made a community, they have thereby made that community one body, with a power to act as one body, which is only by the will and determination of the majority. For that which acts [for] any community, being only the consent of the individuals of it, and it being necessary to that which is one body to move one way; it is necessary the body should move that way whither the greater force carries it, which is the consent of the majority: or else it is impossible it should act or continue one body, one community, which the consent of every individual that united into it, agreed that it should; and so everyone is bound by that consent to be concluded by the majority" (163).

22. Dickinson's approach to liberty is consistent with the general demand for vigilance in maintaining individual freedoms conveyed by John Stuart Mill in *On Liberty*: "There is a limit to the legitimate interference of collective opinion with individual independence: and how to find that limit, and maintain it against encroachment, is as indispensable to a good condition of human affairs, as protection against political despotism" (14).

Chapter 1

1. As recently as May 24, 2003, Harold Bloom has written that "Emerson remains the central figure in American culture, informing our "politics, as well as our unofficial religion" (5). In *Individualism and Its Discontents: Appropriations of Emerson, 1880–1950*, Charles M. Mitchell effectively outlines the terms of the debate over Emerson's politics, especially in his introduction (1–11). T. Gregory Garvey's *The Emerson Dilemma: Essays on Emerson and Social Reform* specifically addresses the range of scholarly interpretations that inform the arguments of Sacvan Bercovitch and John Carlos Rowe that I touch on later in this chapter.

2. I am not overlooking Agnieszka Salska's excellent book *Walt Whitman and*

Emily Dickinson: Poetry of the Central Consciousness in which her opening chapter is titled "Whitman, Dickinson, and American Literary Individualism." Salska's focus, however, is not on the political implications of Emersonian individualism and its influence on Dickinson. As the following passage indicates, Salska is more interested in Dickinson's dedication to the private self: "Dickinson denied the relevance of the social self for man's spiritual biography. Just as in her daily life she almost gave up relations with the external world, she cut off the public aspect of the self because it seemed distracting" (21). Valerie Ann DeBrava's 2001 dissertation, "Authorship and Individualism in American Literature," is also worth mentioning as a possible exception to scholarly neglect. My comments here relate to Dickinson's absence in the many books and scholarly articles that have looked at the politics of individualism in nineteenth-century American literature.

3. Betsy Erkkila and Domhnall Mitchell have both published influential works that charge Dickinson with apolitical elitism. I discuss their positions in what follows.

4. For an excellent description of the political atmosphere of the Dickinson family home, see Coleman Hutchison's "'Eastern Exiles': Dickinson, Whiggery, and War" (7–10) and the "House Politics" section of Erkkila's essay "Dickinson and the Art of Politics" (138–144).

5. For good summaries of the political and civic lives of the Dickinson men, see Erkkila ("Class" 1–2), Wolff (545–546n45), and Mitchell (*Monarch* 62–63).

6. John Stuart Mill's midcentury comments on individuality in *On Liberty* provide a useful supplement to Tocqueville and Emerson by conveying both the positive benefits of individualism and the curbs on personal liberty necessary to ensure a balance of individual and collective interests: "As it is useful that while mankind are imperfect there should be different opinions, so is it that there should be different experiments of living; that free scope should be given to varieties of character, short of injury to others; and that the worth of different modes of life should be proved practically, when any one thinks fit to try them. It is desirable, in short, that in things which do not primarily concern others, individuality, should assert itself" (101–102).

7. Capps provides evidence that Emerson's prose as well as his poetry were visible influences on Dickinson (113–119). He also points out that Dickinson received an 1847 edition of Emerson's *Poems* from Benjamin Newton when she was nineteen (113). Lena Koski points out that Newton was a law student who worked in Edward Dickinson's law office "from 1847 to late 1849" and that he was one of Dickinson's early teachers (209). Koski usefully summarizes Newton's role, drawing particular attention to Dickinson's 1854 letter to Edward Everett Hale in which Dickinson described Newton as "teaching me what to read" as well as "what authors to admire."

8. For a good general overview of individualism, particularly in relation to Emerson, see Bercovitch's *The Rites of Assent*, especially 308–346. John Carlos Rowe makes Emerson's influence the central focus of his study in *At Emerson's Tomb: The Politics of Classic American Literature*. In that work, he concentrates on the Emer-

sonian tradition of *"aesthetic dissent"* that he defines as, "the romantic idealist assumption that rigorous reflection on the processes of thought and representation
constitutes in itself a critique of social reality and effects a transformation of the
naïve realism that confuses truth with social convention" (1). In what follows, I treat
Rowe's concern with the psychological focus of Emersonian dissent as part of the
often-remarked tendency within individualism to elevate the interior, private, and
ahistorical over the exterior, public, and historical. Accordingly, I take the position
that when Rowe objects of Emerson's writings that they "represent an internal contra-
dictoriness between the anticommunal, ahistorical aspects of his philosophy and the
demand he placed upon that philosophy to effect social reform" (40), Rowe is also objecting to that expression of American individualism for which Emerson is the leading exponent.

9. In *Individualism and Its Discontents,* Mitchell makes clear the extent that
Emerson is at the heart of ongoing debates over the politics of individualism: "If, as
I believe, Emerson is the most articulate and representative expounder of American
individualism, it is because his own work so clearly reflects the contradictions and
paradoxes inherent in democratic individuality. In the over one hundred years since
his death, Emerson has been claimed by back-to-the-landers and industrial capital-
ists, Nietzche and Nike footwear" (3). Mitchell explains that Emerson's currency is the
result of the fact that "Emerson confronted in his own work the issues that were and
remain at the core of American democracy." Bloom echoes Mitchell's comments on
the broad political applicability of Emerson's thought when he describes the "paradox
of Emerson's influence" as the emergence of "Peace Marchers and Bushians alike"
who qualify equally as "Emerson's heirs" (5). Today, Bloom notes, America has "Emer-
sonians of the left (the post-pragmatist Richard Rorty) and of the right (a swarm of
libertarian Republicans, who exalt President Bush the second)" (4).

10. A full account of all the monarchical terms mentioned in the previous two
sentences gives a further sense of the way these terms proliferate in the poems: variants of "royal" appear twenty-two times (Rosenbaum 636); variants of "crown" appear twenty-seven times (162); variants of "queen" appear nineteen times (605); and
variants of "emperor" appear eight times (222).

11. See 99–104 in *Representational Democracy.* In these pages Ankersmit spells out
what he means about the ways continental and American forms of democracy differ
over the role of absolute authority. The following passage represents his general position: "In contrast to continental democracies, in Anglo-Saxon democracy the absolute monarch is still present insofar as the possession of political power and having
an absolute majority in the representative body go together there" (102).

12. For a full account of Hamilton's presentation, see Madison's notes in volume
1 of *The Records of the Federal Convention of 1787,* edited by Max Farrand, 281–293.

13. Jefferson clearly accuses Hamilton of monarchism in his January 8, 1825, letter to William Stott. See Appleby and Ball, *Jefferson: Political Writings,* 462.

14. In his October 28, 1813, letter to John Adams, Jefferson first affirms that "there
is a natural aristocracy among men" and then asserts, "that that form of government

is best, which provides the most effectually for a pure selection of the natural aristoi into the offices of government" (Appleby and Ball 187).

15. See Davidson's "Literacy, Education, and the Reader" chapter (55–79) in *Revolution and the Word*.

16. Robert Dahl points out in *After the Revolution* that a failure to accurately associate "the people" of democratic discourse with the actual populations supposedly represented has been a familiar feature of writing about democracy. "Strange as it may seem to you," he writes, "how to decide who legitimately make up 'the people'—or rather *a* people—and hence are entitled to govern themselves in their *own* association is a problem almost totally neglected by all the great political philosophers who write about democracy" (46). See also 64–65.

17. Tocqueville's most famous statement about equality in America comes in the opening sentence of his "Author's Introduction" to the first volume of *Democracy in America:* "No novelty in the United States struck me more vividly during my stay there than the equality of conditions" (9). Writing specifically of New England, Tocqueville states, "the colony came more and more to present the novel phenomenon of a society homogeneous in all its parts" (39). Of the United States at the time he viewed it, he notes, "the last traces of hereditary ranks and distinctions have been destroyed" (54). He concludes his commentary on equality in "Social State of the Anglo-Americans" with these words: "Men there are nearer equality in wealth and mental endowments, or, in other words, more nearly equally powerful, than in any other country of the world or in any other age of recorded history" (56).

18. In "Hawthorne and His Mosses," Melville writes of the need to create a literary supremacy that will match the global political supremacy that he anticipates for America in the near future: "While we are rapidly preparing for the political supremacy among the nations . . . in a literary point of view, we are deplorably unprepared for it" (248). There are also numerous passages where Melville expresses disdain for a public incapable of comprehending literary genius (240, 244–247, 251).

19. Whitman also discusses the "Supremes" in his 1855 preface to *Leaves of Grass.* There he speaks for "great poets" as he invites "each man and woman" to "Come to us on equal terms" (14). He clearly promotes what might be thought of as democratic access to the sphere of the Supremes, but he persists in using hierarchical language. For instance, he urges individual recognition of "supremacy within" and mastery "of nature and passion and death, and of all terror and pain" (14–15). In language of this kind, Whitman distinguishes between the equality of access and the inequality of achievement, so that greatness is invested with qualities of the divine. The link to an aristocratic past is further established when, in the next paragraph, he writes of "American bards" who "shall not be careful of riches and privilege . . . they shall be riches and privilege" (15).

20. Erkkila forthrightly asserts that Dickinson's use of monarchical language places her in direct opposition to the democratic aims of those writers Matthiessen discusses in this work: "Dickinson returned to a pre-Revolutionary and aristocratic language of rank, titles, and divine right to assert the sovereignty of her self as ab-

solute monarch. Not only does she set herself against what F. O. Matthiessen calls 'the possibilities of democracy' invoked by other writers of her age (ix), but at a time when a woman, Victoria, was the queen of England, Dickninson's royalist language also bears witness to the political irony that it is under an aristocratic order of hereditary and divine right rather than under a democratic order of contract and inalienable rights that a woman was entitled to political power and to rule" ("Class" 15–16).

21. In "Her Own Society: An Acrostic for Emily," Alicia Ostriker elegantly clarifies the way the opening lines of Dickinson's poem, especially the words "divine Majority," establish Dickinson's concern with politics: "Emily reproduces, rhythmically, the careful intentionality of selection and its / Conclusion. / Then she brings politics into it, but sideways. Divinely, / 'Soul' outvotes all opposition. Majority rules. Soul as majority? How improbable!" (18).

22. I provide a detailed discussion of the relationship Dickinson's dashes have with voice and speaker in *Inflections of the Pen: Dash and Voice in Emily Dickinson*, especially 14–23. Also see my essay on "Dickinson's Dialogic Voice" in *The Emily Dickinson Handbook*.

23. The linking of sun and noon with male power has been well established in Dickinson criticism. The most-famous example appears in Dickinson's June 1852 letter to Susan Huntington Gilbert where she describes married life in terms of flowers submitting to the "man of noon" and appearing "with their heads bowed in anguish before the mighty sun" (*L* 210). See also my discussion of this letter in *Inflections of the Pen* (25; 119–120).

24. James R. Guthrie presents the only other extensive reading of this poem in "Darwinian Dickinson: The Scandalous Rise and Noble Fall of the Common Clover." In his carefully mounted Darwinian analysis, Guthrie arrives at a set of conclusions very different from mine. Where I propose that the poem is designed for a skeptical readership who questions the achievements of the "Purple Democrat," Guthrie concludes that her progress is on the whole admirable, despite her somewhat scandalous beginnings. His reading frames the "Purple Democrat" in terms that neatly conform to achievement as defined by capitalist individualism: "Dickinson presents her as someone who rises within a class-bound social hierarchy by dint of her own merits, rendering her comparable to an upwardly mobile business woman who has shown herself to be particularly adept at managing her clientele" (83). As will become increasingly clear, my reading treats the poem as riddled with irony and far less transparent than Guthrie would have us believe.

25. This facsimile of the first edition presentation of the poem appears without the original title in *Emily Dickinson: Collected Poems*, 55–56.

26. Emerson refers to an underlying divine or spiritual order throughout his works. The following passage from *Nature* outlines the way in which the individual gives expression to this order: "behind nature, throughout nature, spirit is present; one and not compound, it does not act upon us from without, that is, in space and time, but spiritually, or through ourselves: therefore that spirit, that is, the Supreme

Being, does not build up nature around us, but puts it forth through us, as the life of the tree puts forth new branches and leaves through the pores of the old" (*Prose and Poetry* 50).

27. Loeffelholz's analysis of this poem in "Etruscan Invitations: Dickinson and the Anxiety of the Aesthetic in Feminist Criticism" looks far more closely at the role of romance and false knowledge than I do. Her essay is well worth reading for this reason and for the care with which she situates her analysis within the context of feminist theory and criticism.

28. If the speaker here is viewed as male, then he would have to be an emasculated and thus feminized male who in fact understands his political position as degraded to a state roughly equating with that assigned to women. My reading of the speaker as female in part derives from my belief that doing so makes more sense from a practical point of view than imagining that Dickinson would crate a male speaker for the purpose of feminizing him.

Chapter 2

1. This is not to say that Dickinson ceases to betray her class identity through references to class-based privilege. Indeed, Dickinson's presentation of herself in terms of the robin's secure home in combination with the public display of the phoenix can certainly be interpreted as an expression of class prerogative. My point is that this chapter examines a rhetorical practice that places Dickinson in the company of other writers who sought to promote a fluid democratic self through their writing and therefore represents a feature of her poems that should be considered in addition to class identity.

2. Cmiel provides a helpful definition of what is meant by the concept of "unified soul": "In Aristotle's *Ethics*... the man of virtue is a 'unified soul,' the 'whole body and soul pull him in a single direction, toward restraint.' By the Roman era, Michel Foucault observed, there was a concerted search for a 'morality of style,' a refined way of life that would be 'common to different areas of conduct.' In the classical world, Foucault observed, 'one's ethos was seen by his dress, by his bearing, by his gait, by the poise with which he reacts to events. . . .' Cicero claimed that decorum was 'nothing more than uniform consistency in the course of our life as a whole'" (26). Cmiel concludes by arguing that this focus on consistency in style persisted through the early modern period and began to collapse in the eighteenth century, at which time "*ethos*" began to give way to "*persona*" (27).

3. Elizabeth Petrino's commentary on the roles of robin and queen in "The Robin's my Criterion for Tune –" (Fr 256) provides an illuminating parallel discussion of Dickinson's dedication to the self's role-playing capacity. Petrino focuses on the way Dickinson's speaker, who sees "New Englandly," conflates rural and royal subjectivities: "Seeing 'provincially' therefore applies not only to aspects of her daily, rural life but also to the individual's subjective perspective, leveling social distinctions and elevating the speaker: 'The Queen, discerns like me – / Provincially –'" (202).

4. The following passage conveys the rationale behind Messmer's observation: "Not quite public published documents ('literature') in the conventional sense, the mailed-out letters and letter-poems (especially in the form of double mailings) nonetheless challenge the boundaries of exclusively private missives and become—quite literally—a private form of publication, or a literary form of correspondence" (48). I will explore Messmer's argument in greater detail in chapter 4, where Dickinson's correspondence is examined as her chosen form of literary circulation.

5. Ruttenburg's definition of "personality" is useful for clarifying what she means when she uses the term, as well as establishing its use in this study of Dickinson's democratic writing. Ruttenburg defines "personality" as a historically conditioned balancing act within which "its meanings have consistently encompassed the apparent opposition between individual specificity and general personhood, and between an authentic trait of selfhood (who one is) and a performed or factitious one (how one acts)" (8). In this sense, personality corresponds to the mix of internal and external, conscious and unconscious forces that combine in the conduct of particular people. Personality embraces both deliberate, consciously controlled features of Dickinson's writing and the cultural influences that impinged on her writing without her conscious knowledge.

6. Messmer usefully points out the increased literariness of Dickinson's later letters, where Dickinson "increasingly omits one or both references to date and place" (41). The point I am making here is that even if these coordinates are de-emphasized by Dickinson, they still function as components of the letters in general.

7. I am leaving out Newman's *A Practical System of Rhetoric* because it has not attracted the same level of scholarly interest as have the other three texts. Lowenberg does include a passage from the introduction to Newman's work, however, that tends to support the idea that rhetoric should serve the aims of expressing a distinct personality rather than reinforcing class distinctions: " 'It should ever be impressed upon the student, that, in forming a style, he is to acquire a manner of writing to some extent, *peculiarly his own, and which is to be the index to the modes of his thinking*—the development of his intellectual traits and feelings' " (80). Such a statement would perhaps position Newman with Whately and Parker in opposition to the artificiality of Porter's fixed system of elocutionary marks but does not represent the more radically democratic position Parker espouses when he encourages a rhetoric that can accommodate the spontaneous effusions of the individual genius.

8. Commenting on the centrality of this poem within Dickinson's work, Cynthia Griffin Wolff usefully identifies Dickinson's manner of presenting Jacob's conduct as admirable without at the same time framing that conduct as a pattern of behavior readers could adapt to their own lives: "Jacob's wrestle, conducted as it was face to face, could not show subsequent nations how to fight" (152). Wolff's point is that Dickinson urges her readers to form a gymnastic habit of mind like that modeled by Jacob, a habit characterized by an intellectual willingness to enter the immediate circumstances life offers as arbiters of their own destinies. It is Jacob's wily form of grappling rather than the specific action he takes that is meant to inspire readers: "the

fact that Jacob was an artful strategist is most significant because it can be applied even to our universal plight" (152).

9. Lawrence Buell describes Emerson's understanding of history as functioning like "a key to all mythologies" that reveals "a deep moral-spiritual-ideational coherence to all human history" (*Emerson* 170). Emerson expresses this view in "History," where he writes that "all the facts of history preexist in the mind as laws. Each law in turn is made by circumstances predominant, and the limits of nature give power to but one at a time" (*Prose* 105). He then describes the individual's power to discern a pervasive order in history: "Genius detects through the fly, through the caterpillar, through the grub, through the egg, the constant individual; through countless individuals the fixed species; through many species the genus; through all genera the steadfast type; through all the kingdoms of organized life the eternal unity" (109). In language resembling Emerson's, David S. Reynolds affirms Whitman's dedication to the idealism of progressive science, particularly as expressed by Alexander von Humbolt, that influenced nineteenth-century thought at midcentury: "One thinks especially of the famous Section 5 of 'Song of Myself,' where, after lying on the grass with his soul, the 'I' contemplates the vast creation and then turns his attention to ever-smaller things: the limitless leaves drooping in the fields, the brown ants underground, heaped stones, mullein and pokeweed. For Whitman as for Humbolt, 'cosmos' signified both the order of nature and the centrality of human beings" (*America* 244–245).

10. Agnieszka Salska provides a helpful way of thinking about the interrelationship of Emerson, Whitman, and Dickinson by positioning all three writers within a "dialectic of faith and doubt" that she traces as far back as the period of Puritan settlement (17). Whitman most neatly fits the faith component of the dialectic through his expression of Romantic vision described by M. H. Abrams as a "'fus[ing] history, politics, philosophy and religion into one grand design, by asserting Providence—or some form of natural teleology.'" Salska presents Emerson as besieged by doubt in his private journals but projecting faith in his published essays. Dickinson most fully embodies the doubt component of the dialectic (17–22).

11. Nina Baym draws attention to the double bind faced by women writers who sought to affirm the rising power of women by identifying the political accomplishments of women in the past while also distancing themselves from a male-dominated past. Baym sums up the dilemma women faced as they attempted to locate a usable past: "if women were to figure in history," they would "be entirely unlike prominent men of the past. Indeed, they would also be entirely different from prominent women of the past—but of course there *were* no prominent women of the past! How could there have been, if brute force had always held sway?" (*American Women Writers* 215). Murray and Fuller also struggled with this double bind, but each also found ways of incorporating women from history. Murray, Baym notes, "mined" history "for example of women equally as capable of enduring hardships as men, equally ingenious, resourceful, heroic, brave, patriotic" and so on because she believed that "'in this younger world [America], "the Rights of Women" begin to be understood'" (220, 221). In her analysis of Fuller, Baym observes that one of the primary historical

accomplishments of *Woman in the Nineteenth Century* is that "it catalogs historical women as evidence of what women have always been capable of" (229).

12. Virginia Jackson also discusses the way Dickinson's writing on printed commercial documents anchors the writing in the historical moment: "rather than turning privacy public, her work tended to take all kinds of public and private, artificial and natural materials into the everyday life of a private person" (53). Jackson argues that the pronounced historical contingency of these documents "emphasize[s] our distance from the time and place of her practice—of her culture."

13. Webster's 1828 *American Dictionary of the English Language* defines "manufacturing" as "Making goods and wares from raw materials." The emphasis on "goods" made for public consumption is even clearer in the language used to define "manufacture": "The operation of making cloth, wares, utensils, paper, books, and whatever is used by man."

14. The misdirection identified in "The Suttee" takes place on a small scale, as the poem's superficial deflection of concern with domestic injustice is achieved within the confines of a particular poem. I should acknowledge that what might be thought of as large-scale misdirection also takes place when women writers surround poems offering subversive critiques with poems that are clearly conventional. Sigourney's "Death of an Infant" and "The Mother of Washington" can in this sense be understood as distracting attention from poems like "To a Shred of Linen" that challenge conventional values. Like Dickinson, Sigourney and other women writers presented inconsistent political views that demanded independent thought on the part of readers. But for these other women writers, reader choice did not achieve the central role apparent in Dickinson's writing. Unlike Dickinson, most women writers were compelled to write for a broad audience and therefore were limited in their ability to depart openly from social conformity. For Dickinson, however, politically divergent voices could play a far more prominent role, as she was free to challenge readers directly, without feeling pressured to reach a mass audience or satisfy editorial expectations. This may be one of the main reasons politically divergent points of view are much more visible in individual poems as well as across the body of her writing.

15. The widespread popularity of Sigourney's writing is worth mentioning here as a reminder to modern readers that social commentary was a generally accepted feature of women's writing in the nineteenth century. In *Achievement in American Poetry, 1900–1950*, Louise Bogan describes Sigourney as inhabiting the role of America's "outstanding ... woman 'singer'" for much of the century. Lawrence Buell goes even further in describing Sigourney as the "period's best-selling poet" (*New England Literary Culture* 60).

16. Ostriker further develops her point in language that applies directly to "The Suttee": "Inflated, exclamatory rhetoric is a device employed when a poet is supposed to seem natural and impulsive but is obliged to repress awareness of her body and her ego" (*Stealing* 33).

17. Petrino has usefully argued that in "Found Frozen" Jackson presents the epitaph's failure to convey an accurate sense of the dead woman's life as part of a larger effort by the poet to criticize conventional female roles: "Jackson hints dissatisfaction

with the prescribed role for women when she writes that the woman's family erected 'some common record which they thought was true'… implying that the typical encomium on the deaths of wives and mothers is not equal to the actual experiences of their lives" (192).

18. Petrino points out that "'Found Frozen' might be a new epitaph for the woman's tombstone, since its title evokes many of the Victorian monuments of the dead, which provide a short poetic record of the dead's life or a caption of only a word or two, sometimes with no name" (192). This analysis opens the possibility that the speaker is modeling exemplary behavior, and to a degree she undeniably is. The problem with such a reading is that it assumes the displacement of the epitaph described in the poem, and the speaker provides no reason to believe that her words about the departed will ever appear above a specific grave. Until that happens, the language of the poem remains unhinged from any specific person and thus performs at best as a broad general gesture that has no bearing on concrete historical events. As a model, then, the speaker can only suggest through her incomplete act the sort of conduct that readers must imagine completing for themselves. Unlike Emerson or Whitman, Jackson does not here provide her readers with fully realized acts.

19. This letter is not in Dickinson's hand and therefore subject to any alterations Lyman may have intentionally or unintentionally imposed. See Sewall, *Letters,* 69–71.

20. I would also argue that Dickinson's separation of self and body in the Lyman letter functions in a highly specialized philosophical sense, as Dickinson is referring specifically to her father's impression that "his life has been passed in a wilderness or on an island" (Sewall, *Letters,* 70). The idea that persons are perpetually isolated to some degree or another from others is very different indeed from the politics of liberty that claim only to represent the *effort* to unite the interior self with the external world.

21. I should mention that the poem opens the possibility that the referent for "Thee" is someone who was compelled by law to serve in the military, or who risked imprisonment as a result of participation in military conflict. In such a reading, the speaker could easily be a woman whose lover or brother was killed in war. Such a reading reinforces the general point I make here, which is that the speaker's commendable wish to experience liberty through the redress of worldly injustice does not logically coincide with the voluntary ending of her life.

Chapter 3

1. Mary Loeffelholz provides a valuable analysis of Dickinson's view of nature as cultural construction in *Dickinson and the Boundaries of Feminist Theory.* There she draws attention to Dickinson's "realization that 'Nature,' as such, and the languages drawn from 'her' are—to put it as generally as possible—the creations of human power-relations, or, as we now say, ideologically motivated constructions" (19–20). Of the many Dickinson poems illuminating the discrepancy between social expectation and actual female experience, those dealing with marriage may provide the

starkest examples. "I'm 'wife' – I've finished that –" (Fr 225), "He put the Belt around my life –" (Fr 330), and "She rose to His Requirement – dropt" (Fr 857) are representative of this category of poems.

2. In "Veiled Ladies: Dickinson, Bettine, and Transcendental Mediumship," for example, St. Armand opens by observing of Dickinson that "one of the poses she assumed was that of a spiritualist medium" (1) and goes on to assert that in her "nervousness, her timorousness, her shrinking sensitivity, and her childlike naiveté and simplicity we see all the outstanding symptoms of the typical nineteenth-century female clairvoyant" (8). "By donning the veil of the medium," St. Armand writes, "Dickinson allied herself . . . with other women in the nineteenth century who sought an outlet for their stifled sensitivity and longing for acclaim in the vocation of Spiritualism" (18).

3. St. Armand's assertion of an idealized natural world is clearly conveyed in "Veiled Ladies": "Above the physical creation hovers the spiritual archetype, the Veiled Eidolon, the Platonic Form, that urges the artist onward and upward" (37). According to this construction of the medium, Dickinson, like other mediums, sought to make herself a vehicle for the transmission of eternal truth, thus drawing personal authority from affiliation with cosmic order rather than from personal choice.

4. Lease astutely responds to St. Armand's assertion that Dickinson joined other women who "sought [through Spiritualism] an outlet for their sensitivity," arguing that Dickinson and other women were "less interested in outlets for sensitivity and longing for acclaim than they were in reaching for truths no longer accessible to them . . . within the confines of a male-dominated church" ("'This World'" 49).

5. Higginson declares that he owes much to spiritualism: "It is not a little thing, and if I may speak personally, if there is anything which I owe to spiritualism, it is a more healthy and deep reverence for human life and less indifference to premature death; I value men's lives more not less for being a spiritualist" (18). He also associates the advent of spiritualism with spiritual growth both individually and collectively. "Many a man who can bear very well to go on in his sins with God looking at him is raised to a higher grade of moral existence, if you make him feel for an instant that his pure child, his sainted mother, his wife, his friend who was dearest on earth, is with clearer eyes watching him from the eternal world" (20). He proclaims the advantages for the whole of humanity in his closing words: "The tendency of humanity is onward; it has gone onward even without the vivid and daily consciousness of immortality, even without the presence and intercourse of the beloved departed; and if without this there has been progress made, what accelerating progress must come with the knowledge of this!" (21).

6. Verena Tarrant, the daughter of a mesmeric healer and herself a trance-medium in Henry James's *The Bostonians,* is perhaps the best-known medium to appear in American literature. Suffragist and 1870 presidential candidate Victoria Woodhull is the most sensational of the female spiritualists to employ her powers as a medium to promote a political agenda. For a full account of Woodhull's role in the spiritualist movement, see Goldsmith.

7. See Braude's chapter titled "The Meaning of Mediumship" for the fullest de-

scription of the types of mediumship and the popularity of mediums in American culture.

8. See Braude (23, 83) on the femininity of the medium. Carroll (38, 93–94) lists the political figures who spoke through mediums.

9. The displacement of the medium by the spirit visitant could result in sexual contact with the medium's body that would be attributed to the spirit and not the medium. As Alex Owen has noted in *The Darkened Room: Women, Power and Spiritualism in Late Victorian England*, "Even those spiritualists who denounced any hint of debasement in mediums could accept a pronounced degree of eroticism in visitors from the other world" (221). Owen provides a detailed discussion of the medium's relationship to sexual norms and the market appeal of sexually active spirits in her chapter on "Spiritualism and the Subversion of Feminity."

10. This frequently discussed poem supports a wide range of interpretations. See Gilbert and Gubar's *The Mad Woman in the Attic* for a discussion of whiteness and associations with female literary characters who wore white (613–625). They discuss forms of haunting in Dickinson poems on 621–625.

11. I use the words "timid," "mystic," and "come back" in this stanza as these are the words Franklin uses in his variorum edition of the poem, despite the fact that he uses the words "hallowed," "purple," and "return" in his reading edition. Dickinson's fascicle holograph presents "hallowed" and "purple" as variants that appear underlined and above "timid" and "mystic," while "return" appears underlined and to the right of "come back" (*MBED* 289). Dickinson also presents "vest" as underlined and placed to the right of "breast" in the penultimate line of the poem, and Franklin includes this variant in his reading edition (290). Franklin's decision to reject these variants in his variorum edition show that he accepted Johnson's earlier rejection of these four variants in his edited version of the poem. Franklin (in both print editions) and Johnson both exclude the word "glimmering" that appears after the word "fog" in the holograph, though both mention the variant in the textual apparatus that accompanies their variorum editions. I don't think the exclusion of these variants necessarily changes the meaning of the poem, though I do think that knowing that they exist increases reader awareness of Dickinson's intermingling of medium and author roles in the second stanza. The word "hallowed" magnifies the sacred or spiritual dimension of the speaker's contemplated action that is not conveyed by the word "timid" and the word "purple" suggests the color of the writer's ink well plus the royalty of divine authority that is not connoted by the word "mystic." The word "glimmering" at the end of the third stanza may also be seen as enhancing the ghostly implications of "hovering" and "fog."

12. It is also worth noting that line twelve is the only line in the poem that deviates from the alternating six- and eight-syllable pattern that otherwise characterizes the poem. The deviation signaled by an additional syllable may be read as drawing attention to the speaker's break with the familiar pattern of her life as she makes the transition from "ponder[ing] how the bliss would look" to actually assuming the expanded perspective of the medium that is the subject of the final stanza.

13. Franklin identifies "spies" as a variant for "sees" in line six and presents the following variant for line seven: "has views of Bridles and of Barns." Two variants appear for line eight: "That would expand us all –" and "[That would] betray us all – ." These final two variant lines, especially, reinforce the way the poem focuses attention on an expanded view of conventional life that results from the medium's glimpse of what lies beyond.

14. Franklin lists the following variants, all of which enhance the interpretation I propose: "Phantasms] fictitious," "scantily] cautiously," "disburse –] express –" or "afford," "defer –] demur – ."

15. Howard Kerr usefully presents this awareness of a primary spiritual reality as "adopting the tone of millennial expectancy already familiar in the various apocalyptic and utopian movements of the 1840's. The Fox sisters were instructed to awaken the world to 'the dawn of a new era,' and believers thought that the fact that their century had been singled out for enlightenment indicated that the material and spiritual realms were drawing ever closer together" (11–12).

16. R. Laurence Moore similarly affirms the spiritualist fusion of natural and supernatural realms: "One of the claims spiritualists were proudest of was that they rejected the distinction between natural and supernatural" (24).

17. In light of the *Webster's* definition of "witchcraft" as "Power more than natural" that appeared in the Dickinson family dictionary, Dickinson's understanding of witchcraft would have embraced expressions of the supernatural in the past as well as the experiences of spiritualists in the world around her.

18. Dickinson's poems also contain references to mediumistic practices resembling the "spirit pen" that appears in this letter. A relatively early poem, "A single Screw of Flesh" (Fr 293), presents a speaker who refers to a "Vail [*sic*]" of the sort frequently used by spiritualist mediums. This speaker goes on to describe the visitation of a "Soul" she "witnessed of the Gauze," as if seen in a trance state. Then, in words reminiscent of the telegraphic communication commonly associated with spirit rappings, or the automatic writing of the spirit pen, she describes the departure of the soul whose "name is put away / . . . as if no plight / Had printed yesterday, // "In tender – solemn Alphabet." The mention of a "plight" would be consistent with spirit messages like the one famously received by the Fox sisters, whose first spirit communication was with the "ghost of a murdered peddler" (Kerr 4). A much-later poem, "Cosmopolites without a plea" (Fr 1592), invests the popular Christian image of Christ knocking at the heart with spiritualist significance. In this case, the "Cosmopolites" of the first line perform as spirit visitants who "Alight in every Land." Their "Theology," the poem tells us, is "Knock and it shall be opened."

19. St. Armand describes this precise reference to a "spirit pen" in Dickinson's letter as an instance when Dickinson "posed as the equivalent of a medium" ("Occult" 345). Kerr identifies "spirit-writing" as one of the most-common spirit manifestations associated with the medium (5).

20. See Ackmann for a succinct account of Dickinson's brush with conversion at Mt. Holyoke ("Mt. Holyoke" 199–200). For a full account of Dickinson's relationship

to conversion at Mt. Holyoke and later at Amherst when her father converted in 1850, see Wolff, 98–104.

21. Wolff observes that though "Dickinson did not leave any evidence of any desire to side with the women of Seneca Falls," she "certainly had mutiny on her mind by this time" (123).

22. These lines are the first stanza of "The only news I know" (Fr 820) that appears in Fascicle 40. Capitalization for "news" and "Day" differ in the fascicle poem (*MBED* 975).

23. The dashes disappear from Dickinson's letters between 1844 and 1849 or 1850, reappearing in Dickinson's 1849 Valentine's Day letter to William Cowper Dickinson (*L* 75–76), but are most pronounced in her January 1850 letter to Joel Warren Norcross (*L*77–81). As only two letters from 1849 survive, it is difficult to state with certainty how frequent Dickinson's use of the dash was in that year. What is certain is that the dash was a regular feature of letters from her April 1850 letter to Jane Humphrey until her death in 1886. For more on the dashes in Dickinson's letters, see Paul Crumbley's *Inflections of the Pen: Dash and Voice in Emily Dickinson,* especially 70–77.

24. Cristanne Miller succinctly defines the dash's contribution to disjunction in her "Disjunction, as a Characteristic" entry in *An Emily Dickinson Encyclopedia:* "Dashes disrupt rhythm, syntax, and a sense of conclusiveness, hence have a particularly disjunctive effect in the poetry" (85).

25. Poems like "In Ebon Box, when years have flown" (Fr 180) and "Essential Oils – are wrung –" (Fr 772B) refer to the discovery of poems by future readers, lending further credibility to the possibility that Dickinson deliberately prepared for the eventual discovery of her poems by the reading public.

26. For more information on Austin's comments and their application to Dickinson's letters, see Richard Sewall's *The Life of Emily Dickinson* (538, 555). See also Wolff on Austin's view of Dickinson's posing (258). For more information on Mabel Loomis Todd's reference to Dickinson as "the Myth," see Sewall 216. For information about the impression Dickinson made on her neighbors through eccentric behavior, see MacGregor Jenkins's *Emily Dickinson: Friend and Neighbor.* For more on Dickinson's performance during Higginson's 1870 visit, see chapter 4 in this volume.

27. The Franklin reading edition of Dickinson's poems uses the variant "halt" in place of "shut." Both words support my reading of the poem.

28. Richard Brantley usefully identifies Dickinson's translation of the commonplace into the miraculous that takes place in this poem: "Nature self-produces to the point of making the commonplace miraculous and obviating, *pace,* Wadsworth, the highest ecclesiastical court of the Presbyterian Church" (109).

29. Carroll's chapter on "The Structure of the Spirit World" provides a comprehensive overview of spiritualist belief in growth after death. Carroll describes the "Spiritualist emphasis on gradual spiritual growth" as part of a larger " 'kinetic revolution' in nineteenth-century Western culture and thought in which the world was conceived in developmental terms and motion became increasingly accentuated at the expense of stasis" (62–63).

30. Daneen Wardrop provides an illuminating analysis of Dickinson's treatment

of the haunted house as a central metaphor in *Emily Dickinson's Gothic: Goblin with a Gauge*. She concludes her chapter on "The Haunted House" with language that corresponds closely to my own sense of the aesthetic importance of haunting: "If 'Nature is a Haunted House – but Art – a House that tries to be haunted' (L 554), then Dickinson's House of Poetry aspires to exactly this type of house that tries to be haunted. Her famous aesthetic condition recognizes the eeriness in nature and the attempt at eeriness that artifice performs" (49).

31. Margaret Homans's description of this speaker's inability to contain nature in language complements my own analysis, even though she does not address Dickinson's use of spiritualist discourse: "The terms 'her ghost' and 'her haunted house' demonstrate the difficulty that even the sardonic speaker has in writing any account of nature. They implicate her in the same error made by 'The ones that cite her most,' because to separate matter from spirit is to impose on her an artificial system" (190). Homans points to the disembodied character of language that attempts to capture the absent presence of nature when she writes that "nature escapes and leaves language a husk."

32. Dickinson sent a variant of "What mystery pervades a well!" (Fr 1433) to Susan in which she altered the final two stanzas by replacing the reference to "nature" with the name "Susan" (Fr 1433C). Such a substitution reinforces the argument that Dickinson associates the unknowable in nature with the insubstantiality of human personality. Reference in the variant to "her Ghost" also positions Susan as medium, while simultaneously affirming Susan's ghostly presence.

33. The fascicle version of the poem that is the basis for Fr 773B includes the words "Report Him" as a variant for the words "esteem Him" that appear in the penultimate line of the poem (*MBED* 898). This variant may be significant because the word "report" suggests a connection with the medium's role as vehicle for reports about the spirit world.

34. See especially Heginbotham's introduction.

35. Susan Howe, one of the most influential commentators on the visual features of Dickinson's holograph manuscripts that pose particular problems for the editors of print editions, identifies the connection between the manuscript record and the incompleteness of writing and thought that I have in mind: "What Dickinson may be increasingly representing in her writing is *process* itself" ("Experience" 36). "I go to Emily Dickinson's poems, letters, and aphorisms because in them I recognize the right of a woman who is a poet to enter the domain of philosophy and philology at the same time that she acknowledges the necessarily incomplete character of all theorization" (37).

Chapter 4

1. Martha Nell Smith has described Dickinson's circulation of poetry in her correspondence as "a consciously designed alternative mode of textual reproduction and distribution" (*Rowing* 1–2). This chapter can be understood as an elaboration of her observation that "Dickinson found the printed transformations of her work dissat-

isfying" and chose "not to distribute her work in the mass-produced ways to which most unknown authors aspire." I also build on the observations of Marietta Messmer, who acknowledges Smith's foundational work and extends it to the world of politics and society: "an additional reason for Dickinson's choice to 'publish' her poems in epistolary format may also lie in the sociocultural and political connotation of these two genre in a nineteenth-century context" (47). In what follows, I make the case that gift culture provides one of the most significant means Dickinson employs not only to distribute her poetry but to expand a politically subversive community of readers. My treatment of gift exchange is also a response to Domhnall Mitchell's wish for "the historical context that can help us better appreciate" how with Dickinson "even refusal can be thought of as a form of relation, a social stance" (*Monarch* 2). I also draw on Mary Loeffelholz's response to Mitchell in *From School to Salon* where she suggests that Dickinson's poetry fits into "a place of tension" between bourgeois art and social art that emerges in the second half of the nineteenth century by means of a "double refusal: of the official honors, fame, and financial success attached to bourgeois art, on the one hand, and of social art's 'demand that literature fulfill a social or political function,' on the other" (*School* 135). See Loeffelholz's chapter " 'Plied from Nought to Nought': Helen Hunt Jackson and the Field of Emily Dickinson's Refusals" in *From School to Salon* for a complete discussion of her response to Mitchell's treatment of refusal in Dickinson and her analysis of the Dickinson-Jackson correspondence.

2. Cynthia Griffin Wolff's observation that Dickinson's "self-imposed labor was to question God's authority and to free language from the tyranny of His definitions" (429) is one of the most-prominent examples of Dickinson's attack on complacency. See also Cristanne Miller's statement that Dickinson "writes antagonistically . . . in opposition to an existing order" and that the "disruptions of her style . . . mark her rejection of the conditions of thought and action in which she has been raised" (*Grammar* 184).

3. Kete's treatment of "little societies" parallels the concept of counterpublics that I drew from Michael Warner in the previous chapter and that I allude to in the opening paragraph of this chapter. Warner describes these counterpublics as forming part of an ongoing, circular process that shapes notions of what a larger public is. See especially "Publics and Counterpublics" (65–124).

4. Logan Esdale has identified the collaborative nature of Dickinson's correspondence when viewed from the standpoint of ownership: "In some ways, Dickinson must have regarded her work as a collaboration, or at least dependent on the response and the initiative of others" (14). Hewitt approaches the issue of collaboration as part of an ongoing process of social negotiation that takes place in Dickinson's letters: "Moreover, Dickinson's deliberate combination of the lyrical with the epistolary reveals her understanding of the ways in which human intercourse requires the perpetual negotiation of social attachments even as such social attachments are never guaranteed" (162).

5. Messmer acknowledges Dickinson's epistolary fusion of public and private writing in *A Vice for Voices:* "Not quite public published documents ('literature') in

the conventional sense, the mailed-out letters and letter-poems (especially in the form of double mailings) nonetheless challenge the boundaries of exclusively private missives and become—quite literally—a private form of publication" (48).

6. The wishes of the woman writer, Aarona Moncrief, are never unambiguously stated. What I treat as the strongest support for the notion that she sought the collaboration of gift-based circulation rather than the fame of print publication is her decision to destroy all her manuscripts after the male writer lies to her about having successfully published the dramatic work she gave him. These she refers to as her "'poor dear children'" that she prefers to have "'depart with me—unread, as I have been'" (268).

7. Elizabeth Petrino usefully explains the obstacles Dickinson faced in her correspondence with Jackson in *Emily Dickinson and Her Contemporaries.* Commenting specifically on Dickinson's failure to return the 1875 literary gift that Jackson returned for clarification, Petrino states the following: "Dickinson withheld it, perhaps because she lacked confidence that Jackson was her best audience" (164).

8. See Susan Coultrap-McQuin's commentary on Jackson's efforts to mentor Dickinson in *Doing Literary Business* (151–153).

9. Dickinson repeats her request for Higginson's assistance in a "*late October 1876*" letter (*L* 566).

10. This letter was written immediately following the fourth adult meeting of the two women and appears to build on the publishing scheme Jackson had promoted during that meeting. Vivian K. Pollak identifies four adult meetings in Amherst: 1860, 1868, 1876, and 1878 ("American Women Poets" 330–331).

11. Loeffelholz describes Jackson as having "managed to smuggle one of Dickinson's poems into the No-Name Series" (*School* 132).

12. See also Petrino 172.

13. Writing specifically of "A Route of Evanescence," Esdale notes, "Dickinson copied this poem again and again, sending it to people (Jackson, Todd, Niles) she knew wished that her work would reach a wider audience" (17).

14. That Dickinson is interested in extending her gift-based system to Niles is made even clearer in 1883 when she sent him what she described as "a chill Gift – My Cricket and the Snow" in response to his having sent her Mathilde Blind's *The Life of George Eliot* (*L* 768). As part of their previous correspondence, Dickinson had sent him an edition of Brontë poems. The cricket and snow references apply to the poems "Further in Summer than the Birds –" (Fr 895E) and "It sifts from Leaden Sieves –" (Fr 291E). Franklin indicates in his notes that both of these poems were written about thirteen years previously and were sent to numerous other correspondents. Virginia Jackson has identified Dickinson's prior departure from Niles's business model of exchange when she sent him a volume of the Brontë sisters poems in the spring of 1883: "In the context of the exchange with Niles, Dickinson seems to have transgressed his sense of the decorum that separated gift and business exchange when she sent him her own copy of the Brontë sisters poems" (254n27). See Dickinson's *Letters* 768–770.

15. The following is the 1828 *Webster's* definition of "requisition": "Demand; ap-

plication made as a right." Dickinson's use of the term clearly reflects her sense of having been pressured by Jackson.

16. This is the only time the word "loyally" appears in Dickinson's letters (MacKenzie 448).

17. Eberwein and Capps both note that Dickinson consistently viewed Shakespeare as a contemporary (Eberwein 264; Capps 24). Sewall describes Dickinson as discovering "re-creative power, joy, and refreshment" in Shakespeare (*Life* 700).

18. Dickinson would have been aware of scholarly and popular debate about editing Shakespeare through the Shakespeare Club and the editorial commentary that appeared in the family edition of Shakespeare that her father purchased with great deliberation (Leyda 277, 352). Jay Leyda's discussion of Emily Fowler's letter describing the Shakespeare Club pays particular attention to Dickinson's insistence that the girls have access to unexpurgated Shakespeare texts, thus providing one instance of her awareness that the public willingly edited these texts (478). In this case, her disapproval of editorial choices urged by male tutors in effect affirmed her own alternative editorial position.

19. Hart and Smith describe "the late 1850s on" as a period during which "Emily shares her poems with Susan, regularly sending drafts and inviting feedback" (64). They conclude "that this relationship is reciprocal, and that Susan sends Emily her own poems for critiques as well" (64).

20. The number of letters and letter-poems I include here is based on the entries Hart and Smith include in *Open Me Carefully*. Johnson and Ward list a smaller number in their appendix of recipients (964–965). They identify approximately 156 letters and eighteen prose fragments. I prefer the Hart and Smith edition because it isolates Dickinson's correspondence with Susan, makes it easier to see the contours of their relationship in letters, and provides more individual examples of the correspondence. I also accept their account as the most complete scholarly analysis of Dickinson's correspondence with Susan.

21. From this point on, in parenthetical citations I refer to page numbers in the Hart and Smith edition, *Open Me Carefully*, with the abbreviation *OMC* followed by the number. I will return to the Thomas and Ward edition when I discuss Dickinson's correspondence with Higginson.

22. There are numerous examples of the collaboration between Susan and Emily. The clearest presentation of evidence is in *Open Me Carefully*; see especially Susan's contributions to "Safe in their Alabaster Chambers –" (97–100) and examples of collaborative writing (152–153; 174–177). The most-detailed analysis of Dickinson's correspondence with Susan appears in Smith's *Rowing in Eden: Rereading Emily Dickinson*. See especially chapters 5 and 6.

23. Hewitt joins Hart and Smith in acknowledging that Dickinson understood her relationship with Susan as "part of a larger literary project" (153). For more on Dickinson's distinction of poetry from prose, see "They shut me up in Prose –" (Fr 445) and "I dwell in Possibility –" (Fr 466).

24. A certain understandable confusion surrounds Dickinson's stance regarding

print publication that may be clarified by reference to the practice within gift culture of empowering receivers of gifts to treat the gift in a manner they deem appropriate. When, for example, Susan happily proclaims the publication of poems in this instance, she may expect Dickinson's approval for taking her own initiative, even though Susan has done what Dickinson herself would not do. Similarly, in the obituary Susan wrote in memory of her friend, she writes that Dickinson "never published a line" and that "now and then some enthusiastic literary friend would turn love to larceny, and cause a few verses surreptitiously obtained to be printed" (*OMC* 267). In this instance, Susan might quite logically include herself in the category of larcenous friends, as her purpose is to focus on Dickinson's attitude toward publication, not her own. Susan would almost certainly have been aware of the position Dickinson conveyed to Higginson in 1866 when she wrote that the recently published version of "A narrow Fellow in the Grass" "was robbed of me" (*L* 450). Dickinson's strong language here reflects her concern that upon reading the print version of the poem that she had sent him earlier, Higginson would mistakenly conclude that she had deceived him when she previously stated that she did not print: "I had told you I did not print." To distance herself further from the print version of the poem, Dickinson draws Higginson's attention to changes in punctuation that appear in the third line: "defeated too of the third line by the punctuation." Her aim here is to make clear that she did not choose to enter print. Sue's reference to larceny in the obituary is consistent with Dickinson's reference to robbery, in the sense that both women use these words to magnify Dickinson's choice not to print. It is worth noting that at no point does Dickinson criticize Sue or anyone else for publishing one of her poems. In the case of her letter to Higginson, Dickinson may be understood as expressing her exasperation at appearing to have desired print publication when in fact the print poem represents the efforts of another.

25. Franklin points out that if Susan did not provide the manuscript used for the 1864 *Brooklyn Daily Union* publication, it must have come from one of the several other Amherst residents with connections to the paper. He holds out the possibility that the source manuscript is lost because the appearance of " 'Requireth' in line 4 deviates from the three [existing] holographs" (*Poems* 145).

26. Hewett makes an important point about reciprocity in Dickinson's correspondence through her analysis of "This is my letter to the World" (Fr 519). Treating that poem as "exemplifying the association between the epistolary genre and Dickinson's *ars poetica*" (149), Hewett concludes, "the poem depicts a scene of social reciprocity—relations between 'countrymen'—that graphically describes just how messy and incomplete correspondence must be" (150). Though Hewitt is not concerned with gift exchange, she identifies the logic of reciprocity that runs through gift culture: that the reception of the gift is itself a gift. Reciprocity is therefore achieved by means of reception and any formal response is understood as redundant. This is why Dickinson so often complicates her expressions of gratitude, stating that gratitude is unnecessary or beyond her powers of expression. This is not to say that Dickinson never writes a simple thanks; it is to say that her letters to Susan and others with whom the

subject of poetry is a primary subject characteristically express the gift-culture view that reciprocity is redundant.

27. Here is the other four-line response: "Despair is treason / toward Man / And blasphemy / to Heaven" (*OMC* 153). As with the other four lines, that may or may not be half of a single eight-line response, these lines represent a response and perhaps even a gloss on Dickinson's letter-poem. Susan's aim here seems to be that of affirming the meaning she derives from Dickinson's words.

28. Elizabeth Horan provides a succint discussion of Susan's efforts to publish Dickinson poems shortly after Dickinson's death. Horan quotes an unpublished memoir by Martha Dickinson Bianchi that recounts Susan's contact with an editor from *Scribner's* who examined the manuscripts Susan possessed and agreed that about " 'a hundred or more should be put together for publication' " (91). Bianchi describes typing about fifty poem manuscripts with her brother Ned's assistance and " 'under Susan's direction' " before Lavinia collected the poems for a reading at her home, after which they were never returned (91). If Bianchi's recollection is accurate, Susan must have either lost interest in the approach she was then pursuing or agreed with Lavinia's decision that the editor's selection was, in Bianchi's words, too " 'conservative.' "

29. Sue's December 1890 letter to Higginson, in which she describes the "rather more full, and varied" volume that she had been envisioning, also explains that she had intended to consult Higginson before going forward (Bingham 86). She tells Higginson that her plans were "subject to your approval of course, with an introduction by yourself, to make the setting perfect." Later in the letter, she admits that she "shrank from going contrary to your practical opinion in the matter." This reliance on Higginson and her pronounced anxiety about going forward without his support makes even clearer Sue's wariness about going public with such a daring project.

30. As Petrino rightly affirms, the Emerson quotation reveals that Higginson "put [Dickinson's] poems into print apologetically, as if their unfinished surface reflected on him" (38).

31. Messmer's analysis of Dickinson's correspondence with Higginson centers on what she identifies as two citation practices, references to titles and revisions of his published works, that serve to sustain a balance of authority: "an oscillation between her role as 'pupil' (who attempts to please her preceptor and displays her familiarity with and respect for his works by regularly quoting his titles) and that of 'poet' (who competes creatively with him as 'fellow author' by rewriting some of his texts)" (153). Situating these aspects of the correspondence in the context of gift culture emphasizes the collaborative character of Dickinson's engagement with Higginson's writing, so that the emphasis shifts from critique of the other to increased mutual understanding.

32. Martha Nell Smith provides the best analysis of Dickinson's distinction between the word "print" and the word "publish" in *Rowing in Eden*: "we need to be aware of the distinction Dickinson and her sister-in-law emphasized between the

often synonymously used terms *publish* and *print*. Dickinson did not say, 'I had told you I did not *publish*'; she said, 'I had told you I did not *print* [emphasis added]'" (15). Smith clarifies even further: "Surrounded by lawyers (Dickinson's father and brother), these women are somewhat legalistic in their differentiations, using *publish* in the special sense 'to tell or noise abroad' (*OED*)."

33. Dickinson also writes to Higginson in November 1880 requesting that he advise her regarding publication of three poems that she has promised to the Mission Circle (*L* 680). Referring specifically to this letter, Higginson writes the following in "Emily Dickinson": "Sometimes . . . her verses found too much favor for her comfort, and she was urged to publish. In such cases I was sometimes put forward as a defense; and the following letter was the fruit of some such occasion" (555). Higginson quite clearly understands that Dickinson used him as a means to avoid fulfilling her promise. In the letter Dickinson writes Higginson to thank him for his advice, she states, "I shall implicitly follow it" and then explains that when her poems were first requested the person appealing to her said that her donation "might 'aid unfortunate Children'" (*L* 682). Dickinson then describes the use of "the name of 'Child'" as "a snare to me," implying that she felt trapped and is grateful to Higginson for releasing her. Her words, plus his, suggest that she did not send the poems and once again avoided this form of publication. Johnson and Ward conclude that "Higginson advised her to offer one or more," but no clear evidence of this exists.

34. Messmer provides a useful commentary on Dickinson's reference to "spectral power" in this letter: "Dickinson suggests that the imaginative power of 'the mind alone' is unencumbered by any form of (biological or cultural) determinism and thus free to create nonexisting ('spectral'), revisionist 'thought[s]'/realities disentangled from prevailing sociocultural configurations" (116).

35. Mabel Loomis Todd's famous letter to her parents in which she describes Dickinson as the "*character* of Amherst," "a lady whom the people call the *Myth*," and "the climax of all the family oddity" shows that by November 6, 1881, Dickinson had achieved an ample measure of notoriety (Sewall, *Life* 216).

36. The "terror – since September" (*L* 404) that Dickinson alludes to in her April 25, 1862, second letter to Higginson could well refer to the struggle with fascicle construction that Franklin describes in the introduction to his variorum edition.

37. Franklin is struck with the new energy Dickinson brings to fascicle production: "She returned to fascicle making with high energy, once again obtaining large quantities of stationary and, beginning with Fascicle 16, producing twenty-six new ones in a steady rush" (*Poems* 24).

38. In his 1891 essay on Dickinson that appeared in the *Atlantic*, Higginson admits, "even at this day I still stand somewhat bewildered" ("Emily Dickinson" 545). With language that closely resembles his much-earlier 1869 letter, Higginson elaborates further on the level of concentration Dickinson demanded and the surprises she conferred: "She was much too enigmatical a being for me to solve . . . I could only sit still and watch, as one does in the woods; I must name my bird without the gun, as recommended by Emerson" (559).

39. Messmer's overview of the ways Dickinson cites Higginson's writing in her own is far more complete than what I can offer here. See especially 152–160.

40. Writing Higginson in the spring of 1876, Dickinson describes her discovery of two of his unsigned reviews: "I inferred your touch in the Papers on Lowell and Emerson – It is delicate that each Mind is itself, like a distinct Bird –" (L 551).

41. Cynthia Griffin Wolff provides solid historical and cultural context for Dickinson's association with Jacob in *Emily Dickinson,* especially 144–159. Wolff places particular stress on Dickinson's setting "herself apart from the great tradition of the religious lyric" (146) and usurping the power of deity: "The poet must stand alone, and the poet's word shall be *itself* a blessing" (159). The sense of daring confrontation with religious conventions would have certainly have been clear to Higginson. In my reading, though, Dickinson is not purely interested in proclaiming her poetic sovereignty; she is also inviting Higginson to proclaim his.

42. Loeffelholz's analysis of Dickinson's correspondence with Higginson and her treatment of "Decoration" is far more extensive than my own and well worth reading. Of particular interest is Loeffelholz's interpretation of "Because that you are going" (Fr 1314B), the poem Dickinson sent Higginson after his second visit in 1874. Loeffelholz sees this poem as expressing "a narrative of private and finally public vindication of worth as a writer" (674) that corresponds closely with my own analysis of Dickinson's relationship with Higginson. Loeffelholz differs, though, in her conclusion that the poem marks the end of Dickinson's "imagined relationship to publication and public recognition" that she desired to achieve with Higginson's assistance.

43. Loeffelholz points out that the epigraph for Higginson's poem, " '*Manibus date lilia plenis*' [give me lilies with both hands]" (" 'Decoration' " 665), further substantiates Higginson's deliberate incorporation of Dickinson's 1870 welcome into his poem. Noting that the epigraph is from both Virgil and Dante, Loeffelholz observes that for Virgil "the object of mourning . . . is a young man, whereas Dante . . . adapts it to the coming of Beatrice" (666). This analysis of the sexual ambiguity of the epigraph magnifies the gender fluidity that was part of the Dickinson-Higginson correspondence and that Higginson trades on when he assumes Dickinson's role as the bearer of the lilies.

44. Here are the lines from the Higginson poem "Decorations," together with the preceding stanza:

Never gleamed a prouder eye
In the front of victory,
Never foot had firmer tread
On the field where hope lay dead

Than are hid within this tomb,
Where the untended grasses bloom;
And no stone, with feign'd distress,
Mocks the sacred loneliness. (Franklin, *Poems,* 1248–1249)

45. It must be noted that Dickinson wrote Higginson another letter-poem in April 1886 in which she also responds to his sonnet. In a discarded draft of that letter, Dickinson begins by stating, "No 'Sonnet' had George Eliot. The sweet Acclamation of Death is forever bounded" (*L* 904). These words imply the impropriety of Higginson's conventional gesture of mourning. However, the letter she actually sent him is much warmer, as if an effort to replace her pugilistic attitude with an affirmation of friendship. "The beautiful Sonnet confirms me," she writes. The two verse passages that follow respond to Higginson's sonnet by expressing the uncontainable and immortal spirit of the departed and in that way open the door his sonnet shuts. She still collaborates.

46. Loeffelholz argues that the public response to poetry changed significantly in the second half of the nineteenth century and that this change accounts for the positive reception of Dickinson's poetry. She describes Dickinson as "enter[ing] . . . literary history . . . rather as Sarah Bernhardt was said to have descended a spiral staircase: 'she stood still and *it* revolved about her'" (*School* 131). Higginson's surprise suggests that he was not aware such a change had taken place.

Chapter 5

1. Dickinson's willingness to interrogate the apparent separation of "public" from "private" has particular importance within the context of democratic considerations of the public sphere. As Mary Ryan makes clear in *Women in Public: Between Banners and Ballots, 1825–1880,* how the term "public" is defined has from the time of Aristotle played an important role in determining the extent that women are granted a voice in political discourse (9–14). Within her overview of politics and the public sphere, Ryan stipulates that female participation in public politics depends upon establishing a highly flexible and open concept of the public, one actively pursued by feminist political theorists. Of special significance for the ensuing discussion of Dickinson's view of the public sphere is Ryan's promotion of a heterogeneous public sphere "fully accessible to women, attentive to the concerns that they embody in any given historical moment, and open to the full range of social differences that inhere in any complex society" (12).

2. For an overview of public awareness of and interest in copyright debates, see Melissa Homestead's *American Women Authors and Literary Property, 1822–1869,* especially 4–11.

3. Concern with the political outcomes of copyright legislation as expressed by Rice and, I will argue, by Dickinson, reflects sensitivity to tensions widely viewed as inherent within the legal establishment of literary property. This is a point stressed by L. Ray Patterson and Stanley W. Lindberg in the early pages of *The Nature of Copyright: A Law of Users' Rights.* They state first that "the primary purpose of copyright . . . is to promote the public welfare by the advancement of knowledge" and second that from "its statutory beginnings in early-eighteenth-century England, copyright has been the product of a precarious attempt to balance the rights of creators—and those of publishers—with the rights of users, present and future" (2).

In what follows, I outline the way Dickinson illuminates the tendency among authors and within the reading public to forget the precariousness of the balance struck between private and public interests. I present Dickinson as concerned about the ease with which private and authorial legal rights take precedence over public and communal interests to the detriment of American democracy. By drawing attention to this concern within Dickinson's writing, I hope to show that while her *approach* to copyright and literary ownership may be distinctive, her *conclusions* place her in the company of other writers, politicians, and citizens.

4. What I am describing here is the importance of Locke in establishing the legal status of the author as perceived in terms of possessive individualism. In *The Political Theory of Possessive Individualism: Hobbes to Locke,* C. B. MacPherson describes the essential makeup of the possessive individual: "As with Hobbes, Locke's deduction starts with the individual and moves out to society and the state, but, again as with Hobbes, the individual with which he starts has already been created in the image of the market man. Individuals are by nature equally free from the jurisdiction of others" (269). Gillian Brown affirms the crucial role of Locke in *Domestic Individualism: Imagining Self in Nineteenth-Century America* where she writes that "by the mid-eighteenth century the notion of individual rights promulgated in the political philosophies of Hobbes and Locke comprised an article of cultural faith" (2).

5. In forwarding an argument that represents Dickinson as a writer concerned with the public character of ostensibly private forms of writing, I clearly raise questions about the accuracy of assertions like the following from "Revising the Script: Emily Dickinson's Manuscripts," in which Mitchell affirms the private nature of Dickinson's writing: "when we give privately produced papers a public significance, we should be aware that we are doing something that Dickinson herself did not do" (731). My aim is not to challenge Mitchell, but rather to question the widespread assumption of privacy that he correctly presents.

6. There are many poems in the Dickinson corpus that explore the disappearance of stories, the way that prominent cultural narratives are not accessible to women, or the extent that gender-specific narratives simply don't address the real lives of women. Almost all of them direct attention to yet-to-be-told stories that more accurately speak to actual experience. In my first chapter, I looked at "Unto like Story – Trouble has enticed me –" (Fr 300) and "I play at Riches – to appease" (Fr 856) as examples of the appeal of primary cultural narratives that female speakers are drawn to but which they ultimately defer or reject as unsuitable to their status as women. I have repeatedly identified "This is my letter to the World" (Fr 519) as a poem in which the speaker asserts that she is writing a letter to the world because the world never wrote to her. She specifically states that nature's "Message is committed / To Hands I cannot see – ." "We talked as Girls do –" (Fr 392) communicates the reflections of a woman who recalls how during childhood she and her female friends "parted with a contract / To cherish, and to write" only to have "Heaven" make "both, impossible." In this case, the stories girls anticipated writing were ended ere they began due to some form of divine intervention. All these poems provoke readers to imagine stories yet to be told.

7. The fascicle version of "Ended, ere it begun –" is the only manuscript version of the poem, though Franklin writes that a manuscript was "said to have been sent to Susan Dickinson, but no such copy is known" (*Poems* 925). What should be noted about the fascicle version is that several line breaks in the manuscript may be significant. I mentioned the way the phrase "perished from Consciousness" is placed on its own line and therefore gives greater emphasis to both the meter and content of the phrase. The line break separating "scarcely told" from "The Title was," in line two, may also add to the poem by magnifying the speaker's sense of suddenly losing control of the story. In the second stanza, the words "print," "read," and "our privilege" are also situated on their own lines in a manner that visually emphasizes these words and may be seen as reinforcing my reading of the poem's concern with the public possession of literary works.

8. In *Sex and Citizenship in Antebellum America*, Nancy Isenberg provides an informative analysis of the logic linking paternalism to the legal definition of "women's economic dependence under coverture" (27).

9. Hyde's assertion of inherent domination echoes the position taken earlier by MacPherson in *The Political Theory of Possessive Individualism* where he argues that "the result of Locke's work was to provide a moral basis for a class state from postulates of equal individual natural rights" (250). Despite challenges leveled at MacPherson's assessment of Locke's intentions, his concern with class structure still applies to discussions of literary property. As Mark Rose has noted in *Authors and Owners: The Invention of Copyright*, "what Locke may have meant is of less concern here than how his writings came to articulate a certain discourse of property" (4n5).

10. Dickinson's concern with the intricacies of the legal determination of property and ownership has been noted previously by James Guthrie in "Law, Property, and Provincialism in Dickinson's Poems and Letters to Judge Otis Phillips Lord." The "Legal Imagery" entry in *An Emily Dickinson Encyclopedia* also acknowledges the importance of Dickinson's use of legal language, especially as "a weapon against limitation and orthodoxy" (Dietrich 173).

11. One of the best nineteenth-century literary examples of editorial blindness is that provided by Ruth Hall's brother, Hyacinth, in Fanny Fern's *Ruth Hall*. In that work, the poverty-stricken Ruth Hall appeals to her well-established brother for assistance publishing in his magazine. He responds by writing that she has "no talent" and advising her to "seek some *unobtrusive* employment" (116). Ruth refuses to accept his judgment as final and declares her defiance in words that may have had a special resonance for Emily Dickinson: " 'At another tribunal than his will I appeal.' " Dickinson would write to Higginson in 1862 that she has "no Tribunal" (*L* 409). Tamara Plakens Thornton's analysis of handwriting in *Handwriting in America: A Cultural History* presents handwriting itself as a medium within which women writers "were rendered culturally illegible" (61). Thus, the difficulties Dickinson and the fictional Ruth Hall faced may have been doubly complicated by cultural restrictions that made female handwriting unreadable as disciplined artistic expression in either holograph or print formats.

12. Dickinson's two most famous responses to advice from Higginson both come

in letters she wrote to him in 1862. In the first, dated June 7, she writes the following: "You think my gait 'spasmotic' – I am in danger – Sir – You think me 'uncontrolled' – I have no Tribunal" (*L* 409). In the second, written in August, she offers the following equivocal observation that seems to hold Higginson responsible for shortcomings, as if they exist in his mind alone: "You say I confess the little mistake, and omit the large – Because I can see Orthography – but the Ignorance out of sight – is my Preceptor's charge" (*L* 415). Dickinson's reference to a tribunal closely resembles the use of that term by Ruth Hall as described in the previous note.

13. Ryan describes her research into women's voices within nineteenth-century newspapers as yielding "the most meager and disturbing results" (17). "Women appear irregularly and surrounded with the most distortion. Yet the female citizens of nineteenth-century cities battered at the walls of the public sphere, relentlessly and with a variety of ingenious tools. . . . Their efforts can tell us something of the process, pitfalls, and possibilities that women encounter in our continuing quest for a secure and equal place in the public sphere."

14. This is a point of special interest to Rice, who seeks to deconstruct "the historical binary of censorship and the free press" by arguing that "while the lapse of censorship and the explosion of print culture in the last half of the eighteenth century may have freed writers from the threat of persecution from church and state, they did so only by transforming printed texts from a practical means for assertive sociopolitical commentary into the more inert medium of property and commodity" (4).

15. Mary Kelley's *Private Woman, Public Stage: Literary Domesticity in Nineteenth-Century America* examines the discrepancy between literary representation and the real lives of literary women. Kelley states that her aim is that of "answering the question of how the literary domestics could have been so visibly onstage in their own time and yet remain invisible to the historical audience" (xii). In *Novels, Readers, and Reviewers: Responses to Fiction in Antebellum America,* Nina Baym responds to the discrepancy between public and private experiences of women by concluding that "even if women had experience and knowledge, the state of their relation to society as a whole requires them to suppress the expression of it" (257). Similarly, Susan Coultrap-McQuin observes in *Doing Literary Business: American Women Writers in the Nineteenth Century* that "the position of woman writers in the mid-nineteenth century—say, from the 1840s to the 1880s—was paradoxical: they had a place in the literary world, yet that world often rendered them invisible" (7). All three of these observations underscore the message I see Dickinson communicating in this poem.

16. Read as poetic mobilizations of voicing possibilities concealed within the possessive self, this and many other Dickinson poems provide the reconceptualization of democracy that Nancy Ruttenburg describes in *Democratic Personality: Popular Voice and the Trial of American Authorship.* Ruttenburg understands democracy as arising through "a theater of verbal (symbolic) action, an experiential ground whose materializations, both historical and literary, would ultimately foster the development of a recognizably democratic (polycentric) cultural semiotic" (15).

17. In "Authority and Authenticity: Scribbling Authors and the Genius of Print

in Eighteenth-Century England," Marlon B. Ross provides an instructive parallel example of the irony Dickinson presents here in his discussion of the confusion of private and public knowledge within medieval religious scholarship. Ross argues that for "the scholar to claim that the knowledge he gleans is solely his own, he would have to deny implicitly the ultimate source of all worthy knowledge outside the fallen flesh" (236). The logical consequence of such an impossibility is the conclusion that "knowledge is by definition communal, just as authority is by definition external and resistant to privatization; all experiences that derive merely from the self are diversions and exceptions" (236). This is essentially the position I see Dickinson urging in her poem.

18. Isenberg describes the way state constitutions replaced the concept of natural law with the concept of vested interest that elevated property above natural law and by this means further removed property from any clear ontological foundation: "Instead of instituting consent of the governed in order to protect natural rights and ensure a just government, state constitutions acknowledged that the right of property superseded natural law and all other fundamental rights" (26–27).

19. The concentration on aesthetic appeal that I am underscoring here parallels features of the argument Terry Mulcaire makes in "Public Credit; or, The Feminization of Virtue in the Marketplace." Mulcaire makes the case that public response is provoked by admittedly imaginary desires that have little to do with ontological considerations but rather correspond to "the way such imaginary desires promise to produce real ideological consequences" (1039). According to my argument about Dickinson, these "real ideological consequences" take the form of stories that both promote and challenge hegemonic cultural assumptions.

20. It is worth noting that in making what may appear to be a bold statement about the duties of democratic authorship Dickinson is in actuality entering a prominent cultural debate while also affirming a meaning inherent within the etymological history of "property." Hyde's etymological analysis in *Bodies of Law* makes plain the way Dickinson's concern with the public character of property reflects a dimension of the word's history that has been overshadowed by the term's specialized function in legal discourse. "The central pun involved in every invocation of 'property,'" he observes, "is inherent in its name: *property*, however defined, always mimetically represents both a supposed private, individual, isolated self (*propre*, one's own), and, at the same time, the proper, as defined publicly or socially through the social conventions that give us *propriety, propre* (clean)" (54).

21. Benjamin Friedlander's essay on "Publication – is the Auction," "Auctions of the Mind: Emily Dickinson and Abolition," provides a careful exploration of the poem's treatment of publication as a form of slavery. Though his conclusions differ from mine, he effectively outlines the social and economic dimensions of the poem.

22. Mitchell presents a much-different interpretation of Dickinson's approach to authorial ownership in *Measures of Possibility*. There he writes, "in the same way that the Divine Author gives life (and perhaps even imaginative ideas) to humans,

the human author—the genius or originator—passes these meanings on to the reader, who 'bears' but does not own or originate them" (286). Mitchell presents Dickinson as standing in opposition to the utilitarian position I have been describing and concludes that in "Publication – is the Auction" Dickinson argues that authorial ownership should extend to the ideas themselves and not the particular embodiment or expression of those ideas. Central to his interpretation of the poem is his belief that originating power somehow passes from the divine to the poet but stops there and does not pass from poet to reader. I read the poem as claiming that originating power is never transferred from the divine source to the poet or to the reader; instead, it circulates through them equally. For a fascinating presentation of a completely different way to read this poem in light of copyright legislation, see 267–270. See also 78–83 in *Monarch of Perception* where Mitchell acknowledges a broader range of interpretive possibilities for this poem though he arrives at the same ultimate conclusion.

23. Ross establishes the precedent for displacement of the message by the medium as far back as the medieval scribal practice of textual embellishment. Because embellishment "brings attention to the prideful self with its intrinsically fallible apprehension of divine authority and its constant yearning to claim God's authority as its own," "the scribe's unpaid labor for the profit of salvation contains within itself the tendency to degenerate into paid labor for mere profit, whether it be worldly fame or monetary gain" (234).

24. There are a great many Dickinson poems that stress the importance of the poet as vehicle for a message that lives on in readers and is not to be confused with the person of the legal author. "The Poets light but Lamps –" (Fr 930), "A word is dead, when it is said" (Fr 278), "A word made Flesh is seldom" (Fr 1715), "To pile like Thunder to it's close" (Fr 1353), and "I would not paint – a picture –" (Fr 348) are but a few prominent examples.

25. In her book on women's clubs, *Intimate Practices: Literacy and Cultural Work in U.S. Women's Clubs, 1880–1920,* Anne Ruggles Gere explains the central role given to literacy as an agent of cultural change: "although they enacted a variety of cultural practices, including pageants, banquets, and musical productions, clubwomen's most common and effective means for expressing and shaping their world appeared in their literary practices" (5). In her preface to Karen J. Blair's *The Clubwoman as Feminist: True Womanhood Redefined, 1868–1914,* Annette K. Baxter clarifies the political agenda prosecuted by women's clubs when she describes their members as holding "a middle ground between women like Charlotte Perkins Gilman, whose analysis of their plight would have mandated a radical break with social norms, and the overwhelming majority of their sex who contentedly played out their conventional roles or suffered in silence" (xiv–xv). Similarly, Blair makes the argument at the beginning of *The Clubwoman as Feminist* that woman's clubs paradoxically used the belief in woman's duty to disseminate domestic values "as a loophole whereby [women] not only could but had to leave the home and exert influence on the public sphere" (7). In *The Sound of Our Own Voices: Women's Study Clubs, 1860–1910,* Theodora Penny Martin provides a history of American woman's clubs that presents Anne Hutchin-

son as the original model for weekly female gatherings (5) and argues that the American Revolution served as a major source for the "egalitarian ideology" of women's clubs (15).

26. See Margaret Maher's "Deposition for the Commonwealth of Massachusetts, Hampshire County, Superior Court of Equity, for 28 May 1897." In that document Maher testified that Dickinson "kept" in "my trunk" certain "small booklets, probably 12 or 14 tied together with a string" (13). For further analysis of Maher's relationship to Dickinson and the manuscripts, see Aife Murray's "Miss Margaret's Emily Dickinson" in *Signs* (Spring 1999): 697–732.

27. For an analysis of Louise Norcross's account, see Gary Scharnhorst's "A Glimpse of Dickinson at Work"; for a description of Frances Norcross's account, see Marisa Anne Pagnattaro's report on Martha Ackmann's conference paper in "Dickinson in Historical Contexts" in the *Emily Dickinson International Society Bulletin*.

28. Ellen Louise Hart and Martha Nell Smith describe the way certain of the materials Dickinson sent to Susan bore signs of wear, including the sorts of pin holes that would indicate that Sue kept them in her own scrapbook. This would suggest that even if Dickinson did not herself keep a portfolio composed of the writing of other people that she did in fact knowingly contribute her work to the scrapbook of another. Hart and Smith's *Open Me Carefully: Emily Dickinson's Intimate Letters to Susan Huntington Gilbert Dickinson* is the best source for clear evidence of the collaborative character of Dickinson's writing. See also Smith's discussion of Dickinson's correspondence in *Rowing in Eden: Rereading Emily Dickinson* for a detailed analysis of the inclusion of published materials in the letters, especially 118–122.

29. In his description of the portfolio genre in "New Poetry," Emerson expresses the way the lack of formal finish betrays both the writer's trust in his or her own perception and an independence that liberates the reader to respond honestly and variously to the writing: "the poet's trust in his own genius [has reached] that degree, that there is an absence of all conventional imagery, and a bold use of that which the moment's mood had made sacred to him, quite careless that it might be sacred to no other" (223). This sentence also mentions a willingness on the part of the poet to focus on the mood of a moment that has special application to the writing of Dickinson's later years when the record shows that she composed poems on the scraps closest to hand. This may have been her practice from a much-earlier stage of her life, but if so it must also be the case that her earlier practice included the destruction of what she may have at that time considered rough drafts of poems. In "Dickinson's Advertising Flyers: Theorizing Materiality and the Work of Reading," Melanie Hubbard concludes that these later poems "demand that the reader enter into the creative process" in order to respond to Dickinson's compositional combination of "accident and choice" (32). In *Rowing Eden*, Smith describes the reader's participation as creator or coauthor as reflective of the "dialogic drama" (53) that grows out of "Dickinson's awareness that she is not in control of the reader's responses" (52).

30. Hart and Smith point out Susan's practice of keeping Dickinson's poems in her own "scrapbooks" in *Open Me Carefully* (xxvii). This and the existence of a

book of Susan's in which she kept such things as poems and clippings makes it clear that Dickinson would have been familiar with the tradition that St. Armand and Socarides describe.

31. To be fair to Mitchell, I should acknowledge that when he points to the indeterminacy of visual features, his aim is to discount their importance by contrasting them with more predictable attributes, such as meter and rhyme, that he sees as more forcefully and predictably shaping the reader's experience of the poem. Mitchell probably goes further than any other scholar in establishing core features of what might be thought of as the nucleus of Dickinson's poetic practice in *Measures of Possibility* where he justifies the editorial normalization of irregularities such as line breaks that conflict with meter and capitalization. He does this by treating consistency and predictability as primary defining features of her writing. "Rigorous and sustained cross-referencing," he writes, "provides us with a set of procedures, a critical apparatus, by which to measure the extent to which contemporary critical approaches to Dickinson's autograph procedures can accurately be formulated as corresponding to the poet's own purposes" (55). As he readily acknowledges, Mitchell is motivated by a desire to limit the role of reader choice by directing attention to the most-stable features of Dickinson's text and reducing the energy readers give to the contemplation of textual gestures that can't be linked to patterns identified in other poems: "Such gestures can be seen as democratically enlarging the territory within which choice might be exercised . . . or as prompting the reader to find intentions for manuscript features that may well be casual—and thus placing a greater burden of responsibility on the reader than is necessary" (271–272). The argument that I have been making does not approach reader choice as an unfortunate burden but rather as a crucial element of Dickinson's poetics that coincides with the more-predictable features of Dickinson's writing that Mitchell so admirably identifies. The difference is that I approach Dickinson as a reader-oriented writer whose irregularities enhance reader choice and increase the democratic circulation of texts, whereas Mitchell understands Dickinson as an author-oriented writer who is far more monarchical than democratic when it comes to controlling the meanings of her texts.

Works Cited

Ackmann, Martha. "Mount Holyoke Female Seminary." *An Emily Dickinson Encyclopedia*. Ed. Jane Donahue Eberwein. Westport, Conn.: Greenwood Press, 1998. 199–200.

Ankersmit, F. R. *Political Representation*. Stanford, Calif.: Stanford University Press, 2002.

Appleby, Joyce, and Terence Ball, eds. *Jefferson: Political Writings*. New York: Cambridge University Press, 1999.

Bakhtin, Mikhail A. *The Dialogic Imagination: Four Essays by M. M. Bakhtin*. Trans. Caryl Emerson. Ed. Michael Holquist. Austin: University of Texas Press, 1981.

———. *Problems with Dostoevsky's Poetics*. Ed. and Trans. Caryl Emerson. Minneapolis: University of Minnesota Press, 1984.

———. *Speech Genres & Other Essays*. Trans. Vern W. McGee. Ed. Caryl Emerson and Michael Holquist. Austin: University of Texas Press, 1986.

Bardes, Barbara, and Suzanne Gossett, eds. *Declarations of Independence: Women and Political Power in Nineteenth-Century American Fiction*. New Brunswick, N.J.: Rutgers University Press, 1990.

Barnes, Elizabeth. *States of Sympathy: Seduction and Democracy in the American Novel*. New York: Columbia University Press, 1997.

Barthes, Roland. "The Death of the Author." *Image Music Text*. Trans. Stephen Heath. New York: Noonday, 1977.

Baym, Nina. *American Women Writers and the Work of History, 1790–1860*. New Brunswick, N.J.: Rutgers University Press, 1995.

———. *Novels, Readers, and Reviewers: Responses to Fiction in Antebellum America*. Ithaca, N.Y.: Cornell University Press, 1984.

———. "Reinventing Lydia Sigourney." *Feminism and American Literary History*. New Brunswick, N.J.: Rutgers University Press, 1992. 151–66.

Baxter, Annette K. Preface. *The Clubwoman as Feminist: True Womanhood Redefined, 1868–1914*, by Karen J Blair. New York: Holmes & Meier, 1980.

Bennett, Paula Bernat. "Emily Dickinson and her American woman poet peers." *The Cambridge Companion to Emily Dickinson.* Ed. Wendy Martin. Cambridge: Cambridge University Press, 2002. 215–35.

———, ed. *Nineteenth-Century American Women Poets: An Anthology.* Malden, MA: Blackwell Press, 1998.

———, ed. *Palace-Burner: Selected Poetry of Sarah Piatt.* Chicago: University of Illinois Press, 2001.

———. *Poets in the Public Sphere: The Emancipatory Project of American Women's Poetry, 1800–1900.* Princeton, N.J.: Princeton University Press, 2003.

Bercovitch, Sacvan. *The Rites of Assent: Transformations in the Symbolic Construction of America.* New York: Routledge, 1993.

Bingham, Millicent Todd. *Ancestor's Brocades: The Literary Debut of Emily Dickinson.* New York: Harper & Brothers, 1945.

Blair, Karen J. *The Clubwoman as Feminist: True Womanhood Redefined, 1868–1914,* New York: Holmes & Meier, 1980.

Bloom, Harold. "The Sage of Concord." *The Guardian Review* (May 24, 2003): 4–6.

Bogan, Louise. *Achievement in American Poetry, 1900–1950.* Chicago: Regnery, 1951.

Bourdieu, Pierre. *The Field of Cultural Production: Essays on Art and Literature.* Ed. Randal Johnson. Cambridge, England: Polity Press, 1993.

———. *Outline of a Theory of Practice.* Trans. Richard Nice. New York: Cambridge University Press, 1977.

Brantley, Richard E. *Experience and Faith: The Late-Romantic Imagination of Emily Dickinson.* New York: Palgrave, 2004.

Braude, Ann. *Radical Spirits: Spiritualism and Women's Rights in Nineteenth-Century America.* Boston: Beacon Press, 1989.

Brodhead, Richard H. *Cultures of Letters: Scenes of Reading and Writing in Nineteenth-Century America.* Chicago: University of Chicago Press, 1993.

Brown, Gillian. *The Consent of the Governed: The Lockean Legacy in Early American Culture.* Cambridge, Mass.: Harvard University Press, 2001.

———. *Domestic Individualism: Imagining Self in Nineteenth-Century America.* Berkeley and Los Angeles: University of California Press, 1990.

Brown, Thomas. *Politics and Statesmanship: Essay on the American Whig Party.* New York: Columbia University Press, 1985.

Buckingham, Willis J., ed. *Emily Dickinson's Reception in the 1890s: A Documentary History.* Pittsburgh: University of Pittsburgh Press, 1989.

Buell, Lawrence. *Emerson.* Cambridge, Mass.: Harvard University Press, 2003.

———. *New England Literary Culture: From Revolution through Renaissance.* New York: Cambridge University Press, 1986.

Bumiller, Elisabeth. "Quietly, the First Lady Builds a Literary Room of Her Own." *New York Times,* October 7, 2002: A1, A14.

Burstein, Andrew. *Sentinental Democracy: The Evolution of America's Romantic Self-Image.* New York: Hill and Wang, 1999.

Bushell, Sally. "Meaning in Dickinson's Manuscripts: Intending the Unintentional." *Emily Dickinson Journal* 14.1 (2005): 24–61.

Cameron, Sharon. *Choosing Not Choosing: Dickinson's Fascicles*. Chicago: University of Chicago Press, 1992.

———. *Lyric Time*. Baltimore: Johns Hopkins University Press, 1979.

Capps, Jack L. *Emily Dickinson's Reading, 1836–1886*. Cambridge, Mass.: Harvard University Press, 1966.

Carroll, Bret E. *Spiritualism in Antebellum America*. Bloomington: Indiana University Press, 1997.

Cheal, David. *The Gift Economy*. New York: Routledge, 1988.

Chéroux, Clément, Andreas Fischer, Pierre Apraxine, et al. *The Perfect Medium: Photography and the Occult*. New Haven, Conn.: Yale University Press, 2004.

Cisneros, Sandra. *The House on Mango Street*. New York: Vintage Books, 1984.

———. "Notes to a Young(er) Writer." *American Review* 15.1 (1987): 74–76.

Cmeil, Kenneth. *Democratic Eloquence: The Fight over Popular Speech in Nineteenth-Century America*. New York: William Morrow and Co., 1990.

Conway, Hugh. *Called Back*. Chicago: Belford, Clarke & Co., 1883(?).

Cott, Nancy F. *The Bonds of Motherhood: "Woman's Sphere" in New England, 1780–1835*. New Haven, Conn.: Yale University Press, 1977.

Coultrap-McQuin, Susan. *Doing Literary Business: American Women Writers in the Nineteenth Century*. Chapel Hill: University of North Carolina Press, 1990.

Crumbley, Paul. "Dickinson's Dialogic Voice." *The Emily Dickinson Handbook*. Ed. Gudrun Grabher, Roland Hagenbüchle, and Cristanne Miller. Amherst: University of Massachusetts Press, 1998. 93–109.

———. *Inflections of the Pen: Dash and Voice in Emily Dickinson*. Lexington: University Press of Kentucky, 1997.

Dahl, Robert. *After the Revolution: Authority in a Good Society*. New Haven, Conn.: Yale University Press, 1990.

Davidson, Cathy N. *Revolution and the Word: The Rise of the Novel in America*. New York: Oxford University Press, 1986.

Davis, Andrew Jackson. *The Harmonial Man; or, Thoughts for the Age*. Boston: Bela March, 1853.

DeBrava, Valerie Ann. "Authorship and Individualism in American Literature." Ph.D. Dissertation, College of William and Mary, 2001.

Decker, William Merrill. *Epistolary Practices: Letter Writing in America before Telecommunications*. Chapel Hill: University of North Carolina Press, 1998.

"Declaration of Sentiments and Resolutions." *Report of the Woman's Rights Convention, Held at Seneca Falls, N.Y., July 19th and 20th, 1848*. Rochester, N.Y.: John Dick, at the North Star Office, 1848.

Deppman, Jed. *Trying to Think with Emily Dickinson*. Amherst: University of Massachusetts Press, 2008.

Derrida, Jacques. "The Double Session." *A Derrida Reader: Between the Blinds*. Ed. Peggy Kamuf. New York: Harvester Wheatsheaf, 1991.

———. *Limited Inc.* Evanston, Ind.: Northwestern University Press, 1977.

Dickie, Margaret. *Lyric Contingencies: Emily Dickinson and Wallace Stevens.* Philadelphia: University of Pennsylvania Press, 1991.

Dickinson, Emily. *Emily Dickinson: Collected Poems.* Philadelphia: Running Press, 1991.

———. *The Letters of Emily Dickinson.* 3 vols. Ed. Thomas H. Johnson and Theodora Ward. Cambridge, Mass.: Belknap of Harvard University Press, 1958.

———. *The Lyman Letters: New Light on Emily Dickinson and Her Family.* Ed. Richard B. Sewall. Amherst: University of Massachusetts Press, 1965.

———. *The Manuscript Books of Emily Dickinson.* Ed. R. W. Franklin. Cambridge, Mass.: Harvard University Press, 1981.

———. *Open Me Carefully: Emily Dickinson's Intimate Letters to Susan Huntington Dickinson.* Ed. Ellen Louise Hart and Martha Nell Smith. Ashfield, Mass.: Paris Press, 1998.

———. *The Poems of Emily Dickinson: Including variant readings critically compared with all known manuscripts.* 3 vols. Ed. Thomas H. Johnson. Cambridge, Mass.: Belknap of Harvard University Press, 1955.

———. *The Poems of Emily Dickinson: Variorum Edition.* 3 vols. Ed. Ralph W. Franklin. Cambridge, Mass.: Belknap of Harvard University Press, 1998.

Dietrich, Deborah. "Legal Imagery." *An Emily Dickinson Encyclopedia.* Ed. Jane Donahue Eberwein. Westport, Conn.: Greenwod Press, 1998. 172–73.

Dixon, Edward H. *Woman and Her Diseases, from the Cradle to the Grave: Adapted Exclusively to Her Instruction in the Physiology of Her System, and All the Diseases of Her Critical Periods.* 10th ed. Philadelphia: John E. Potter and Co., 1866.

Dobson, Joanne. *Dickinson and the Strategies of Reticence: The Woman Writer in Nineteenth-Century America.* Bloomington: Indiana University Press, 1989.

Eberwein, Jane Donahue. *Dickinson: Strategies of Limitation.* Amherst: University of Massachusetts Press, 1985.

Emerson, Ralph Waldo. *The Complete Works of Ralph Waldo Emerson.* Vol. 3. New York: Sully and Kleinteich, 1883.

———. *Emerson's Prose and Poetry.* Ed. Joel Porte and Saundra Morris. New York: W. W. Norton & Co., 2001.

———. *Essays and Lectures.* Ed. Joel Porte. New York: Literary Classics of the United States, 1983.

———. "New Poetry." *The Dial* (October 1840): 220–32.

———. *Selections from Ralph Waldo Emerson.* Ed. Stephen E. Whicher. Boston: Houghton Mifflin, 1957.

Erkkila, Betsy. "Dickinson and the Art of Politics." *A Historical Guide to Emily Dickinson.* Ed. Vivian Pollak. New York: Oxford University Press, 2004. 133–74.

———. "Emily Dickinson and Class." *American Literary History* 4.1 (Spring 1992): 1–27.

———. *The Wicked Sisters: Women Poets, Literary History & Discord.* New York: Oxford University Press, 1992.

Esdale, Logan. "Dickinson's Epistolary 'Naturalness.'" *Emily Dickinson Journal* 14.1 (2005): 1–23.

Farrand, Max, ed. *The Records of the Federal Convention of 1787.* Vol. 1. New Haven, Conn.: Yale University Press, 1966.

Fern, Fanny. *Ruth Hall and Other Writings.* Ed. Joyce Warren. New Brunswick, N.J.: Rutgers University Press, 1986.

Foucault, Michel. "What Is an Author?" *Textual Strategies: Perspectives in Post-Structuralist Criticism.* Ed. Josue V. Harari. Ithaca, N.Y.: Cornell University Press, 1979. 141–60.

Franklin, Ralph W., ed. *The Manuscript Books of Emily Dickinson.* Cambridge, Mass.: Harvard University Press, 1981.

———, ed. *The Poems of Emily Dickinson: Reading Edition.* Cambridge, Mass.: Harvard University Press, 1999.

Friedlander, Benjamin. "Auctions of the Mind: Emily Dickinson and Abolition." *Arizona Quarterly* 54 (Spring 1998): 1–25.

Fuller, Margaret. *Woman in the Nineteenth Century.* Ed. Larry J Reynolds. New York: W. W. Norton & Co., 1998.

Fulton, Alice. *Feeling as a Foreign Language: The Good Strangeness of Poetry.* Saint Paul, Minn.: Graywolf Press, 1999.

Garvey, T. Gregory. *The Emerson Dilemma: Essays on Emerson and Social Reform.* Athens: University of Georgia Press, 2001.

Gere, Anne Ruggles. *Intimate Practices: Literacy and Cultural Work in U.S. Women's Clubs, 1880–1920.* Chicago: University of Illinois Press, 1997.

Gilbert, Sandra M., and Susan Gubar. *The Madwoman in the Attic: The Woman Writer and the Nineteenth-Century Literary Imagination.* 2nd ed. New Haven, Conn.: Yale University Press, 2000.

———. *No Man's Land: The Place of the Woman Writer in the Twentieth Century.* Vol. 1. New Haven, Conn.: Yale University Press, 1988.

Giles, Paul. "Transnationalism and Classic American Literature." *PMLA* 118.1 (2003): 62–77.

Godbout, Jacques T. *The World of the Gift.* Trans. Donald Winkler. Ithaca, N.Y.: McGill-Queen's University Press, 1998.

Goldsmith, Barbara. *Other Powers: The Age of Suffrage, Spiritualism, and the Scandalous Victoria Woodhull.* New York: Alfred A. Knopf, 1998.

Guthrie, James. "Law, Property, and Provincialism in Dickinson's Poems and Letters to Judge Otis Phillips Lord." *Emily Dickinson Journal* 5.1 (1996): 27–44.

———. "Darwinian Dickinson: The Scandalous Rise and Noble Fall of the Common Clover." *Emily Dickinson Journal* 16.1 (2007): 73–91.

Habegger, Alfred. *My Wars Are Laid Away in Books: The Life of Emily Dickinson.* New York: Random House, 2001.

Hamilton, Alexander. "'Publius,' The Federalist I, October 27, 1787." *The Debate on the Constitution: Federalist and Anti-Federalist Speeches, Articles, and Letters During the Struggle over Ratification.* Ed. Bernard Bailyn. Vol. 1. New York: Literary Classics of the United States, 1993. 219–23.

Hardinge, Emma. *Modern American Spiritualism. A Twenty Years' Record of the Communion Between Earth and the World of Spirits.* New York: The author, 1870.

Harris, W. C. *E Pluribus Unum: Nineteenth-Century American Literature and the Constitutional Paradox.* Iowa City: Iowa University Press, 2005.

Hart, Ellen Louise, and Martha Nell Smith, ed. *Open Me Carefully: Emily Dickinson's Intimate Letters to Susan Huntington Dickinson.* Ashfield, Mass.: Paris Press, 1998.

Heginbotham, Eleanor Elson. *Reading the Fascicles of Emily Dickinson: Dwelling in Possibilities.* Columbus: Ohio State University Press, 2003.

Herndl, Diane Price. *Invalid Women: Figuring Feminine Illness in American Fiction and Culture, 1840–1940.* Chapel Hill: University of North Carolina Press, 1993.

Hewitt, Elizabeth. *Correspondence and American Literature, 1770–1865.* New York: Cambridge University Press, 2004.

Higginson, Thomas Wentworth. "Emily Dickinson." *The Magnificent Activist: The Writings of Thomas Wentworth Higginson (1823–1911).* Ed. Howard N. Meyer. New York: Da Capo Press, 2000. 543–64.

———. "Preface." *Emily Dickinson: Collected Poems.* Philadelphia: Running Press, 1991.

———. "A Letter to a Young Contributor." *The Magnificent Activist: The Writings of Thomas Wentworth Higginson (1823–1911).* 528–42.

———. "The Results of Spiritualism, A Discourse Delivered at Dodsworth Hall, Sunday, March 6, 1859, by Thomas Wentworth Higginson." Phonographically Reported. New York: S. T. Munson, 1859.

———. "To the Memory of H. H." *Century Magazine* (May 1886): 47.

Hirschorn, Norbert. "New Finds in Dickinson Family Correspondence." *Emily Dickinson International Society Bulletin* 7.1 (May/June 1995): 5–6.

Homans, Margaret. *Women Writers and Poetic Identity: Dorothy Wordsworth, Emily Brontë, and Emily Dickinson.* Princeton, N.J.: Princeton University Press, 1980.

Homestead, Melissa J. *American Women Authors and Literary Property, 1822–1869.* New York: Cambridge University Press, 2005.

Hooker, Richard. *The Laws of Ecclesiastical Polity.* Book VIII. *The Works of Richard Hooker in Eight Books.* 3 vols. London: 1821.

Horan, Elizabeth. "To Market: The Dickinson Copyright Wars." *Emily Dickinson Journal* 5.1 (1996): 88–120.

Howe, Daniel Walker. *The Political Culture of the American Whigs.* Chicago: University of Chicago Press, 1979.

Howe, Susan. "Experience Is the Angled Road." *Emily Dickinson Journal* 15.2 (2006): 34–37.

———. *The Birth-mark: Unsettling the Wilderness in American Literary History.* Hanover: Wesleyan University Press, 1993.

Hubbard, Melanie. "Dickinson's Advertising Flyers: Theorizing Materiality and the Work of Reading." *Emily Dickinson Journal* 7.1 (1998): 27–54.

Hutchison, Coleman. "'Eastern Exiles': Dickinson, Whiggery, and War." *Emily Dickinson Journal* 13.2 (2004): 1–26.

Hyde, Alan. *Bodies of Law.* Princeton, N.J.: Princeton University Press, 1997.

Isenberg, Nancy. *Sex and Citizenship in Antebellum America.* Chapel Hill: University of North Carolina Press, 1998

Jackson, Virginia. *Dickinson's Misery: A Theory of Lyric Reading.* Princeton, N.J.: Princeton University Press, 2005.

James, Henry. *The Bostonians.* New York: Thomas Y. Crowell Co., 1974.

Jefferson, Thomas. *Jefferson: Political Writings.* Ed. Joyce Appleby and Terence Ball.

Jehlen, Myra. "Introduction: Beyond Transcendence." *Ideology and Classic American Literature.* Ed. Sacvan Bercovitch and Myra Jehlen. New York: Cambridge University Press, 1986.

Jenkins, MacGregor. *Emily Dickinson: Friend and Neighbor.* Boston: Little, Brown and Co., 1930.

Jones, Kathleen B. *Compassionate Authority: Democracy and the Representation of Women.* New York: Routledge, 1993.

Kamuf, Peggy, ed. *A Derrida Reader: Between the Blinds.* New York: Columbia University Press, 1991.

Kelley, Mary. *Private Woman, Public Stage: Literary Domesticity in Nineteenth-Century America.* New York: Oxford University Press, 1984.

Kerber, Linda K. *Women of the Republic: Intellect and Ideology in Revolutionary America.* Chapel Hill: University of North Carolina Press, 1980.

Kerr, Howard. *Mediums, and Spirit-Rappers, and Roaring Radicals: Spiritualism in American Literature, 1850–1900.* Urbana: University of Illinois Press, 1972.

Kete, Mary Louise. *Sentimental Collaborations: Mourning and Middle-Class Identity in Nineteenth-Century America.* Durham, N.C.: Duke University Press, 2000.

Knight, Charles. "Advertisement." *The Comedies, Histories, Tragedies and Poems of William Shakespeare.* 8 vols. Boston: Little, Brown and Co., 1853.

Knott, Stephen F. *Alexander Hamilton and the Persistence of Myth.* Lawrence: University Press of Kansas, 2002.

Koski, Lena. "Newton, Benjamin Franklin." *An Emily Dickinson Encyclopedia.* Ed. Jane Donahue Eberwein. Westport, Conn.: Greenwood Press, 1998. 209.

Lang, Amy Schrader. *The Syntax of Class: Writing Inequality in Nineteenth-Century America.* Princeton, N.J.: Princeton University Press, 2003.

Laski, Harold. *A Grammar of Politics: Democratic Socialism in Britain.* Vol. 6. London: Pickering & Chatto, 1996.

Lease, Benjamin. *Emily Dickinson's Readings of Men and Books: Sacred Soundings.* New York: St. Martin's Press, 1990.

———. "'This World is not Conclusion': Dickinson, Amherst, and 'the local conditions of the soul.'" *Emily Dickinson Journal* 3.2 (1994): 38–55.

Left, Sarah. "Anti-war poest force scrapping of White House symposium." *Guardian,* January 30, 2003. http://www.guardian.co.uk/politics/2003/jan/30/antiwar.uk1 (accessed April 15, 2003).

Lindberg-Seyersted, Brita. *Emily Dickinson's Punctuation.* Oslo: American Institute, University of Oslo, 1976.

Locke, John. *Two Treatises of Government.* Ed. Mark Goldie. North Clarendon, Vt.: Everyman, 1993.

Loeffelholz, Mary. *Dickinson and the Boundaries of Feminist Theory.* Urbana: University of Illinois Press, 1991.

———. "Dickinson's 'Decoration.'" *ELH* 72 (2005): 663–89.

———. "Etruscan Invitations: Dickinson and the Anxiety of the Aesthetic in Feminist Criticism." *Emily Dickinson Journal* 5.1 (1996): 1–26.

———. *From School to Salon: Reading Nineteenth-Century American Women's Poetry.* Princeton, N.J.: Princeton University Press, 2004.

———. "'Plied from Nought to Nought': The Field of Dickinson's Refusals." Unpublished essay.

Lombardo, Daniel. *A Hedge Away: The Other Side of Emily Dickinson's Amherst.* Northampton, Mass.: Daily Hampshire Gazette, 2004.

Looby, Christopher. *Voicing America: Language, Literary Form, and the Origins of the United States.* Chicago: University of Chicago Press, 1996.

Lowenberg, Carlton. *Emily Dickinson's Textbooks.* Ed. Territa A. Lowenberg and Carla L. Brown. Lafayette, Calif.: West Coast Print Center, 1986.

———. *Musicians Wrestle Everywhere: Emily Dickinson and Music.* Berkeley, Calif.: Fallen Leaf Press, 1992.

Lutz, Donald S. *Popular Consent and Popular Control: Whig Political Theory in the Early State Constitutions.* Baton Rouge: Louisiana State University Press, 1980.

MacKenzie, Cynthia. *Concordance to the Letters of Emily Dickinson.* Boulder: University of Colorado Press, 2000.

MacPherson, C. B. *The Political Theory of Possessive Individualism: Hobbes to Locke.* Oxford: Clarendon Press, 1962.

Madison, James. "Monday, June 18, 1787." *The Record of the Federal Convention of 1787.* Vol. 1. Ed. Max Farrand. New Haven, Conn.: Yale University Press, 1937.

Maher, Margaret. "Deposition of Margaret Maher, Witness Called by Plaintiff." *Lavinia N. Dickinson vs. Mabel Loomins Todd, et al. The Commonwealth of Massachusetts, Hampshire, In the Superior Court, In Equity. 28 May 1897.*

Margolis, Stacey. *The Public Life of Privacy in Nineteenth-Century American Literature.* Durham, N.C.: Duke University Press, 2005.

Martin, Theodora Penny. *The Sound of Our Own Voices: Women's Study Clubs, 1860–1910.* Boston: Beacon Press, 1987.

Matthiessen, F. O. *American Renaissance.* New York: Oxford University Press, 1985.

McIntosh, James. *Nimble Believing: Dickinson and the Unknown.* Ann Arbor: University of Michigan Press, 2000.

Melville, Herman. *The Piazza Tales and Other Prose Pieces, 1839–1860.* Ed. Harrison Hayford, Alma A. MacDonald, and G. Thomas Tanselle. Chicago: Northwestern University Press, 1987.

Messmer, Marietta. *A Vice for Voices: Reading Emily Dickinson's Correspondence.*
Amherst: University of Massachusetts Press, 2001.

Michaels, Walter Benn. *The Shape of the Signifier: 1967 to the End of History.*
Princeton, N.J.: Princeton University Press, 2004.

Mill, John Stuart. *On Liberty.* London: Longmans, Green, Reader and Dyer, 1874.

Miller, Cristanne. "Disjunction, as a Characteristic." *An Emily Dickinson Encyclopedia.* Ed. Jane Donahue Eberwein. Westport, Conn.: Greenwood Press, 1998.
84–86.

———. *Emily Dickinson: A Poet's Grammar.* Cambridge, Mass.: Harvard University
Press, 1987.

Mitchell, Charles E. *Individualism and Its Discontents: Appropriations of Emerson,
1880–1950.* Amherst: University of Massachusetts Press, 1997.

Mitchell, Domhnall. "Emily Dickinson and Class." *The Cambridge Companion to
Emily Dickinson.* Cambridge: Cambridge University Press, 2002. 191–214.

———. *Emily Dickinson: Monarch of Perception.* Amherst: University of Massachusetts Press, 2000.

———. *Measures of Possibility: Emily Dickinson's Manuscripts.* Amherst: University
of Massachusetts Press, 2005.

———. "Revising the Script: Emily Dickinson's Manuscripts." *American Literature*
70 (December 1998): 705–37.

Moore, R. Laurence. *In Search of White Crows: Spiritualism, Parapsychology, and
American Culture.* New York: Oxford University Press, 1977.

Morgan, Edmund S. *Inventing the People: The Rise of Popular Sovereignty in England and America.* New York: W. W. Norton & Co., 1988.

Mulcaire, Terry. "Public Credit; or, The Feminization of Virtue in the Marketplace."
PMLA 114 (October 1999): 1029–1042.

Murray, Aife. "Kitchen Table Poetics: Maid Margaret Maher and Her Poet Emily
Dickinson." *Emily Dickinson Journal* 5.2 (1996): 285–296.

———. "Miss Margaret's Emily Dickinson." *Signs* (Spring 1999): 697–732.

Murray, Judith Sargent. *Selected Writings of Judith Sargent Murray.* Ed. Sharon M.
Harris. New York: Oxford University Press, 1995.

Nash, Kate. "Liberalism and the Undecidability of 'Women.'" *Essex Papers in Politics and Government: Sub-Series in Ideology and Discourse Analysis* 6 (April
2006).

Newman, Samuel P. *A Practical System of Rhetoric, or the Principles and Rules of
Style. . . .* 7th ed. Andover: Gould and Newman, 1839.

Olds, Sharon. "I Think Emily Dickinson Would Have Been Political Today."
Titanic Operas: a Poet's Corner of Responses to Emily Dickinson. Internet.
6/26/01. http://www.emilydickinson.org/titanic.

Ormsby, R. McKinley. *A History of the Whig Party.* Boston: Crosby, Nichols & Co.,
1860.

Ossowski, Stanislaw. *Class Structure in the Social Consciousness.* London: Routledge
& Kegan Paul, 1963.

Ostriker, Alicia Suskin. "Her Own Society: An Acrostic for Emily." *Emily Dickinson Journal* 15.2 (2006): 18–19.

———. *Stealing the Language: The Emergence of Women's Poetry in America.* Boston: Beacon Press, 1986.

Owen, Alex. *The Darkened Room: Women, Power and Spiritualism in Late Victorian England.* Philadelphia: University of Pennsylvania Press, 1990.

The Oxford English Dictionary: Complete Text Reproduced Micrographically. Oxford: Oxford University Press, 1971.

Pagnattaro, Marisa Anne. Report on Martha Ackmann's conference paper in "Dickinson in Historical Contexts." *Emily Dickinson International Society Bulletin* 7 (November–December 1995): 11.

Parker, Richard Green. *Aids to English Composition Prepared for Students of All Grades. . . .* Boston: Robert S. Davis, 1844.

Patterson, Annabel. *Critical Terms for Literary Study.* Eds. Frank Lentricchia and Thomas McLaughlin. Chicago: University of Chicago Press, 1995. 135–46.

Patterson, L. Ray, and Stanley W. Lindberg. *The Nature of Copyright: A Law of Users' Rights.* Athens: University of Georgia Press, 1991.

Petrino, Elizabeth A. *Emily Dickinson and Her Contemporaries: Women's Verse in America, 1820–1885.* Hanover, N.H.: University Press of New England, 1998.

Pinsky, Robert. *Democracy, Culture and the Voice of Poetry.* Princeton, N.J.: Princeton University Press, 2002.

Pollak, Vivian. "American Women Poets Reading Dickinson: The Example of Helen Hunt Jackson." *The Emily Dickinson Handbook.* Ed. Gudrun Grabher, Roland Hagenbüchle, and Cristanne Miller. Amherst: University of Massachusetts Press, 1998. 323–41.

———. *Dickinson: The Anxiety of Gender.* Ithaca, N.Y.: Cornell University Press, 1984.

Pollitt, Katha. "Poetry Makes Nothing Happen? Ask Laura Bush." *The Nation* (February 24, 2003): Online 2. www.thenation.com/doc.html?I=20030224&s=pollitt.

Porter, Ebenezer. *The Rhetorical Reader; Consisting of Instructions for Regulating the Voice, with a Rhetorical Notation. . . .* 23rd ed. New York: Dayton and Saxton, 1841.

Price, Monroe E., and Malla Pollack. "The Author in Copyright: Notes for the Literary Critic." *The Construction of Authorship: Textual Appropriation in Law and Literature.* Ed. Martha Woodmansee and Peter Jaszi. Durham, N.C.: Duke University Press, 1994. 439–56.

Prothero, Stephen. "From Spiritualism to Theosophy: 'Uplifting' a Democratic Tradition." *Religion and American Culture* 3.2 (1993): 197–216.

Reynolds, David S. *Walt Whitman's America: A Cultural Biography.* New York: Alfred A. Knopf, 1995.

Rice, Grantland S. *The Transformation of Authorship in America.* Chicago: University of Chicago Press, 1997.

Richards, Eliza. *Gender and the Poetics of Reception in Poe's Circle.* New York: Cambridge University Press, 2004.

Romero, Lora. *Home Fronts: Domesticity and Its Critics in the Antebellum United States*. Durham, N.C.: Duke University Press, 1997.

Rose, Mark. *Authors and Owners: The Invention of Copyright*. Cambridge, Mass.: Harvard University Press, 1993.

Rosenbaum, S. P. *A Concordance to the Poems of Emily Dickinson*. Ithaca, N.Y.: Cornell University Press, 1964.

Ross, Marlon B. "Authority and Authenticity: Scribbling Authors and the Genius of Print in Eighteenth-Century England." *The Construction of Authorship: Textual Appropriation in Law and Literature*. Ed. Martha Woodmansee and Peter Jaszi. Durham, N.C.: Duke University Press, 1994. 231–57.

Rowe, John Carlos. *At Emerson's Tomb: The Politics of Classic American Literature*. New York: Columbia University Press, 1997.

Ruttenburg, Nancy. *Democratic Personality: Popular Voice and the Trial of American Authorship*. Stanford, Calif.: Stanford University Press, 1998.

Ryan, Mary. *Women in Public: Between Banners and Ballots, 1825–1880*. Baltimore: Johns Hopkins University Press, 1990.

St. Armand, Barton Levi. *Emily Dickinson and Her Culture: The Soul's Society*. New York: Cmabridge University Press, 1984.

———. "Emily Dickinson and the Occult: The Rosicrucian Connection." *Prairie Schooner* 51 (1977–78): 345–57.

———. "Veiled Ladies: Dickinson, Bettine, and Transcendental Mediumship." *Studies in the American Renaissance* (1987): 1–51.

Salska, Agnieszka. *Walt Whitman and Emily Dickinson: Poetry of the Central Consciousness*. Philadelphia: University of Pennsylvania Press, 1985.

Sanborn, Geoffrey. "Keeping Her Distance: Cisneros, Dickinson, and the Politics of Private Enjoyment." *PMLA* 116.5 (October 2001): 1334–48.

Sanchez-Eppler, Karen. *Touching Liberty: Abolition, Feminism, and the Politics of the Body*. Berkeley and Los Angeles: University of California Press, 1993.

Scharnhorst, Gary. "A Glimpse of Dickinson at Work." *American Literature* 57 (October 1985): 483–85.

Scheurer, Erika. " 'Near, but remote': Emily Dickinson's Epistolary Voice." *Emily Dickinson Journal* 4.1 (1995): 86–107.

Scholes, Robert. *The Rise and Fall of English: Reconstructing English as a Discipline*. New Haven, Conn.: Yale University Press, 1998.

Sewall, Richard B. *The Life of Emily Dickinson*. New York: Farrar, Straus and Giroux, 1980.

———. *The Lyman Letters: New Light on Emily Dickinson and Her Family*. Amherst: University of Massachusetts Press, 1965.

Smith, Martha Nell. "Because the Plunge from the Front Overturned Us: *The Dickinson Electronic Archives* Project." *Studies in the Literary Imagination* 32 (Spring 1999): 1–19.

———. "By Way of an Introduction: American Women's Poetry & Dickinson's

Legacy." *Titanic Operas: A Poet's Corner of Responses to Dickinson's Legacy.* Internet. 17/09/2002.

———. *Rowing in Eden: Rereading Emily Dickinson.* Austin: University of Texas Press, 1992.

Smith-Rosenberg, Carroll. *Disorderly Conduct: Visions of Gender in Victorian America.* New York: Oxford University Press, 1985.

Socarides, Alexandra. "Rethinking the Fascicles: Dickinson's Writing, Copying, and Binding Practices." *Emily Dickinson Journal* 15.2 (2006): 69–94.

Stoddard, Elizabeth. *The Morgesons and Other Writings, Published and Unpublished, by Elizabeth Stoddard.* Ed. Lawrence Buell and Sandra A. Zagarell. Philadelphia: University of Pennsylvania Press, 1985.

Stonum, Gary Lee. *The Dickinson Sublime.* Madison: University of Wisconsin Press, 1990.

Thornton, Tamara Plakens. *Handwriting in America: A Cultural History.* New Haven, Conn.: Yale University Press, 1996.

Titanic Operas: A Poet's Corner of Responses to Emily Dickinson. http://jefferson.village.virginia.edu/dickinson/titanic.

Tocqueville, Alexis de. *Democracy in America.* Trans. George Lawrence. Ed. J. P. Mayer. New York: HarperCollins, 2000.

Tonkovich, Nicole. *Domesticity with a Difference.* Jackson: University Press of Mississippi, 1997.

Tucker, Susan, Katherine Ott, and Patricia P. Buckler, eds. *The Scrapbook in American Life.* Philadelphia: Temple University Press, 2006.

Vaidhyanathan, Siva. *Copyrights and Copywrongs: The Rise of Intellectual Property and How It Threatens Creativity.* New York: New York University Press, 2001.

Vanderberg, Susan. "'Coming to grips with the World': Susan Howe's Reading of Emily Dickinson." *Emily Dickinson International Society Bulletin* 7.1 (May–June 1995): 12–13.

Walker, Cheryl, ed. *American Women Poets of the Nineteenth Century: An Anthology.* New Brunswick, N.J.: Rutgers University Press, 1992.

———. *The Nightingale's Burden: Women Poets and American Culture before 1900.* Bloomington: Indiana University Press, 1982.

Wardrop, Daneen. *Emily Dickinson's Gothic: Goblin with a Gauge.* Iowa City: University of Iowa Press, 1996.

Warner, Michael. *The Letters of the Republic: Publication and the Public Sphere in Eighteenth-Century America.* Cambridge, Mass.: Harvard University Press, 1990.

———. *Publics and Counterpublics.* New York: Zone Books, 2002.

Warren, O. G. "Dialogues." *The Sacred Circle* 2 (1855): 5–14.

Webster, Noah. *An American Dictionary of the English Language.* 2 vols. New York: S. Converse, 1828.

Weisbuch, Robert. "Prisming Dickinson; or, Gathering Paradise by Letting Go." *The Emily Dickinson Handbook.* Ed. Gudrun Grabher, Roland Hagenbüchle, and Cristanne Miller. Amherst: University of Massachusetts Press, 1998. 197–223.

Welter, Barbara. "The Cult of True Womanhood: 1820–1860." *Locating American Studies: The Evolution of a Discipline*. Ed. Lucy Maddox. Baltimore: Johns Hopkins University Press, 1999. 43–66.

Werner, Marta L. *Emily Dickinson's Open Folios: Scenes of Reading, Surfaces of Writing*. Ann Arbor: University of Michigan Press, 1995.

Whately, Richard. *Elements of Rhetoric, Comprising the Substance of the Article in the Encyclopedia Metropolitana. . . .* Cambridge: James Munroe and Co., 1834.

Whitman, Walt. *Leaves of Grass and Other Writings*. Ed. Michael Moon. New York: W. W. Norton & Co., 2002.

———. *Walt Whitman: Complete Poetry and Collected Prose*. New York: Literary Classics of the United States, 1982.

Wolff, Cynthia Griffin. *Emily Dickinson*. New York: Alfred A. Knopf, 1986.

Wolosky, Shira. "The Claims of Rhetoric: Toward a Historical Poetics (1820–1900)." *American Literary History* 15.1 (Spring 2003): 14–21.

———. "Dickinson's Emerson: A Critique of American Identity." *Emily Dickinson Journal* 9.2 (2000): 134–41.

———. "Emily Dickinson: Being in the Body." *The Cambridge Companion to Emily Dickinson*. Ed. Wendy Martin. Cambridge: Cambridge University Press, 2002. 129–41.

Woodmansee, Martha. "On the Author Effect: Recovering Collectivity." *The Construction of Authorship: Textual Appropriation in Law and Literature*. Ed. Martha Woodmansee and Peter Jaszi. Durham, N.C.: Duke University Press, 1994. 15–28.

Woolson, Constance Fenimore. *Women Artists, Women Exiles: "Miss Grief" and Other Stories*. Ed. Joan Myers Weimer. New Brunswick, N.J.: Rutgers University Press, 1988.

Index of First Lines

Index of Letters Organized by Date

The abbreviation L *indicates letters from* The Letters of Emily Dickinson, *edited by Thomas H. Johnson and Theodora Ward.* OMC *indicates letters from* Open Me Carefully *edited by Ellen Louise Hart and Martha Nell Smith.* Letter *indicates letters from* The Lyman Letters *edited by Richard B. Sewell.*

Index